A Short History
of Irish Literature

A BACKWARD LOOK

A Short History of Irish Literature

A BACKWARD LOOK

by Frank O'Connor

G. P. PUTNAM'S SONS New York

FOR MY CHILDREN

look back to look forward

ACKNOWLEDGEMENTS

The author and publishers wish to thank the following, who have kindly given permission for the use of copyright material: Messrs. Jonathan Cape Ltd. and The Viking Press Inc. for the extract from *A Portrait of the Artist as a Young Man*, by James Joyce (copyright 1916 by B. W. Huebsch Inc., 1944 by Nora Joyce); Messrs. Putnam & Co. Ltd. for the extracts from *The Gaol Gate* and *Dervorgilla* by Lady Gregory; and Mr. M. B. Yeats for the extracts from *The Only Jealousy of Emer* and *The Collected Poems of W. B. Yeats*.

Contents

Publisher's Note

After Frank O'Connor had completed the present work he had some new thoughts on the interpretation of the texts discussed in the chapters on early Irish story-telling. These he had hoped to incorporate with the present volume, but his death, on 10 March 1966, prevented this.

Fortunately, these fresh ideas were expressed in lectures he gave at Trinity College, Dublin, and at St. Patrick's College, Maynooth, a few weeks before his death. These lectures are so significant and illuminating that, despite some repetition of material in the early chapters, they are printed in their entirety as an appendix to this volume.

Introduction

I

This book is based upon a series of lectures delivered in Trinity College, Dublin, which was suggested by the professors of Irish and English, David Greene and Philip Edwards. What form they wished the lectures to take I do not know, though both may have had in mind a question that has frequently occurred to myself: 'Is there such a thing as an Irish literature, or is it merely two unrelated subjects linked by a geographical accident?'

It should be a fairly easy one to answer, but even while I was delivering the lectures I was not at all certain what the answer might turn out to be. The abandonment of every mark of cultural identity by the Irish people during the nineteenth century has left a historical gap that is hard to span. Ours is probably the only civilized country which has no such thing as a chair of national literature; thousands of students pass through our universities each year with less knowledge of their own culture than one would expect to find among American students. The literature of the past is simply ignored; the literature of our own time is either ignored or banned by law. At the beginning of the present century the Irish theatre was world-famous, but since effective control of it passed into the hands of the State it is impossible to study its history in Ireland itself: the student has better opportunities for doing so almost anywhere else. As for our archaeological and architectural monuments, they scarcely bear thinking of.

Having completed the work, I have little doubt that there is such a subject or that the title of the book, which I chose merely as a description, is also by way of being a definition. Irish literature is literature of a peculiar kind because it has been created by a unique set of historical circumstances. Its origins are in an extraordinary mass of tradition with which British and continental missionaries were faced on their arrival in Ireland in the fifth century — a closely knit system of orally transmitted medicine, law, religion, and history that in many ways takes us back to the very childhood of Indo-European civilization. Everywhere else, except in the remoter corners of Britain, it had been extinguished altogether, and even there some of its principal manifestations had disappeared. In Ireland itself by the medieval period native medicine had disappeared before Arabic medicine, and religion had been obscured by its Christian recorders; but the sheer bulk of what remained was such that it imposed itself upon the imagination of early Christianity as its mere shadow imposed itself upon the much more sophisticated imagination of the later nineteenth century. One may sometimes regret this obsession with the past and wish that Ireland could have come into the Middle Ages or the Renaissance without this dead weight of tradition : one may even sympathize occasionally with the literary critic who recently asked in a Jesuit review : 'Is our past so unique that we must always be gazing back lovingly on it?'; but we cannot ignore it. Our attitude must be rather that of the twelfth-century scribe of 'The Cattle Raid of Cooley', who added wistfully to his text : 'But I who wrote this history or rather fable put no trust in this history or fable, for some of these things are the feats of devils, some poetic figments, some apparently true, some not, and some for the delectation of fools.'

In the first few chapters I have tried to describe a few characteristic specimens of early Irish literature, but I must emphasize how few these are by comparison with what remains and how very little remains of the vast quantity that once existed. For a people whose own traditions were almost entirely oral, the early Irish wrote apparently without ceasing, but the total native manuscript production in Irish from 600 to 1100 has been completely wiped out, and what survives of that period in later manuscripts has been so mishandled by ignorant transcribers that it is often difficult even to guess what the original text was like.

That is, if there ever was what one could call an original text. One of the principal sources of confusion — and this, I suspect, even before the bad compilers of the post-Norse period got to work — was that saga was still regarded as history, and though this attitude was weakened by the lives of the saints, which treated history as historical romance, it persisted; the sagas were looked on not as works of literature written by individual men of genius in individual monasteries, but as fragments of history, so that they developed into a series of introductions and sequels; the beginning of one story being attached to the end of another and its end to the beginning of a third.

Something of this kind certainly happened to the story of Conchobar's death. An introductory story, 'The Siege of Howth', begins with a rambling bit of folk-lore about the avaricious Ulster poet, Athirne the Exacting, who demands the eye from one man's head, the wife from another's bed, etc., and having plagued the Leinstermen sufficiently goes to the border at Dublin where an Ulster escort awaits him. Ulster and Leinster men fight, and the Leinstermen are defeated. Here, the narrative line breaks down for the Ulstermen are hindered by a tabu from pursuing, but Conall Cernach ('Cernunnos') follows up Mess Gegra, the Leinster king, on his own, to avenge his two brothers, one of whom we have not heard of previously. At this point the whole style changes to a magnificent narrative prose, which in style and treatment recalls a similar passage in 'The Death of Cú Chulainn' — Thurneysen's statement that it is an imitation is not convincing. Mess Gegra, while his charioteer is asleep, fishes a big nut from the river and keeps half for the charioteer, but when asked about it by the charioteer says jokingly that he 'lessened it first'. The charioteer chops off Mess Gegra's hand, which is holding the nut, and when he discovers his mistake falls on his sword. As I have said in Chapter Four the chopped-off-hand theme and the classical suicide — the latter unknown elsewhere in Irish literature except in another saga which I suspect is of Leinster origin — suggest some Latin school, such as that of Kildare.

The story trails off in the last paragraph when Conall instructs his charioteer to extract Mess Gegra's brain and mix it with lime, but at the beginning of 'The Death of Conchobar' Cet mac Mágach of Connacht steals the brain ball from Emain Machae and later uses it as a sling-shot to strike down Conchobar. Conchobar recovers, but with the shot still in his head, and when on the first Good Friday a druid tells him of the crucifixion, the shot bursts from his head and he dies.

I have no doubt that the second half of 'The Siege of Howth' and the first half of 'The Death of Conchobar' were originally one story, because the author of the pious Christian climax was not sufficiently careful to cover up his tracks, and the language indicates that Conchobar in one version did *not* recover but was buried where he was struck down. Unfortunately, this really explains nothing, because the Christian episode is much older in style than the humanist one, and if the author of that splendid scene was anything, he was an interpolator rather than the author of the original story.

The truth is that scholars — and as a result we who must only fumble after them — cannot get out of their minds that somewhere, at some time, there was an original text if only they could discover it. All our great scholars have been good classicists, and whenever a story contained blatant repetitions and contradictions they resorted to the concept of an A and B text with a stemma, rather as Thurneysen does with the text of 'The Cattle Raid of Cooley', which I have tried to analyse in Chapter Three. I doubt if there ever was such a thing as an original in our sense of the word, because apart from legal texts and a small group of religious poems, which were regarded as having magical significance and were glossed instead of being rewritten, Irish men of letters in the early Middle Ages had no conception of authorship or of a text as a thing in itself, and felt perfectly free to add, subtract, and rewrite as they later did when they translated from Latin. Conscientious scribes could merely note that 'other books say differently' and, like the scribe of 'The Destruction of Dá Derga's Hostel', add hopefully 'and they are probably truer'. Like modern scholars they never really lost hope of seeing 'Truth dawn ere morning'.

I am not, of course, arguing against textual criticism, merely suggesting that it will be more successful when it takes into account the minds of the men who wrote these remarkable stories, and the circumstances in which they wrote them. Part of their mystery is that they were never beaten into shape by any dominating literary intelligence who could impose his versions on his successors along with his name written on the title-page. Though they are literature, composed by men who were rarely without a pen in their hands, they retain the wavering, uncertain quality of folklore with its innumerable, forgotten authors.

I I

The secret of what I have called 'the backward look' is probably the existence at the very origin of Irish literature of this immense mass of tradition, the sheer mystery of which overwhelmed the simple imagination of educated people in early Christian times. In the great monastic codices it stood side by side with the new learning, and though it was influenced by this, it influenced the new learning far more. Literature suffered from it as well, for, as Thurneysen makes clear in the passage I have quoted as my text, though you might have a great vernacular literature you could not at the same time have an Eriugena or a Bede. The Irish had the choice between imagination and intellect, and they chose imagination.

When the worst of the Norse invasion was over, the tradition revived, but the erection of large Romanesque monasteries and the Norman invasion between them terminated its period of greatness, and by the year 1200 lyric poetry in the old manner and good prose were no longer being written. Yet, even though it was no longer a creative force, though the medical schools silently abandoned the old medicine and the law schools (which *did* preserve the old law texts) were themselves subject to quite different laws, the tradition continued in a sort of sullen suspension. The old stories were rewritten in a dull prose and an even duller narrative technique, but they delighted both Norman and native. When Chaucer's contemporary, Desmond, was imprisoned in the O'Brien stronghold of Kincora with an old woman for wardress, he wrote an amusing poem, comparing her with Conchobar's serving-woman, Leborcham, and even in the seventeenth century, when some aristocratic poet wrote an enchanting lyric on the history of love, he embarrassed his present-day translator by referring to sagas and to versions of sagas which have now disappeared forever.

> *Macaomh eile tug annsacht*
> *Do mhnaoi do bhantracht na Gréige,*
> *Cú Chulainn na gcleas n-iongnadh,*
> *Is leis do rinneadh an sméideadh.*

Lá dá raibh i ndiaidh seilge
 Go bhfuair Deirdre ag dul 'na brógaibh,
 Naoise, an fear fial fosaidh,
 Isé do thosaigh na póga. . . .[1]

While Ulster's Hound as well,
 When a Greek girl went by,
 Falling beneath her spell
 Was first with the glad eye.

Naisi, home from the chase,
 Weary, inspired by bliss,
 Seeing Deirdre don her trews,
 Endowed us with the kiss. . . .

By this time Geoffrey Keating was collecting such of the old stories as he could find and fitting them as he believed into a framework of genuine history. In the following century Keating himself was being translated into the language of the Conqueror, and Charlotte Brooke was trying to render Irish poetry into English verse. Indeed, there is practically no time in our history when some equivalent of a Jesuit quarterly might not have asked sadly: 'Is our past so unique that we must always be gazing back lovingly on it?'

That perseveration becomes most obvious in the nineteenth century when the language was almost gone and the population largely dispersed, because the tradition was literally fighting for its life, and only a handful of people, like Petrie and Ferguson were even aware of its existence. Sometimes one gets the impression that all the vital political issues of the time were unimportant compared with the task of bringing the name of Cú Chulainn into English literature. This was finally achieved by a combination of great Celtic scholars and the literary genius of Yeats and his circle, and by the year 1910 it could be said that Irish literature again existed in something like the way in which it had existed about the year 800.

Surely, this must be a unique thing in the history of literature, and in dealing with Irish literature, as I have had to do, from age to age, and often myself confused by its vagaries as well as by

[1] T. F. O'Rahilly, *Dánta Grádha* (Cork, 1926), 8.

my own lack of academic scholarship, I have had no alternative
but to conclude that if it is not a real subject, then all the subjects
of our criticism are likewise dreams.

III

Why it should be so is a different matter and one I find almost
impossible to explain. The survival of ancient traditions in places
geographically remote is a familiar enough phenomenon, and the
folk-tales, songs and superstitions of western districts, which
resembled those of the Scottish islands, provided Yeats with a very
valuable second string to his bow. Something is also due to the
fact that among the Irish as among other subject races foreign
rule has produced a certain stubbornness about the past. But neither
of these provides anything like a complete or convincing explanation. Nothing in the least resembling what has happened in Ireland
has happened in Scotland or Wales or Brittany. Yeats was uneasily
conscious of something out of the ordinary in the whole subject
in his later years, as when he wrote:

> When Pearse summoned Cuchulain to his side,
> What stalked through the Post Office? What intellect,
> What calculation, number, measurement replied?

That the founder of a new literature and the founder of a new
state should both be saturated in the legends of Cú Chulainn was
something peculiar enough to suggest that both of them were
being used by some force outside themselves. It is true that both
were fortunate in their periods, Yeats because his coincided with
a general disillusionment regarding the values of Victorian life
and literature, Pearse because the time was ripe for a whole series
of national independence movements. In Ferguson's time it is hard
to imagine anyone doing more than he did, and Davis could
certainly not have achieved what Pearse achieved.

Yet there is an obvious link between the literary movement and
the Rising of 1916 and between both and the saga tradition. It
would almost seem to be a question of the scale on which Ireland
has inherited the remains of Indo-European civilization — a scale

which invests it with mystique that has made us, for the most part unwillingly, a People of the Book. It is as though we could no more escape from the burden of tradition than the Jews have been able to escape from the Pentateuch, and perhaps we can escape it only as they are now attempting to do, by confronting it and so robbing it of its mystique.

I am greatly indebted to Professor Greene and Professor Edwards for having made the book possible. I am particularly indebted to Professor Greene and Professor Binchy, whose patience with literary theorizing on a subject they have made their own has given the earlier chapters whatever semblance of coherence they may have. Most of the texts of early Irish poetry are from *A Golden Treasury of Irish Poetry*, which Professor Greene and myself have edited; where footnote references are given to alternative sources, these are to other, easily available texts.

In the discussion of these poems with Professor Greene I have long ceased to remember whose ideas I have put forward, his or my own. Where they are wrong they may, with perfect security, be debited to my account.

FRANK O'CONNOR

Dublin, 1965

CHAPTER ONE

Early Ireland

In reviewing a ninth-century Irish handbook of grammar and rhetoric Rudolf Thurneysen made a striking criticism of the Irish type of mind that goes straight to the heart of my subject.

The Irishman sees the grammatical schemas as concrete realities. There are few documents that give us so deep an insight into the mind of the early Irish — so completely different from our own — as these tracts, and yet they spring from the learned classes, acquainted with the Latin grammarians. Only by comparison with them can we judge the powerful intellectual achievement a Johannes Eriugena has accomplished in the 9th century, schooled of course by the translation of Dionysius the Areopagite; he too erects a similar pyramidal construction, though it is logically built on a capacity for abstraction learned from the Greeks, without any loss of the Irish capacity for concreteness. Such a work in the Ireland of his day would have been impossible and remained incomprehensible. Apart from their piety the Irish certainly brought abroad with them their inclination to scholarship, which was not very wide-spread on the continent, and made them welcome as schoolmasters; but to develop their reasoning powers was something they could only do in closer proximity to the Mediterranean.[1]

Thurneysen is discussing scholarship and philosophy, but he might have said with equal truth that a book like Bede's *History of the English Church* would in the Ireland of that time have been impossible and remained incomprehensible. In fact, with certain qualifications, everything he says is equally relevant to Irish literature. He does not discuss why things were so, which is part of my story.

When Irish history begins — with the arrival of Christian missionaries from Gaul and Britain in the fifth century — Ireland must have been a peculiarly desolate and undeveloped country.

[1] *Zeitschrift für celtische Philologie*, XVII.

The population consisted of the original Stone Age inhabitants, an overflow of Celts from Britain (principally in the north and east), and finally the Féni, the continental Celts, who are the Irish proper and who may be assumed to have invaded the country about the beginning of the Christian era. One group of them occupied Munster; another invaded Connacht and later a considerable part of Leinster from the Boyne to the Liffey. For the purpose of this work they may be regarded as inhabitants of O'Connell Street, while at our side of the Liffey lived the Lagin, the original inhabitants of all Leinster, who were probably British Celts. North of the Boyne (and at the comparatively late period I write of still farther north) lived the Ulaid, the original inhabitants of Ulster. They, too, were probably British Celts.

The total population must have been exceedingly small. Naturally one guesses, but my own guesses falter at the quarter of a million mark, which probably means they should have stopped sooner. A great part of the country was filled with woodlands, and, generally speaking, it remained so until the seventeenth century, when the cutting of the woods and the change from an economy that was largely pastoral sent the population soaring in an unmanageable way. The standard of living was low. Until the building of Cormac's Chapel in 1134 there was no monument as grandiose as the Neolithic tombs near Slane, which were built three thousand years before Christ. There were no towns, which does not mean the same thing as 'the Irish did not live in towns' into which historians translate it. Towns are not a racial characteristic, but a fact of economic geography, and early Ireland did not permit of much in the way of commerce. Towns developed with the rise of monasteries, and by the tenth or eleventh century Armagh must have been a big town indeed. A standard joke of the last thousand years or so has been the simple countryman's equation of his native village with Paris for size and iniquity, and the Middle Irish equivalent was 'Is Ard Macha ar gnáthchi' — 'It's as bad as Armagh with the visitors.'

The country was divided into a hundred or more small kingdoms, many of which were at war with their neighbours, and most of which were loosely linked in provincial federations. The system of warfare was not so much one of conquest, which usually implies superiority in numbers or weapons, as of cattle raiding. This, once more, is not peculiarly Irish, for in 1381 when the English justiciar Desmond writes a lament for his friend, Diarmuid MacCarthy, he does so in terms of a cattle raid, and his fine poem would have been perfectly intelligible to an Irishman of the fifth century.

The social organization was a tribal one with three main classes: nobles, professional men, and peasants. Slaves were not reckoned, though there must have been many thousands of them who formed the nucleus of the early Irish Church and gave us our greatest saint, Patrick. The nobles, as in most tribal societies, were insanely arrogant. One of the standard subjects in early Irish story-telling was their boasting, and the court poetry that was written for them is sometimes comic in its pretentiousness. The professionals were priests, historians, doctors, lawyers, and poets proper. Because of the rudimentary nature of its skills this professional class might be better described as a Church. Its culture was oral, and its common form of expression unrhymed, alliterative verse, almost entirely mnemonic in purpose, which did not often rise above the level of 'Thirty days hath September, April, June, and November'.

If we ask ourselves why we cling to that odd but useful bit of information, we may be able to enter more easily into the Irish type of mind, which is largely the mind of primitive man every-where. To primitive man the greatest possible nightmare is the loss of his identity, which may occur at any time as the result of a loss of memory. If he does not know who his father, grandfather, and great-grandfather were or the names and events associated with the place where they lived he is nobody. In the year 1772 Arthur O'Leary, a colonel in the Austrian army, was killed by English soldiers in Carriganimma, County Cork. His wife was Eileen O'Connell of Derrynane, aunt of Daniel O'Connell, 'the Liberator', and she composed a lament for her husband in which she calls him 'Art O'Leary, son of Conor, son of Cady, son of Lewis O'Leary' and mentions her own family in the same way.

> Dónal Mór Ó Conaill
> Nó Conall a bháigh an tuile,

> Nó bean na sé mblian fichead
> Do chuaidh anonn thar uisge
> Ag déanamh cáirdeasa le rithe. . . .

> Donal Mor O'Connell,
> Conal who died by drowning,
> Or the girl of six and twenty
> Who went across the water
> To be a king's companion. . . .

To us it is a rather tiresome convention, but to Eileen O'Connell it was the essence of the matter because it identified herself and her husband to all who heard the lines. The first and most important thing to remember about Irish literature is that for this particular purpose the Irish never relied on books, always on oral tradition, on 'what the Old Man said'.

As a result the most characteristic social feature of this primitive fear is the hereditary transmission of knowledge. An individual would die, and a school might scatter, but a whole family, protected by law and custom, might endure; and the spells and curses of the priests, the laws and judgements of the lawyers, the genealogies and traditions of the historians would never die.

About the literature I have to assume certain things, but I believe my assumptions are well founded. I have no real evidence that in the seventh and eighth centuries verse was written by particular families of professional poets, but we do know that this was so from the twelfth to the seventeenth century, and it is reasonable to suppose that this was no innovation. I am not certain how the verse of professional poets was composed in the early centuries, but we do know that from the twelfth to the seventeenth it was composed in completely dark rooms; and this, as Osborn Bergin pointed out, can hardly be anything except a survival of ancient practices.

In his famous lecture on 'Bardic Poetry' he quotes first from the *Memoirs* of the Marquis of Clanricarde (1722), describing schools for professional poets.

The said subject (either one or more as aforesaid) having been given overnight, they worked it apart each by himself upon his own bed, the whole next day in the dark, till at a certain hour in the night, lights being brought in, they committed it to writing.

Then he quotes Martin's *Description of the Western Islands of Scotland* (1703) on the making of poetry in Irish-speaking districts at that time.

They shut their doors and windows for a day's time, and lie upon their backs with a stone upon their belly, and plaids about their heads, and their eyes being covered, they pump their brains for rhetorical encomium or panegyric; and indeed, they furnish such a style from this dark cell as is understood by very few.[2]

Bergin himself edited a poem by Fear Flatha O Gnímh, written about the year 1550 and addressed to a poetic blackleg who scorned trade-union rules for the composition of poetry.

> Misi féin dá ndearnoinn dán
> Maith liom — lughaide ar seachrán —
> Bac ar ghriangha um theachta as teagh,
> Leaptha diamhra 'gár ndídean.[3]

When I compose a poem, since it minimizes my lack of recollection, I prefer to hinder sunrays from coming in and a dark bed to shelter me.

There is no mistaking the meaning of these quotations. A thousand years after the introduction of writing Irish, professional poets composed as though it had not been introduced at all. What distinguishes this professional poetry of the later Middle Ages from the amateur poetry produced in the monasteries of the early Middle Ages is that we cannot for a moment believe that the monks composed their verses in dark rooms. They sing more as the bird sings.

> Fom-chain coí menn, medair mass,
> I mbrott glass di dingnaib doss —
> Dé bráth nom Coimmdiu coíma! —
> Caín scríbaimm fo roída ross.[4]

[2] Osborn Bergin, 'Bardic Poetry.' *Invernian Journal*, 1913.
[3] Osborn Bergin, 'Unpublished Irish Poems, X.' *Studies*, June 1920.
[4] W. Stokes and J. Strachan (eds.), *Thesaurus Palaeohibernicus* (Cambridge, 1901), II, 290. *A Golden Treasury of Irish Poetry* (London, 1967), 84. This volume will hereafter be cited as *GT*.

> In a green cloak of bushy boughs
> The cuckoo pipes his melodies —
> Be good to me, God, on Judgement Day!
> How well I write beneath the trees!

Because of their obsession with the oral transmission of knowledge the Irish professional classes aimed at producing not the man with the best brain, but the man with the best memory. This attitude persisted into our own time, and in every Irish-speaking community there was usually someone capable of fabulous feats of memory. A Kerry fisherman recited the three-hundred-odd lines of 'The Lament for Art O'Leary' to D. A. Binchy, though he had heard it only twice in his life, and my old friend Timothy Buckley of Gougane Barra — the hero of a Senate debate on evil literature that went on for a week — could recite stories and poems by the hour without once halting for a word.

I am not suggesting that the Kerry fisherman or Timothy Buckley resembled the Irish scholars Thurneysen was criticizing in anything other than the power of their memory. Much criticism of Irish literature is vitiated by the false assumption that since everything in folk-lore is transmitted orally, everything transmitted orally is folk-lore, and that the great Irish sagas were told twelve hundred years ago in the manner of the stories Timothy Buckley told about the Gárlach Coileánach. (Incidentally, his hero's name is merely a folk corruption of a name for the god Lug — the Ioldánach, or Man of Many Arts.) Nor, in spite of the opinion of scholars I respect, do I think that the sagas were oral compositions, written down after the lapse of centuries by literary monks, because, though I know from experience what traditional story-tellers can remember, as a professional writer I also know what they cannot remember. With some practice I could tell a story more or less as Timothy Buckley would have told it, but to memorize and repeat a page of naturalistic prose narrative by Jane Austen or Tolstoy would be well beyond his powers and mine; and there are too many passages in early Irish prose that have the same sort of inner complexity and could not have been transmitted orally.

Nevertheless, though when I write of Irish literature I mean something written and intended to be read, I do not think we shall

understand it unless we appreciate the considerable part taken in
its composition and preservation by men whose memories were
as highly trained as was the intellect of Eriugena.

One effect of this oral tradition was particularly regrettable.
The development of the memory at the expense of the intelligence
paralyses the critical faculty, since the critical faculty depends as
much on what it forgets as on what it remembers. The mass of
information that was fed into the memory of an Irishman of the
professional classes could produce nothing but a brainstorm.
Psychologists call that sort of brainstorm rationalization. There is
a minor form of rationalization to which the Irish were particularly
addicted — that of false etymology. They may have learned it
originally from Isidore of Seville, but they made their own of it
and carried it to fantastic extremes.

The etymologies in the ninth-century handbook that Thurneysen
was reviewing are a good example of what I mean.

> Masculine gender is, however, *added* gender, or it is *true*
> gender, or it is '*goodman* gender' or it is *male* gender, or it is
> *manly* gender or it is *better than the woman* gender, or it is
> merely *man* gender.[5]

The remarkable thing about this passage is that the writer had a
perfectly good text in front of him and yet etymologized by the
sound of the word exactly as though he had never seen it written
down. He did not bother to look at his manuscript because he
knew that manuscripts were unreliable things, always getting
burned or lost. Only what you had in your head was safe, and even
this was not as safe as it might be. According to a seventh-century
tale, which rationalized the fact that the great 'Cattle Raid of
Cooley' was an epic story so long and elaborate that no professional
story-teller could carry it in his head, Senchán Torpéist, the chief
poet, discovered to his horror that not a single poet in Ireland
knew the complete story, so he sent his two favourite students to
Brittany to see if they could pick it up there. Fortunately one of
them had the sense to pass by the grave of Fergus mac Roich, the
hero of the raid, and call up his ghost. In the space of three days

[5] George Calder, *Auraicept na nÉces*, Edinburgh, 1917.

and nights the dead hero managed to teach it to him, but it was a narrow squeak.

As a result Irish literature never had a critical apparatus. When something went wrong with a text, it did not get corrected, but was rationalized over until it established a minor mythology of its own. The example of this I have quoted to the point of boring myself is the 'childbirth sickness' that is supposed to have afflicted the Ulstermen at the time of the Connacht invasion. This was inflicted on them by the goddess Macha, the Ulster Epona, after they had forced her to race against the king's horses while she was pregnant. The two different legends have become fused by a rationalization and a false etymology. There was no 'childbirth sickness'; the Ulstermen were merely attending a *noinden* — a *nundinae*, which means a holiday gathering — at Emain Machae, but the Latin word was forgotten, and the professional men invented secondary stories on the assumption that *noinden* was really *noídiu*, 'a baby', and reasoned that the Ulstermen were being punished for their impiety to Epona. Later story-tellers took it farther and promoted the Roman holiday to the rank of a war goddess, and even today there are scholars who explain it as a Celtic form of *couvade*, a sort of lying-out hospital for married men.

There is one further remarkable thing about this class, which is that it seems to have been completely supra-tribal and that its members moved freely from kingdom to little kingdom. The facts of this are not in dispute, though the machinery is not easy to understand. From the ninth-century 'Liadan and Cuirithir' it would seem that a Connacht poet going to Munster would pack his poet's uniform in his bag and remove the heads from his spears, while from the contemporary 'Boyish Feats of Cú Chulainn' one would gather that a frontier guard would escort him to the king's residence. The reason that suggests itself for this extra-territoriality is that the country was so thinly populated that few of the tribes could support a group of professional men, but there may be another explanation.

From the very beginning we are faced with a contradiction which seems to call for some such explanation. Politically the country was anarchic, but culturally it was quite homogeneous, more so than Europe in the eighteenth century. Though we know we are dealing with scores of tribes, with different races, perhaps even with different languages, so far as the professional classes are concerned there is only one nationality — Irish, whatever that might mean at any given time — and only one language, and that without a trace of dialect.

One can only assume that the professional classes, particularly the poets, who had to move freely among the warring tribes, all subscribed to a common fiction of racial identity that changed as the dominant race changed, while everything that conflicted with this fiction was suppressed or distorted. This gave the culture immense powers of absorption. It absorbed the invasion of Ulster by the Féni in the fifth century and the rise of the O'Briens, who were not even of Irish blood and so cleverly falsified history that even today our schoolbooks echo O'Brien propaganda of the eleventh and twelfth centuries.

It even absorbed the Norman invasion, and it is amusing to watch the process at work. In the year 1213 an interesting professional poet called Murrough O'Daly had an argument with a Donegal tax-inspector and, like Christy Mahon of later times, split him with a great blow to the breeches belt. Murrough himself could see nothing unreasonable in this, but the prince of Tyrconnell thought otherwise, and Murrough had to fly. As he put it in his elegant way:

> Beag ar bhfala risin bhfear,
> Bachlach do bheith dom cháineadh,
> Mé do mharbhadh an mhoghadh,
> A Dhé, an adhbhar anfholadh?[6]

Small is my disagreement with the man; a rascal abused me and I killed the slave. God, is this matter for quarrelling?

Murrough then threw himself on the mercy of Richard de Burgo, one of the Norman invaders of Connacht, who at that time could scarcely have provided himself with a proper shelter, much less a knowledge of classical Irish. All the same Murrough addresses him and his men in good court verse as 'Foreign Gaelicized people, young, slender and well-born'. Within a generation or two the de

[6] Osborn Bergin, 'Unpublished Irish Poems, XXVI.' *Studies*, June 1924.

Burgos were as Irish as the O'Donnells were and as the O'Briens had become.

Perhaps a people whose minds dwelt so much on the past could not bear to think of it as being no better than the present; and it may be this that gives all Irish literature that characteristic note I have described as 'the backward look'. It is the characteristic that has transmitted itself best to our own times, through Moore's 'Let Erin Remember the Days of Old', Mangan's 'It was in the time, these were the days of Cahal More of the Wine-Red Hand', Magee's 'Long, long ago beyond the misty space of twice a thousand years', to Yeats' 'Caoilte tossing his burning hair and Niamh calling "Away! Come away!"'

CHAPTER TWO

The Beginning of Poetry

An oral tradition is necessarily valueless for literature, but becomes of enormous potential value when it comes into contact with a literary tradition, however rudimentary, because the literary tradition may act as a precipitant. The precipitate is almost bound to have the quality of one of the great primary literatures, like Hebrew or Greek. Later I shall have to discuss what a primary literature is, but for the present it will be enough if I try to illustrate in the work of Thomas Hardy what I mean by the effect of a precipitant. The oral tradition in Hardy is not a very ancient one, nor, I should say, very rich. The written element in his work is inadequate — a jumble of Victorian music-hall songs, novelettes, and melodrama — but in a novel like *The Mayor of Casterbridge* the tradition that a man is entitled to sell his wife submerges the inadequacy of the precipitant and gives us a story that is closer to Greek drama than to the fiction of Trollope.

The literary tradition that acted as precipitant for the oral tradition in Ireland was imported by Christian missionaries in the fifth century, and I doubt if it was much more adequate than the literary tradition Thomas Hardy inherited. Perhaps, to be an effective precipitant, a literary tradition should not be really adequate, for if it were it might take over entirely as Latin seems to have done from Gaulish.

What the missionaries brought to Ireland was a book and the language in which they believed the book was written. By comparison with anything the Irish knew it represented historical truth and ascertained fact, and to depart from these was to be guilty of error — about the only sort of error an educated Irishman could commit, so far as I know. There might be a dozen different accounts of the death of an Irish god, but there could only be one of the death of Christ — how often Irish professional men must have felt they could have written it better themselves.

One might also play about with Irish and invent twenty-five

different cases for the noun and scholarly names to suit them, such as neglective, desidative, fundative, privative, comitative, ascensive, augmentative, ingressive, depositive, parentative, progenitive, circumdative, and trespassive, but you had to be careful with Latin. Partly this was because it was the key to the Holy Scriptures, but besides that it was the only access to the outer, non-Irish world, as English is to us today. It may be significant that the two great periods of Irish literature coincide with the acquisition of a secondary language and the emigration of considerable numbers of the educated classes.

We know very little of the early history of the written tradition. When St. Patrick died, somewhere about the year 500, the episcopal Church that the earlier Roman missionaries and himself had established was breaking up, and its place was being taken by a monastic Church. This was not because the Irish were naturally attracted to the monastic ideal, but because an episcopal Church in a tribal society was a contradiction in terms. No tribe, however small or weak, would accept the authority of a bishop from another tribe; but with a monastic organization, each tribe could have its own monastery, and the larger ones could have as many as they pleased.

One of the best-founded traditions of the early Church was that of the 'white martyrdom', death in exile, which to the poor Irishman meant some outlandish place like Armagh or Lismore. Some exquisite corrupt lines from a poem in Old Irish specify the agony.

> Abb anfine fort,
> Ingnás do chineóil duit co lá th'éco,
> Úir aineóil tarat i forcend do shéto.[1]

The abbot of a strange tribe over you; estrangement from your family to the day of your death and foreign earth over you at the end of your road.[1]

In the same way the Church was given its proper place within the framework of the oral law. Churchmen were treated exactly as though they were poets or druids, and we need scarcely be

[1] W. Stokes, *On the Calendar of Oengus* (RIA MSS, series i, Dublin, 1880), CLXXXV.

surprised if they soon began to act like poets and druids. It was an unsatisfactory compromise, because the Church's tradition was literary, that of the professional classes oral; the Church's outlook was international, and that of the professional classes national (and even this national outlook was, as I have said, a mere fiction); the Church, in theory at least, was democratic, while the professional classes were organized in a tight, hereditary caste system. Of course, by the eighth century the Church itself had become a hereditary profession, and it was as unnatural for a priest's son not to be a priest as it was for a poet's son not to be a poet.

The best illustration of this development is Zimmer's account, quoted in Bergin and Best's edition of the Book of the Dun Cow, of the genealogy of Mael Muire, its principal scribe, who was killed in Clonmacnois cathedral in the year 1106. It seems that in the year 753 Gorman, Abbot of Louth, a subsidiary of Armagh, earned the 'white martyrdom' in Clonmacnois. His family still retained its claim on Armagh, and his son, Torbach, died as Abbot of Armagh in 807. Torbach had a son called Aedagán, who, like his grandfather, was Abbot of Louth. He died in 834. At this point the family reverts to Clonmacnois, for Aedagán had a son called Eogan, who was an anchorite of Clonmacnois and died in 845. His son, Luchairén, was a scribe and anchorite who died in 863, and Luchairén's son, Égertach, died in 893 as Superior of Little Church in Clonmacnois — the tiny church, now represented by the remains of a stone building, which covered the grave of St. Cíarán. He had a son called Dúnchad, Bishop of Clonmacnois, who died in 953, and Dúnchad had one called Joseph, a confessor, who died in 1022. Joseph's son was Conn the Almoner; Conn had one called Célechar, the bishop who died in 1067, and Célechar's son was our hero, Mael Muire. If further information is required, Mael Muire's uncle, Mael Chíaráin, was the abbot who in 1070 paved the two streets in Clonmacnois, parts of which one can still see.

Zimmer was perfectly right in saying that Mael Muire was 'in the line of a great tradition', but I think it would be even more correct to say that he was a member of a most extraordinary branch of the Catholic Church. By the eighth century it had already become a hereditary profession, and Clonmacnois was sometimes at open war with other monasteries — like Birr and

Durrow. At the same time we begin to hear of a reform movement originating in Tallaght and Clondalkin, the Céli Dé, who
referred contemptuously to the 'old churches' and the 'lax
churches'.

This reform must have sprung from the Romanist party of the
seventh century. The Romanists and the people of the older foundations disagreed about the form of tonsure and the dating of Easter,
but this is rather like saying that the Irish Civil War began from
an argument about the Treaty versus Document Number Two. The
real differences, I should say, concerned the question of how far
the Church was to be absorbed by the tribal system. The Romanists
were persecuted by the people of the old foundations; some emigrated, and others, expelled from their monasteries, established
themselves in remote places like the islands. We know that
St. Mo Chota was expelled from the Columban monastery of
Durrow, and on Aran there is a tombstone to the 'VII Romani',
which has given rise to a lot of speculation. I do not think these
were seven Roman priests who dropped in on Aran and liked the
climate, nor do I think the gravestone commemorates the seven
martyred sons of St. Symphorosa. They were probably seven
Romanist monks, expelled from their own monastery, who had
attended to the decree of the so-called 'Second Synod of St.
Patrick' with its moving reflection on the plight of the Irish intellectual in all ages.

One's own country is to be instructed first, after the example
of Our Lord, and later, if this does not succeed, to be abandoned,
after the example of the Apostle. But he who can succeed, even
if he imperil himself, shall teach and show himself everywhere;
and he who cannot, let him be silent and depart.

In those times, nevertheless, the situation must have been more
fluid and the Church more powerful. Its numbers were increased
by British refugees from the Anglo-Saxon invasions and later by
the Anglo-Saxons themselves, and fifty years after St. Patrick's
death we begin to read of shiploads of students arriving from
abroad. The bigger monasteries had developed schools which
became very popular; they were influential, and by the standards

of Irish economics enormously wealthy — too wealthy for their own good and too weak for their own wealth, because material standards still continued to be low. Until the tenth century the monasteries were built entirely of timber. Irish does not even have a word for 'mason', and though carpentry was a well-organized craft the native laws do not recognize the existence of stone buildings.

By comparison with the churchmen, the professional poets, the *filid*, were weaker than they ever were in the later Middle Ages. We read that because of their numbers and rapacity they would have been expelled from Ireland at the Convention of Drom Cet in 575, and though this is no more than a legend set going by clerical propagandists, it represents a historic fact. The powerful monastery schools with their infinitely superior system of education presented the poets with a challenge they could not meet, and it was not a challenge only to their intellectual abilities, but to their claim to supernatural powers, their power to curse and bless. Their children and grandchildren, as well as studying in the old type of school, now had a further education in the monastery schools, like the sons of an old-fashioned bone-setter who study surgery. Within a century or so the churchmen were blessing and cursing as hard as themselves.

We can actually watch this process at work in a few fragments by Colmán mac Léníni, who died in the year 604 as Abbot of Cloyne in County Cork. St. Colmán began life as a professional poet, and the seven scraps of his verse that have been collected by Thurneysen are both secular and religious. Thurneysen is almost certainly correct when he treats the secular verse as early work and accepts the tradition that Colmán underwent conversion.

We see that he was a professional poet accustomed to memorize his verse because it contains chain alliteration — that is to say, for mnemonic purposes he makes the last word of each line alliterate with the first word of the next — in later verse this would be the first *stressed* word. With the formal 'conclusion', which repeats the first word of the poem as its last, and (in longer lines) interior alliteration, he had as good a check as one can have on the correctness of his performance. His poems also contain rhyme, a recent invention of the British or Irish schools. The rhyming is by consonantal groups so carefully distinguished that no modern student of phonetics can better them. This probably began with Latin hymns, for the Latin case-endings were a natural invitation to the rhymester, but even in these phonetic rhyme is the rule rather than the exception.

> *Benchuir bona regúla,*
> *Recta atque divina,*
> *Stricta, sancta, sedúla,*
> *Summa, justa, ac mira.*

> *Munter Benchuir beata,*
> *Fide fundata certa,*
> *Spe salutis ornata,*
> *Caritate perfecta.*

Except from the point of view of a metrist or a historian of literature the fragments of Colmán are of no great interest, and one will do as example. It is from a professional poem in praise of a sword given him as fee by a prince called Domnall, who later became King of Tara.

> *Luin oc elaib,*
> *Ungi oc dírnaib,*
> *Drecha ban n-aithech*
> *Oc ródaib rígnaib;*
> *Ríg oc Domnall,*
> *Dord oc aidbse*
> *Adand oc caindil,*
> *Calg oc mo chailg-se.*[2]

Blackbirds compared with swans, ounces with hundredweights, peasant women's faces with great queens; kings compared with Domnall, yodelling with a choir, a spark compared with a candle is every sword compared with my sword.

Colmán went to school in the second half of the sixth century in the great period of the monastic schools and during the lifetime of St. Colum Cille. A contemporary of his was Dallán Forgaill, who

[2] *Zeitschrift für celtische Philologie,* XIX, 198.

wrote an elegy on Colum Cille's death in 595. Dallán would seem to have been more a traditionalist than Colmán, and, but for the first few lines, the elegy uses alliteration, not rhyme. One would assume that Dallán had not attended a monastery school, for, though his poem is every bit as dull as Colmán's, it is infinitely more tortuous and obscure.

The rampart of Niall is not silent. The great sorrow is not the lamentation of a single plain. A great cry hard to endure is the story when you tell that Colum is without life, without a church. How shall a fool tell of him, even Nera? The prophet of God sitting at the right hand of the God of Sion now lives no more. He does not abide with us. Our sage who has been hidden from us is no help to the soul. He who protected the living is dead. He has gone from us in death who was our leader in time of necessity. He has gone from us in death who was our messenger to the Lord.[3]

Colmán seems to be a link between the professional poetry of the sixth century and that of the seventh, when Irish poetry may really be said to begin. I want to quote you some verses of another poem on St. Colum Cille written — if my identification of a personal name in it is correct — within a couple of years of the Synod of Whitby in 664.

> Fo réir Choluim céin ad-fías
> Find for nime snáidsium secht;
> Sét fri úathu úair no tías
> Ní cen toísech, táthum nert.
>
> Nípu fri coilcthi tincha
> Tindscain airnaidi cassa;
> Crochais, nípu i cinta,
> A chorp for tonna glassa.[4]

While I proclaim myself under the obedience of Colum, may the hero escort me over the seven heavens; when I tread the path of terrors it is not without a leader — I have strength.

It was not on soft beds that he undertook hard vigils; it was not for his sins that he crucified his body on the blue waves.

[3] Quoted by Myles Dillon: *Early Irish Literature* (Chicago, 1948), 172-3.
[4] *GT*, 19.

The syntax of the second line — 'Hero over heavens may he escort me seven' — is that of archaic Irish without the definite article and the conjunction *ocus* (and), and there is the same sort of tentative rhyming that we find in Colmán mac Léníni, that is to say the poet uses perfect rhyme when it comes naturally (which a later poet might have regarded as inartistic), but compromises on a phonetic rhyme when he cannot. In the Bangor hymn the poet rhymes *certa* and *perfecta*, and our author rhymes *secht* (*sept-em*) and *nert*. But he is very much the professional, terrified that he will dry up in the middle of his beautiful poem, and he provides not only chain alliteration but internal alliteration as well.

But while the elegy on St. Colum Cille is merely of local and historic interest, this is the most beautiful of Irish hymns. Professor Greene has not completed his edition, and through some of it I have had to guess my way. I have also had to cheat by using a word to suggest 'Irish', which would have meant nothing whatever to the writer, because when he wrote the professional poets had not yet fully faked the history of the invasion of Ulster by the Tara dynasty and provided the Ulaid with a respectable Irish ancestry. Colum Cille was one of the ruling family of the invaders; the poet belonged to the same race, and the Columban monastery where it was sung must have been as carefully segregated as an Irish kindergarten today.

> Let me, while in Colum's care,
>   Be guarded by the heavenly throng;
> When I tread the path of fear,
>   I have a leader, I am strong.

> It was not on beds of down
>   That Colum learned what heals and saves,
> And not for sin he crucified
>   His body on the blue sea waves.

> In Iona as of right
>   He claimed his marvellous estate;
> In more ways than man has thought
>   God has made him fortunate.

The lone man's strength, the army's might,
  The weak one safe within his ward,
Our fortress and our victory
  We stand secure in Colum's guard.

He conquered in the wars with lust
  And lit a flame that shall not dim;
Well-famed, well-born, and doubly blest
  The mother who once shrieked for him.

Happy, numerous, and safe
  Whirlwinds swept his curraghs home;
Colum, candle of the Gael,
  None like him was ever known.

Priests with angelic energy,
  His sturdy crew, he swept along;
Though they were deaf he gave them ears
  Though they were weak he made them strong.

His sailors stopped above the Glen,
  Colum's crew, that famous band;
They journeyed far, he was their feet,
  They laboured hard, he was their hand.

Men and women of his race
  Share in his blessings stored away;
They have a leader, they are free;
  On the dark path they know the way.

Ireland he left and all besides,
  In ships traversed the home of whales,
A fearless sailor, ruled the tides,
  Flouted the billows with his sails.

He fought the battles of the flesh,
  He studied wisdom with the wise,
Stiffened and sewed the peaks of sails,
  Seaborne, with heaven for a prize. . . .

Even in an unsatisfactory verse translation I think the reader can feel how with the third line the poem becomes airborne. The poet knew it as well for those beautiful lines—

> *Sét fri úathu úair no tías*
> *Ní cen toísech, táthum nert. . . .*

—are repeated in the loveliest of echoes:

> *Ní cen toísech, táthus soer,*
> *Sét fri temel, táthus cíall.*

They are not without a leader; they are free. On the shadowy path they have a sign.

By the middle of the seventh century at least Irish poetry was beginning to discover itself.

CHAPTER THREE

Early Irish Story-telling

We can be sure of one thing about the literature of any primitive people : poetry will come before prose because prose — the literary medium, not the stylized, simplified medium of the folk-story — cannot be memorized.

The history of Irish prose is very significant in this way. There was little or none before the year 700; in the eighth and ninth centuries there was a very good narrative prose; by the tenth or eleventh century this was beginning to give place to the clumsy rhetoric of the later stories; and after the year 1200 there is no prose worth discussing.

Writing in Irish almost certainly began in the way we find it in the continental glosses — as a student's notes of what the professor said some particular passage in Scripture meant. It was probably continued by lawyers who wrote down the laws as they remembered them. Judgments and precedents were originally delivered in archaic Irish verse; they may have been written down as early as the sixth century, and they must have come as a shock to their transcribers, who can only have had vague notions of what they meant. By the year 700 the lawyers had begun to translate them into prose, as we see from a text like the 'Judgments of Blood-lyings', where in the last few pages the legal scholar tires of translating and reverts to archaic verse.[1]

This is how the great early stories must have come into being. Clearly there was some way of telling stories before the eighth-century elaboration of prose, and it is doubtful if this was in the medium of the folk-story. It was probably in verse, either in the standard seven-syllable alliterative verse that was a sort of metrical Jack-of-all-trades with the professional classes or in the free alliterative verse that we find used for dramatic speeches in the earliest stories. Story-tellers may have used both.

At any rate, some time in the seventh century someone composed

[1] D. A. Binchy, *Eriu*, XII, 1.

the first draft of a story now called 'The Cattle Raid of Cooley', that was more ambitious than anything that had so far been attempted in Ireland. We can deduce this from one of those legends which are merely rationalizations of historic facts. When Senchán Torpéist, the principal poet of Ireland, discovered that none of the poets knew 'The Cattle Raid' in full he sent two of his students, Émine and Muirgein, to Brittany to see if they could discover it there. On the way they halted at the gravestone of Fergus mac Roich and Muirgein invoked Fergus' aid. A cloud covered him, and for three nights and days Fergus' ghost recounted the story of the raid.

Now of course the story had not been lost; it was merely a text too long and complicated for the ordinary reciter and had to be written down. There is a further historical fact to be deduced from the legend which I shall have to revert to — that the hero of the original story was not Cú Chulainn, but Fergus mac Roich.

'The Cattle Raid' is a simply appalling text, which I cannot fully read much less interpret, but I have chosen to discuss it first because it has been endlessly scribbled over and accordingly illustrates the development of Irish prose literature from the seventh to the twelfth century. It is a task better suited to an archaeologist than a literary critic, because it is like an excavation that reveals a dozen habitation sites. Some I cannot identify at all, but I think I can isolate a seventh-century sub-stratum in archaic verse; an eighth-century rendering of this in good narrative prose, which more or less corresponds with what the lawyers were trying to do at the same time with the chanted laws; definitely there is a ninth-century layer, very elegant, but less vigorous than the earlier strata; and finally, as the influence of the Norse invasions becomes felt, there is a recrudescence of the oral element, and the narrative prose tends to disintegrate into bombast. The text is a history of Irish literature in the early Middle Ages, which is all the more impressive because it is haphazard and unintentional, and buried under those layers of different centuries is something that was once regarded as a masterpiece.

It is very far from being a masterpiece now. It is a tedious, rambling account of how Medb, Queen of Connacht, accompanied by Ulster exiles under Fergus mac Roich, invaded Ulster in wintertime in quest of a famous bull, the Brown Bull of Cooley, and of how the Ulster hero Cú Chulainn defended the province single-handed while the Ulstermen were in their 'childbirth sickness'. It would seem to be part of the mass of Ulster legends which, according to the various editions of the elegy for St. Colum Cille, was recorded by the poets of Ireland at a spot near Newry at the instance of a King of the Ulaid, a race which by this time had been effectively crushed by the Uí Néill invaders from Leinster.

T. F. O'Rahilly pointed out that the Ulster sagas describe the historical circumstances of the invasion, but this the professional poets entirely ignored. The fiction of racial identity was too strong among them. They slipped up badly when they made Medb Queen of Connacht, for the Irish tribes, unlike the British ones, did not have queens, and Medb was anyhow the tutelary goddess of Tara. (Something similar seems to have happened to the traditions of that other non-Gaelic race that occupied Leinster, because the cycle of legends we associate with Fionn mac Cumhaill are very like the legendary history of the Lagin.)

This had a peculiar effect on the development of the sagas, because by the year 700 the tribal hero of the beaten Ulaid was being taken over as the national hero of Ireland. Still stranger, St. Patrick, who, as D. A. Binchy suggests, was almost certainly the tribal saint of the Ulaid, was being taken over as the national saint in place of the great Uí Néill saint, Colum Cille. This is an extraordinary shift of emphasis for which the historical reasons are anything but clear. We must, of course, remember that Emain Machae, the capital of the Ulaid, which was probably destroyed by the Uí Néill about the middle of the fifth century, is supposed to be Navan Fort, only two miles from Armagh, which is traditionally associated with St. Patrick. But this itself involves a good deal of mystery, because Armagh is a place we never read of in the sagas, exactly as though it were a foundation of St. Patrick, though the fort itself is identical with that at Navan, and within the enclosure has been found a big collection of prehistoric sculpture — four statues of someone I take to be Lug; two of a horned god, presumably Conall Cernach, the Ulster Cernunnos; one of Macha; and some figures that look like animal gods. These can scarcely be later than the fourth century; but why do we not hear of Armagh in the fourth century? Is it perhaps that Emain Machae, which means 'The Twins of Macha', is a general term applied to the twin forts of Armagh?

I must also refer back to the story of Senchán Torpéist and his students. If 'The Cattle Raid of Cooley' at that time was anything like the story we know, why did Muirgein not go to Cú Chulainn's grave rather than to Fergus'? I see no possible explanation except that Cú Chulainn was not the real hero of the original story and did not begin to emerge as such until the eighth century. Now, as it happens, the very oldest layer one can identify, which can scarcely have been composed after the seventh century, is in the still un-translated passages of chant in which the principal characters seem to be Medb, her husband, Ailill, and her lover, Fergus mac Roich.

But if the saga has suffered distortion from a change of hero it has suffered worse from a change of theme. Thurneysen was led astray by a few minor echoes of the *Aeneid* into thinking the original author had Virgil in mind. If he had anything in mind it was more likely to have been the Book of Judges. Fergus' name, 'Manly Energy Son of Stallion', shows that he was originally a fertility god and a suitable substitute for Samson, as Medb, whose name means 'Drunkenness', would have been for Delilah.

This, of course, is mere guess-work, but what is certain is that the purpose of the original author would seem to have been to warn his readers against women, particularly women in positions of authority. Look at what happens to people and armies when they are in a woman's power! he seems to say. Medb's husband is a complaisant cuckold who allows her to start a military campaign so that she can say her property is equal to his. And her lover, Fergus, is a traitor to his own people. 'A woman of ill counsel', he calls her in his last, contemptuous speech, and the real subject of 'The Cattle Raid' can be best described in the title of another work by a great hater of queens, John Knox's *Monstrous Regiment of Women*.

But at once we run into real difficulty. If this story deals with prehistoric Ireland it deals with a period when women had no legal rights at all. The change in the laws that permitted women to have property of equal value with their husbands' can hardly have taken place before the seventh century, and then only because the ecclesiastical families had daughters who became abbesses and who had to be able to inherit property and enter into contracts. Accordingly I can only assume that in spite of its archaic air 'The Cattle Raid' deals with a contemporary situation about which the author had strong feelings.

For the same reason I have to disagree with Thurneysen and other scholars on a second point. The earliest version of 'The Cattle Raid' has lost its opening scenes; the later version in the Book of Leinster has a delightful though garrulous opening in which Medb and Ailill quarrel in bed about the extent of their respective possessions. This is in the Irish of the eleventh century, so Thurneysen regards it as an accretion. So does Professor Greene, though he does admit that when he prepared a version of the saga for broadcasting he felt bound to make use of it. This suggests that scholars who are also men of letters should trust their instincts, because there is no doubt in my mind that this is the original opening.

'It's a true word, girl,' said Ailill, 'that a good man's wife is a lucky woman.'

'True enough,' said Medb. 'What do you mean?'

'I mean you are better off now than you were the day I married you,' said Ailill.

'Ah, I was well enough off before,' said Medb.

'Little I heard or knew of it,' said Ailill, 'except that you were a dependent woman, and the enemies in the lands adjoining yours were stealing and plundering from you.'[2]

The argument as to how well off each of them is continues, but in the accounting Medb loses, because her property has been lessened by the defection of a famous bull, who, scorning to be dependent on a woman, has gone over to her husband's herd. The meaning of this is perfectly clear, because this is what Medb accuses her husband of being, 'dependent on a woman'. The bull has more self-respect than he.

As there is only one better bull in Ireland and that in Ulster, Medb sends a messenger called Mac Roth to get the loan of it for a year, offering, among other rewards, her 'thigh friendship' to the

[2] R. I. Best, O. Bergin, and M. A. O'Brien, *Book of Leinster* (Dublin, 1954), II, 261.

owner. When the owner refuses to give up the bull, Medb has no choice but to undertake a campaign against Ulster. 'There is no need to polish the knots, Mac Roth,' she says in her stately way, 'since I knew that what was not freely given would have to be taken by force; and by force it shall be taken.' I suspect that in this version Mac Roth is really Fergus mac Roich (Mac Roth occurs in no other story known to me), and that he is deliberately humiliated by having to offer the use of his mistress' bed to another man; but there is no mistaking here the rancorous anti-feminist irony that occurs again and again through the story.

Having tried to give the saga back its original opening, we can pass to the earlier text. The first eighteen lines of this are a conventional 'muster' of three battalions of the Connacht hosting. As the first two battalions ride by, Medb says: 'It is not Cormac yet.' It is a typical bit of random interpolation by a dim-witted editor who for some reason felt that Cormac Connlongas, 'Head of the Exiles', was not getting his fair share of the limelight, and whose clumsy duplications occur in other parts of the story.

The next two sections describe Medb's search for omens, and it is in the first of these that Thurneysen finds his echo of the *Aeneid*. The second is merely a verse translation by the gentleman I identify as the 'Bad Poet'. His work is late and *very* bad. But Episode 4 is a different matter altogether, and we are definitely back to the original theme with its cynicism and anti-feminist irony. The Connacht hosting has reached a place called Cúl Sibrinne where Medb reviews the quality of her forces. Originally the scene seems to have described a supper party at which Medb and Ailill sat down with Fergus and Finnabair, the king's daughter, who is being offered as sexual bait to anyone who can help in the raid, but the author of Interpolation 1 insisted on introducing his favourite Cormac Connlongas again.

A quarrel blows up at supper when Medb declares that the whole hosting may as well stay at home if the Leinster contingent — the Gaileóin — is permitted to go.

'What is wrong with the men?' asked Ailill.
'There is nothing wrong with them,' said Medb. 'They are splendid fellows. While the rest were making camp, they had

thatched theirs and cooked their food. When the rest were eating, they had finished their meal and had their harpers playing. It is foolish for them to go. They will seize all the credit for the victory.'

'Well, they are fighting on our side,' said Ailill.

'They are not coming with us,' said Medb.

'Very well,' said Ailill. 'They can stay behind.'

'They will not stay behind,' said Medb. 'They will only attack us from the rear and steal our land from us.'

'What are we to do with them so?' asked Ailill. 'Since it is a matter of indifference to us whether they come or go.'

'Kill them!' said Medb.

'It is no use pretending that that is not a woman's advice,' said Ailill. 'You are being silly.'[3]

Apart altogether from the characteristically harsh tone of the scene we can judge that this is part of the original story because the 'woman's advice' that Medb gives is one of the taunts repeated against her in the archaic verse. She is 'a woman of ill counsel'.

The quarrel grows noisier when Fergus points out that the Gaileóin are under his command and with the aid of the Munster contingent he can protect them from massacre. He suggests as a compromise that the Gaileóin be split up between his own contingent and that of the Munstermen. This is agreed to, but the only result is that next day, when a hundred and sixty deer are roused, all but five are killed by the Gaileóin. Thurneysen may be right when he suggests that the author was a Leinsterman, though I have doubts of this because the Gaileóin, like the 'woman of ill counsel', are part of the archaic verse scenes; but to make too much of it is to miss the significance of what the story-teller is really saying, which is not that Leinstermen are ten times as smart as other people, but that this sort of thing is only what you can expect when you allow a woman to direct an army.

This episode is followed by one which Thurneysen identifies as a duplicate of another, later passage, and is mainly in verse. But with Episode 6 we seem to be back again to something like the original theme. This is where we find the peculiar incident in which Cú Chulainn, having been warned of the invasion by Fergus,

[3] J. Strachan and J. G. O'Keeffe, *Táin Bó Cúailnge* (Dublin, 1912), 8.

goes off to spend the night with Feidelm Noichride at Tara. In this little scene we may have the original historic core of the story — the tradition of some marcher lord from Dundalk who failed to go to the November *nundinae* at Emain Machae because he was spending the night with a girl on the enemy side, so that he was able to learn the invaders' plans and intercept them. But in the story as we now have it this incident is treated in a remarkable way. Fergus, out of old loyalty to Ulster, has betrayed the Connacht plans to Cú Chulainn and led the hosting astray; but instead of taking advantage of this, Cú Chulainn spends the night with a woman. Next morning he says, 'I wish I had not gone there or betrayed the Ulstermen', so Ulster is doubly betrayed, each time because of a woman of light behaviour. Is it possible that this repetition of a theme is really accidental and not a deliberate emphasizing of the story-teller's dislike of loose women?

Then, while the Connacht hosting is halted by Cú Chulainn, the Ulster exiles tell the Connacht chiefs the story of his 'Boyish Feats'. The writing in this section is exceedingly literary; the 'he saids' and 'she saids' are distributed with the mincing precision of a lady novelist ('He has not', said June calmly, lighting a Turkish cigarette, 'yet arrived.') and the long flashback is a purely humanist device beyond the ability and perhaps the interest of the original story-teller. I am certain that Thurneysen is wrong in regarding this interlude as part of the original story; it cannot be anything but the work of an independent author who was also something of a student of classical literature, and at no time could it have been transmitted orally, as Thurneysen assumes the whole story was. A flashback would never have been preserved by professional story-tellers through independent versions, and there are little naturalistic touches like 'This took place in the presence of Bricriu here' and 'I met him in the doorway of the fort after I had been badly wounded', which would not have lasted an hour in any sort of oral version.

In spite of the barbaric fantasy that disfigures his work, the author of this section (whom I call the 'Prose Writer' to distinguish him from the 'Poet' of the archaic verse and the 'Bad Poet' of the later doggerel) was a deliberate and selfconscious artist of the greatest ability. As Professor Greene says with perfect truth: 'These stories, extraneous though they may be to the action of the "Táin" . . . came to form an integral part of it — indeed, to modern taste, by far the most attractive part.'⁴ The Prose Writer had a powerful imagination and the ability to fix it in unforgettable pictorial sequences. His pictures are those of a child: he has no sense of perspective or scale and draws the dog bigger than the man and the man bigger than the house, but the child has genius; the impression is conveyed. The picture of the little boy, Cú Chulainn, leaving his home to cross the mountains to Emain Machae, pucking his ball, tossing his hurley after it, and his dart after both, and then running to catch them before they fall is the picture of every small boy in the world setting out on the great adventure of existence.

All the same — let us be quite clear on this — the Prose Writer *was* a child, and he was handling material that no child, however brilliant, could comprehend. What he produces is very like the *Iliad* as it might have been if rewritten by Hans Christian Andersen. The original story reminds us sharply of this when it re-emerges a few pages later. Again, let us notice that the hero is Fergus.

Then Ailill said to his charioteer, Cuillius: 'Find me Medb and Fergus today. I do not know what has happened to keep them together, and I should like some indication from you.'

Cuillius went where they were in bed together, for the lovers remained behind and the warriors went on. Cuillius crept up on them, and they did not hear the man. It happened that Fergus' sword was near him. Cuillius drew it from its sheath and left the sheath empty. Cuillius went to Ailill.

'Well?' asked Ailill.

'Well!' said Cuillius. 'You know what this token means. As you suspected, that is how I found them — in bed together.'

Then they laughed at one another.

'That is all right,' said Ailill. 'She has to do it; she did it to get his help on the raid. Mind the edge of the sword,' added Ailill. 'Put it under your seat in the chariot with a linen cloth round it.'

Fergus rose to take his sword.

'Oh!' he cried.

'What ails you?' asked Medb.

⁴ Myles Dillon (ed.), *Irish Sagas* (Dublin, 1959), 104.

'A bad turn I did Ailill,' he said. 'Wait here till I go to the wood, and do not wonder how long I may be.' It happened that Medb did not know of the loss of the sword. [Fergus] went out with his charioteer's sword in his hand and made himself a wooden sword in the wood. .

'Let us go on after the others,' said Fergus.

All their contingents met in the plain. Their tents were set up. Fergus was invited by Ailill to play chess. When Fergus went to his tent Ailill began to make fun of him.[5]

This passage introduces the archaic verse scene that is in an Irish so difficult that no one has attempted to translate it yet, which is an embarrassment, because clearly it is one of the central scenes of the original story and reduces most of what has preceded it to the irrelevance and interpolation it almost certainly is. Where the greatest of scholars have given up, it is hardly for a literary man to fill the gap, but so far as I can follow the action, Fergus seems to be still full of premonitions of disaster, referring darkly to the loss of his sword, the threat to the Leinstermen, and the evil counsel of Medb. Ailill lightly reassures him about the sword and about the danger from light women, and then, as they begin to make the first moves in the game of chess, he seems to be mocking him about his possible marriage to Finnabair and his secret affair with Medb. Medb reproves him and reminds him that he is a brave, just, generous man. The archaic verse continues into an argument on the following morning in which Medb mistakenly wishes to force the cattle and women ahead, and Fergus insists that he and the Ulster exiles shall take the lead, along with the cattle, the hosting behind and the woman behind them, but the point is not clear to me. What *is* clear is that the details referred to in the verse — the threat to the Leinstermen at Cúl Sibrinne, the theft of Fergus' sword, and the folly of Medb — are all integral parts of the original story. The sword that Fergus has lost is variously described as 'the sword of Leti', 'the Belgic sword' (or, in the verse, 'Macha', after the Epona of the Ulstermen), but it would seem to be analogous to Samson's loss of his hair, which in one called 'Manly Energy Son of Stallion' can only refer to castration.

This scene is now almost lost in a jungle of accretions, but we

[5] Strachan and O'Keeffe, *Táin Bó Cúailnge*, 35.

can see how it is picked up later in the story when Fergus, armed with nothing but a wooden sword, is shamed into attacking his foster-son, Cú Chulainn. He promises Cú Chulainn that if the young man will run from him now, he will run from Cú Chulainn on a greater occasion, thus preparing the stage for the last great scene in which the Connacht hosting is defeated. Naïve as this is, it is a very effective piece of construction, and it shows that the original 'Cattle Raid' was anything but the amorphous mass it now is.

Then comes the long, late rhetorical effusion that describes the fight between Cú Chulainn and his foster-brother, Fer Diad, which Thurneysen regards as an interpolation. 'Independent composition' would be nearer the mark, because even in this intolerable piece of rhetoric there are half a dozen lines that have all the irony and bitterness of the older tale.

> Then Fer Diad passed by Medb urinating on the floor of the tent.
> 'Are you asleep, Ailill?' she asked.
> 'No,' said Ailill.
> 'Do you hear your new son-in-law saying good-bye to you?' she asked.
> 'Is that what he is doing?' asked Ailill.
> 'It is, indeed,' said Medb, 'but I swear by what my tribe swears that the man who says good-bye will not come back on the same feet.'[6]

In spite of the work of editors who duplicated passages and etymologized every place-name, the last scenes of the story are mainly the work of the Poet, and if these are not great poetry they are grand opera in the Wagnerian manner. Fergus receives back his lost sword and rages through the Ulster lines. Cú Chulainn, who, because of his wounds, has been tied down to keep him from the battle, bursts his bandages and rushes out to meet Fergus, and Fergus, remembering his promise, flees before his foster-son and precipitates the Connacht retreat. The brutal irony of the penultimate scene was too much for the Clonmacnois scribes who omitted it altogether, but we learn from the Book of Leinster version that Medb, as the hosting retreated, began to menstruate and that Fergus

[6] Strachan and O'Keeffe, *Táin Bó Cúailnge*, 87.

was forced to fight a rearguard action to protect her. Later she excuses herself to Fergus by blaming the defeat on 'feuds and factions', but Fergus in a few final lines of verse retorts that 'this is only natural in a drove of horses led by a mare'.

The Connachtmen succeed in driving the Ulster bull back with them, and then the real battle takes place — the battle of the two virilities, the undefeatable bulls. After fighting for a day and night in a Roscommon lake, the Ulster bull emerges triumphant with the wreck of the Connacht bull on his horns, and as he passes, home-sick and dying on his lonely journey across Ireland, he tosses the fragments of the Connacht bull to the four quarters and drops dead on the frontier of his native land.

It is one of the great climaxes of literature. Nowhere else in literature that I know has war been so vividly imaged; yet some sort of murderous irony pursues irony: *Gulliver's Travels* is a favourite children's book; *Ulysses* is becoming the last refuge of crossword-puzzle fiends; and only very serious linguists will ever be able to penetrate properly the jungle of 'The Cattle Raid of Cooley'.

CHAPTER FOUR

Primary Literature

Oral tradition is almost timeless. Thirty years ago I had an opportunity of testing this for myself. I went with a historian friend to a Longford cottage where there was an old man who had traditions of the French invasion of 1798. He had heard them from his grandfather, who had been a boy at the time, and they were extraordinarily factual, exactly like the stories Thomas Hardy had heard in Dorset about the Napoleonic wars. It interested me that when he used French names, proper or place, he usually did so with a French accent. 'Humbert they call him now, but Grandfather always said "U'ber".'

The old man's name was O'Reilly, and he turned from his account of the invasion to the story of an ancestor who had been a United Irishman, escaped from his native place, 'married a lady of title and property in the Isle of France (that's what Grandfather called it)', and 'beat Wellington off the heights over Old Saragossa'. His ancestor, I might add, was a perfectly historical figure, and has his own small place in French history. But then he went back to a seventeenth-century O'Reilly — Myles the Slasher — and according to him Myles was not killed at the Bridge of Finea, but escaped to France and was buried in a graveyard whose name I forget though it was in perfectly recognizable French. I gave up at last when he retreated to a still earlier O'Reilly who in Elizabethan times had a love affair with 'one of the Dunsanys', because what he was telling us was in fact Arnold's *Sohrab and Rustum*, Yeats' *On Baile's Strand*.

When an oral tradition like this comes into contact with a written tradition — preferably one that is not too highly developed — it may produce literature of the highest quality, autonomous and primary in the way of Greek and Hebrew literature.

When I say a literature is primary I mean that it is in the main original, not derivative, and expresses the joys and fears of man confronted with an unfamiliar universe. Only to a limited extent is

this a critical standard because neither French nor English literature is autonomous and primary, but it would be very foolish to
pretend that they were not major literatures.

At the same time there is an element of excellence in all originality. Nothing in any other literature prepares us for the shock of
the Hymn to Man in *Antigone*, even if we read it in translation
as I must do — 'There are wonderful things on earth but none more
wonderful than man.' Yet one might read the whole of Greek
literature without preparing oneself for the shock of the nineteenth
Psalm — 'The heavens declare the glory of God.' Accordingly the
test I propose for Irish literature is not the test of how far it
resembles English or French, because this is something that did
not happen until the sixteenth century, when Ireland shared in a
common Renaissance culture, but of whether or not it gives us
the same sort of shock we get from lines such as those I have
quoted — the shock of man's fundamental experience set down as
though for the first time.

Naturally we shall find that originality expressed most clearly
if we stick to the themes that are common to all primary literatures. One is the relationship of man to the mysterious universe
about him — 'An', as it blowed and blowed, I often looked up at
the sky and assed meself the question — what is the stars, what
is the stars?'

What the early Irish really thought of the stars is something we
may never know; the early missionaries did too good a job of
destruction. I know of only two stories that give any impression of
the gravity of primitive religious thought. One is 'The Voyage of
Mael Dúin', which was cleverly guyed by Tennyson; the other 'The
Wooing of Étaín', which even Tennyson would scarcely have had
the audacity to guy. It is one of the most beautiful stories in the
world and must be older than almost anything else in Irish, for
in it we see the early Celts living among the ruins of the Neolithic
civilization and wondering which gods were those who had occupied the country before them, cut down the woods, built cause-
ways across the marshes, and erected great tombs like Newgrange
for themselves.

According to 'The Wooing of Étaín' Newgrange was originally
the home of one Elcmar (does this mean 'the Evil One'?), whose

wife was called Eithne or Boann (the river Boyne which flows beside it and whose name seems to mean 'the White Cow'). She was loved by the King of Ireland, Eochaid Allfather, otherwise known as the Dagda or 'Good God', who sent Elcmar on a journey that to him appeared to last only twenty-four hours, though in reality it lasted nine months. In that time Eochaid Allfather became the lover of Boann, who bore him a son, Óengus, otherwise In Macc Óc (the 'Maponos' of British legend). Óengus was fostered by a man called Midir in County Longford, and, when he was old enough, introduced to his father, who showed him how to gain possession of Elcmar's palace of Newgrange by a trick. (The trick — borrowing the use of Newgrange for a day and a night and then claiming successfully that this means for all time — has some esoteric meaning which I cannot grasp.) Óengus woos for his foster-father the daughter of an Ulster king — Étaín Echraide, 'Aideen of the horses'. As a bride-price her father insists on the clearing of the great plains and the opening up of rivers, which Óengus, assisted by his father, achieves.

But Midir's wife, Fuamnach, strikes Étaín with a quicken-bough and turns her into a pool of water, which then turns into a worm, and finally into a fly. Fuamnach causes a wind to blow the fly away. After seven years of hardship Étaín alights on the cloak of Óengus, who causes a little bower to be made for her where she grows strong on the fragrance and bloom of herbs. But once again Fuamnach drives her off, and this time she falls into the golden cup of a woman who drinks from it and becomes pregnant with a daughter — Étaín again, but in a new incarnation.

In the second and most beautiful of the three episodes Étaín is married to Eochaid Airem, King of Tara, and his brother, Ailill Anguba, falls in love with her. When Ailill becomes ill, the physician tells him that he has one of the diseases no physician can cure — either love or jealousy. While his brother is away Ailill confesses his love to Étaín, and she agrees to become his mistress, 'not for sin or harm, but that one of the royal family of Ireland should be saved from death'. She will not deceive her husband in his own house and makes an appointment for a near-by hilltop. Ailill falls asleep at the time, but his place is taken by a man who resembles him. Finally, the stranger tells Étaín that he is her real husband of a previous incarnation, Midir, but she refuses to leave Eochaid without his own consent.

This is the theme of the third episode, in which Midir and Eochaid play chess for vast stakes and Midir loses. Once more we have a repetition of the Herculean tasks imposed on Óengus. Midir wins his final stake, which is an embrace and kiss from Étaín, in the midst of which he carries her through the roof in his arms, and they fly off in the form of swans to the fairy mound of Femuin — on Slievenamon, near Clonmel. Eochaid starts to dig up the mound and Midir offers to let Étaín return if Eochaid can recognize her. Fifty women all resembling her are sent to Tara, and Eochaid picks the one who most resembles her. It is only after he has slept with her that he realizes she is not Étaín, but Étaín's daughter, and the daughter she bears him is exposed in the manner of Oedipus and reared by a cowherd.

This story always gives me the same sort of shock, though it is not the shock I get from Greek or Hebrew literature. Clearly it is very old, and perhaps in the story of the love affair between the horse god, Eochaid, and the cow goddess, Boann, we have a legend of reconciliation between the Neolithic inhabitants and the Bronze Age invaders. As Boann is the wife of the Evil One, who is the master of the Irish Elysian Fields, and her son by Eochaid, Óengus, finally dispossesses him, it would seem as though we were also dealing with a resurrection myth. There can be no doubt that the transformation of Étaín first into a pool of water, then into a worm, and finally into a fly is a creation myth. Three doctrines seem to emerge from the legend as fundamental: the relativity of time, the relativity of matter, and the relativity of identity. All three occur again and again in Irish literature and give it a markedly subjective character.

One of the signs that it belongs to a primary literature is its reference to incest. Primitive races were obsessed by two crimes that hit tribal society at its most vulnerable point — incest and parricide, or 'kin-slaying' as the Irish preferred to call it. The shock these caused cannot have been altogether unpleasant, for heroes and even saints were frequently the children of an incestuous relationship. The exposure of Étaín's daughter by her father shows us the historical level at which we are working: the same level as that of the story of Oedipus, who committed the two unforgivable crimes.

There is one Irish story about an Oedipal situation, and it gives us the shock of an experience seen with complete freshness, as though for the first time in the world's history. Clothru, daughter of the King of Connacht, learns that her three brothers are about to kill their father and divide the kingdom between them. Since none of them has a family and she expects disaster as a result of their parricide, she sleeps with each in turn 'so that some good may come of it' as she says. Later she adds: 'Now you have done harm enough by sleeping with your sister, so do not add to it by killing your father.' As it stands, it is a simple incident not treated by any skilled story-teller, but it strikes a chord very deep in us because the author is looking at incest and parricide as no Greek or Jew had done. Incest is evil, but children are good; better that a child should not have incestuous parents, but better a child of incestuous parents than none at all!

There is a variant of the incest theme in the strange and beautiful story of Cú Chulainn and Dervorgilla. I suspect that this and portions of 'The Sick-bed of Cú Chulainn' and the preceding story are really episodes from a much longer romance, dealing with the love affairs of Cú Chulainn and his friend Lugaid of the Red Stripes — the fruit of Clothru's incest with her brothers — of which nothing much remains but the late redaction of 'The Wooing of Emer'.

Dervorgilla is a daughter of the King of Norway; she falls in love with what she has heard of Cú Chulainn and sets off for Ireland with her two handmaids in the form of swans. Cú Chulainn brings Dervorgilla down with his slingshot, and she resumes her own shape, but the stone has penetrated her belly and he has to suck it out. When she tells him that she has come to live with him, he replies, 'The belly I have sucked is not the belly I shall link with', meaning that by sucking her blood he has made her kindred. 'Give me to whom you please so', says Dervorgilla, and he gives her to his friend Lugaid.

One day at the end of winter the men make a big snowman and the women test how far each of them can urinate through it. The implication is that a woman's sexual attraction is related to the size of her bladder. Dervorgilla does not wish to compete because 'she was not lustful', but is compelled to do so and proves the best performer. Then, since the men will love only her, the women turn on her, mutilate her, and leave her dying. From a hill over Armagh Cú Chulainn and Lugaid notice that there is no smoke from her house and hurry home, but when Cú Chulainn calls to her to open the door she replies in a beautiful phrase, 'Cain bláth for ro-scarsam', which means something like 'Let us part under a flowering bough.'

Apart from stories like these, which echo old religious beliefs, we find the originality of Irish literature most often in stories of love and death. The most famous of these, the story of Derdriu, must be very old, older even than the original 'Cattle Raid', because though it is not stated directly that Fergus' reason for being with the Connacht hosting was part of his revenge for the murder of the sons of Uisliu it is clearly implied. The Derdriu story goes back to a period when the great Ulster hero was Fergus mac Roich. In fact, whether because of the difficulty of fitting him in — which would not have disturbed an Irish story-teller unduly — or because he had not yet become the principal figure in the literature, Cú Chulainn is not referred to at all. There are other peculiar features that suggest great antiquity : it seems to deal with a political and social framework that differs from that of the other stories, and does not refer to the wars of the Ulstermen with the Tara dynasty, almost as though it had taken shape before the fall of Emain Machae in the fifth century.

At bottom it is not a heroic story. Alone of the early tales it describes the crude domestic economy of an age of herdsmen; the killing of the calf in the house yard, Noísi's singing to his herds from the ramparts, the strange courtship in the language of cowboy and cowgirl, and the great climax in which Conchobar insults Derdriu in another herdboy joke. It is the only Irish story that gives us the feeling of the herds at evening, the smell of the cowdung and the herdsmen's shouts.

Once the girl's foster-father was skinning a calf on the snow outside the house in winter to cook it for her. She saw a raven drinking its blood and said to Leborcham :

'I should love a man with these three colours — hair like the raven, cheek like the blood and body like the snow.'[1]

In the next scene Noísi is singing to his cattle in the pastures below the fortress, much, I suspect, as a Texas cowboy still does to keep them from stampeding at the scent of a wild beast. When Noísi descends the wall Derdriu runs by him to attract his attention, and he pretends to believe that she is one of his herd that has strayed.

> 'That's a nice little heifer that's going by,' he says.
> 'Heifers should be big where there are no bulls,' she said.
> 'You have the bull of the province,' he said, meaning the King of Ulster.
> 'If I had my choice I'd pick a little young bull like yourself,' she said.
> 'No, not after Cathbad's prophecy,' he said.
> 'Do you mean you don't want me?'
> 'I certainly do.'
> Then she rushed at him and grabbed his two ears.
> 'Then two ears of shame and mockery on you unless you carry me off,' she said.
> 'Ah, get away, woman!' he said.
> 'You'll get it,' she said.
> Then he raised the pitch of his voice.[1]

I am assuming that what Noísi does here, again in the manner of a Texan cowboy, is to change the pitch of his tune to an alarm cry that would make the cattle turn homewards. I do not know what the grabbing of the ears means, though I fancy it refers to the old type of bull-fighting from which we get the phrase 'taking the bull by the horns'. If this is so, Derdriu is implying that Noísi, like Fergus in 'The Cattle Raid', is no bull at all. Not that it matters, for the scene is pure magic. Like the wooing of Masha in Tolstoy's *The Cossacks* it shows us a story-teller watching a pair of lovers without a single recollection of how lovers behave in the best romances. There is the same fidelity to the facts of pastoral life in the climax, which was softened and vulgarized in later redactions.

[1] V. Hull (ed.), *Longes Mac n-Uislenn*, Modern Language Association of America, 1949.

She was a year with Conchobar and never smiled and never took enough food or sleep, or raised her head from her knees.
'What do you hate most of all you see?' Conchobar asked.
'You for certain,' she said, 'and Eogan mac Durthacht.' [This was the man who had killed Noísi.]
'Then you can spend a year with Eogan,' said Conchobar.
So Conchobar passed her on to Eogan. Next day they went to the fair of Emain. She was standing behind Eogan in the chariot. She had sworn that she would never see two of her bedmates on earth at the one time.
'Aha, Derdriu!' said Conchobar. 'Between me and Eogan you look like a sheep between two rams.'
There was a great rock facing them. She dashed her head off the rock and made bits of it and died.[2]

Once more we hear in Conchobar's loutish gibe the bleating of the sheep in an Ulster farmstead at the end of day, but now the herdboy's joke has the smell of death from it. Derdriu's vow, never to see two of her bedmates on earth at one time, has exactly the quality of Étaín's refusal to deceive her husband in his own house, and suggests good manners rather than good morals. It is the vow of a woman who can be degraded, but keeps one small corner of her soul as a last redoubt of self-respect. Self-respect, too, is what the original 'Cattle Raid' was about.

Some slight but perceptible change comes over Irish literature between the ninth and the tenth centuries. This is not entirely attributable to the Norse raids. It had also something to do with the reign of Charlemagne. Some Irish professional poet abroad wrote a famous elegy on him, which could almost be translated directly back into Irish.

A solis ortu usque ad occidua
Littora maris planctus pulsat pectora.

After him what was needed in Europe was no longer missionaries, but teachers, and this seems to me to correspond fairly closely with a slight shift of emphasis in the literature itself from the Bible to the classics. In excavating 'The Cattle Raid' we came upon

[2] Hull (ed.), *Longes Mac n-Uislenn*.

one ninth-century stratum that gave clear evidence of its humanist origin.

In the first half of the ninth century there seems to have been a very good classical school in Kildare, a number of whose students emigrated to the Continent by way of Wales. At the same time there is a group of stories, all produced about this time, all vaguely related to one another and to Leinster, and all with what seem to me slight classical echoes. It is not so much that these still do not represent a primary literature, but that more and more traces of a secondary literature seep in. The best way I can describe this is to show what all of them have in common — a passion for Virgil and a weakness for head-hunting. Two of them also have the classical suicide, which is almost unknown in Irish.

In 'The Death of Cú Chulainn' there is a passage that describes Cú Chulainn's horse weeping as he says farewell to his master. I know that this also occurs in the story of the life of Colum Cille, but both *must* derive from the episode of Mezentius' horse in the *Aeneid*. There is also a reference to a chopped-off hand that reminds me of a passage in the *Aeneid* about a hand that 'seeks its master and whose dying fingers twitch and clutch again at the sword'.

Then Cú Chulainn gathered his guts into his belly and went to the lake. When he reached the lake he drew his hand across his belly and cast away his guts. Then he took a drink and washed himself. He leaped out of the lake and signalled for them to come to him. He went a good distance from the lake before his sight left him. Then he went to a pillarstone on the plain and tied himself to it with his belt, so that he might not die sitting or lying down, but standing. The men came round him, but they did not dare come near him for they thought he was still alive.

'It is a shame for you', said Erc, Cairbre's son, 'not to take that man's head for my father's head that he took and buried in Nia Fer's Neck.' Then the Grey of Macha (Cú Chulainn's horse) went to protect him so long as life was in him and the hero-light lingered round his head. Afterwards birds came and alighted on his shoulder. 'There used to be no birds on that pillar,' said Erc, Cairbre's son.

Lugaid caught up Cú Chulainn's hair from behind and cut off

his head. The sword fell from Cú Chulainn's hand and chopped off Lugaid's hand so that it fell to the ground. They cut off Cú Chulainn's hand in revenge for that. Then the host set out for Tara.[3]

We find the chopped-off hand again only in 'Mac Dathó's Pig' and 'The Siege of Howth', but all of them agree on the head-hunting. 'You have my brothers,' says Conall Cernach in 'The Siege of Howth'. 'Not in my belt,' says Mess Gegra. 'I feel my loaded belt heavy,' says Lugaid in 'The Death of Cú Chulainn'. If we are to believe 'Mac Dathó's Pig', the warrior did not even take off the filthy things at night because Conall Cernach says that he never slept 'without a Connachtman's head under my knee'. When his enemy, Cet, says that things would be different if his brother, Anluan, were there, Conall retorts coolly 'Oh, but he *is*!' and tosses Anluan's head at Cet's chest.

This, it seems to me, is the background of the most popular of the Irish stories — popular, in fact, because it is the most un-Irish — 'Rónán's Kin-slaying'. Essentially it is the story of Phaedra and Hippolytus, and its first editor, Kuno Meyer, regards it as an Irish retelling of the Greek story, while its second editor, my friend David Greene, regards it as an independent story. Either view seems to me equally plausible, though I have no doubt that the author was a classical scholar.

At any rate, for once it does not matter because the Irish story is better than the Greek, and the device by which this is achieved is so simple that one wonders why some Greek did not think of it. Mael Fhothartaig's father, Rónán, an elderly man, marries a skittish young princess from the north of Ireland, who is much more interested in seducing her stepson. He ignores her first hint that he should do her 'a good turn' in the Elizabethan sense — 'the best turn in the bed' — so she instructs one of her maids to do her 'a good turn' with him instead. The girl is frightened, and Congal, Mael Fhothartaig's foster-brother, asks her what is wrong. When she tells him, he warns her not to obey her mistress, but offers to do her 'a good turn' with Mael Fhothartaig instead. The maid becomes Mael Fhothartaig's mistress, and the queen then

[3] Book of Leinster, II, 449. Not edited.

accuses her of not doing her 'a good turn' at all. The phrase is repeated like a death-knell till the girl uses it once again in conversation with Mael Fhothartaig: the shy girl and the slightly vulgar phrase, which translators torture into such models of decorum, have laid the foundations of high tragedy.

Congal exposes the queen and she takes her revenge by telling Rónán that his son had tried to seduce her. To amuse her, Mael Fhothartaig had indulged in the curious game of tossing off half quatrains and allowing her to complete them — an antiphonal feature of early Irish poetry that suggests Japan. Now he tosses off one with a double meaning, and the queen's reply convinces Rónán that she had told him the truth. He orders one of his guard to kill Mael Fhothartaig and Congal.

Congal's brother, Donn, then sets off for Dunseverick in the north, kills the queen's father, son, and daughter-in-law, and on his return tosses the three heads at the queen's chest exactly as Conall Cernach does with Anluan's head in 'Mac Dathó's Pig', and the queen throws herself upon her knife exactly in the manner of the charioteer in 'The Siege of Howth'.

The suicide device in both stories is unquestionably the work of someone who had been educated in a classical school, probably Kildare. One of its scholars was Sedulius of Liège, who emigrated in the first half of the ninth century. Sedulius was obviously a professional poet, though we do not know a single line of his in Irish; indeed, we do not even know his name, though clearly it was Síadal, an Old Irish form of the same Latin name. Professor Carney thinks he wrote the little epigram we find written on the margin of one of his manuscripts abroad.

> Techt do Róim,
> Mór saítho, becc torbai;
> In Rí con-daigi i foss,
> Manim bera latt ní fhogbai.[4]

> To go to Rome
> Is little profit, endless pain:
> The Master that you seek in Rome
> You find at home or seek in vain.

[4] *Thesaurus Palaeohibernicus*, II, 296. (*GT*, 112.)

I suspect he wrote the famous 'Scholar and his Cat', and if he is one of the Leinster scholars who travelled to the Continent by way of the Welsh kingdoms of Gwynedd and Powys he certainly picked up his cat there, for 'Pangur' is a Welsh name.

> Meisse ocus Pangur Bán,
> Cechtar nathar fria shaindán;
> Bíth a menma-sam fri seilgg
> Mo menma céin im shaincheird.
>
> Caraim-se foss, ferr cach clú,
> Oc mo lebrán léir ingnu;
> Ní foirmtech frimm Pangur Bán,
> Caraid cesin a maccdán.[5]

Each of us pursues his trade,
I and Pangur my comrade;
His whole fancy on the hunt,
And mine for learning ardent.

More than fame I love to be
Among my books and study;
Pangur does not grudge me it,
Content with his own merit.

It is the last word in humanist elegance and urbanity, the perfection of the Oxford common-room; and yet it was written by a Latinist who probably came of a family of head-hunters; who may, indeed, as I sometimes think, have been responsible for the marvellous farce of 'Mac Dathó's Pig' and the classical power of 'Rónán's Kin-slaying'. I have quoted it to remind you that behind these stories of the ancient world is the Latin precipitant, the thing 'without which not'. In the earlier stories, where it is not so significant, the precipitant is the Bible; in the later ones, where it is very significant indeed, it is more likely to be Virgil. Certainly the author of 'The Scholar and his Cat' had a Horace close to his elbow.

[5] *Thesaurus Palaeohibernicus*, II, 293. (*GT*, 81.)

CHAPTER FIVE

Sagas and Pseudo-sagas

What I call the period of the Little Monasteries — the eighth and
ninth centuries — is probably the most delightful in Irish history,
at least before the first decade of the twentieth century. As my
friend Professor Greene says, 'they wrote like angels', and on the
whole I think he is right. It is the period of the early religious
poetry edited by Professor Carney, and I do not know much religious poetry anywhere that is better than that. The author of the
verse translation of the 'Apocryphal Gospel of St. Thomas', which
he has edited, was a natural poet, and it comes out in the extraordinary artlessness of his style, which resembles that of the early
English carols. Here is one little story to show how charming and
effortless he can be.

> Imbu maccán cóic blíadnae
> Isu macc Dé bí,
> Sénais dá uiscén deac,
> Arrus-fí di chrí.

> Delbais dá énán deac —
> Paisir a n-anmann —
> Dia Sapaite dos-géni
> di chrí cen madmann.

> Con-said alaile Iudea
> Isu mac Dé máir;
> Dochum a aiti Ioseph
> Do-n-indnacht ar láim.

> 'Ergair do macc, a Ioseph;
> Ní maith a ndo-gni;
> Dia Sapaite dos-rigni
> Delba én di chrí.'

Con-ort Ísu a dí bais,
  A guthán ro-cloth;
Fiad a súilib — ségdae rath —
  Ind énán, fos-mboth.

Ro-clos guthán cain inmain
  For giun Ísu glain:
'Ar fessid ciab dergéni
  Airciub do for ndaim.'

Fásaig alaile co túaith,
  Ba hamrae a scél,
Ro-clossa for luamain
  Garmann inna n-én.[1]

When he was only five years old
  Jesus, son of God,
Made twelve little waterholes
  In the wet mud.

Then he made twelve little birds —
  Passeres as they say;
He made them on the Sabbath
  Faultlessly of clay.

A certain Jew denounced him
  For what he had done,
And by the hand to Joseph
  He took God's only son.

'Correct your son, Joseph,
  For on the Sabbath day
He made graven images
  From the wet clay.'

Jesus clapped his hands;
  His voice was clear and bright;
Before their eyes, a marvel,
  The little birds took flight.

[1] James Carney, *The Poems of Blathmac* (Dublin, 1964), 91. (*GT*, 23.)

And then the voice of Jesus
Was heard to proclaim:
'To show you know who made you
Go back whence you came!'

Another Jew reported
Without a word of lie
That far in the distance
He heard the birds cry.

All the same, even with the author of this and Bláthmacc, the other poet whose work Professor Carney has edited, this is not really the stern Ireland we began with. It is much richer, to begin with. The rulers of the monasteries, having disposed of the Romanist prigs, are no longer the harsh, unworldly men we meet in the pages of Bede, who read nothing but their gospels and Psalmbooks. They are far more like the parsons of Peacock and Meredith — wealthy, worldly, scholarly men, who live in little oases of civilization among the bogs and woods, in comfortable wooden houses, with wine cellars and libraries, with clever sons who will become in their turn abbots or professors of scripture, and clever daughters who will manage big convents or marry among the ruling classes. They are custodians of relics and treasures worth the ransom of a great many kings. In his own house, Domnall, who is a very clever boy, is producing a new universal anthology, where side by side you will find 'The Vision of Adomnán', 'A Description of the Day of Judgement', 'A Description of the Resurrection', 'The Cattle Raid of Cooley', and 'The Wooing of Emer'. Where on earth have we met with this jumble before? Ah, yes, of course, in 'The Bishop orders his Tomb in St. Praxed's Church', with its mixture of Venuses, virgins, and 'mistresses with great smooth marbly limbs'. It is no exaggeration. In a twelfth-century satire there is a delightful description of an abbot appearing, his Wellington boots stuffed with manuscripts: in one 'The Cattle Raid' and 'The Destruction of Dá Derga's Hostel' and in the other 'The Wooing of Emer' and 'The Wooing of Étaín'. There is a lot about it to remind us of the Renaissance; a little perhaps to remind us of the Anglican Church of the eighteenth century — a Church whose members are definitely well heeled and determined on making the best of both worlds.

At the same time it had marked limitations. Churchmen, it is true, had become part of the professional classes and could travel freely and marry in their own class in other little kingdoms; but they did not have the strict discipline of the older professional men with their fiction of national identity. They were still linked to their monasteries, and these were tribal institutions whose patron saints were sometimes old pagan gods. That meant that history — even folk history, which was all that most of them knew — looked quite different according to the monastery from which you viewed it. St. Adomnán, St. Colum Cille's biographer, was a pious and scholarly man, but Adomnán was one of the Uí Néill — the inhabitants of O'Connell Street who had expelled the Lagin from their ancient home — and viewed from the standpoint of Westmoreland Street and points south, could appear a very sinister figure indeed, as he does in the life of the Lagin saint Mo Ling.

Similarly, Feidilmid mac Crimthainn, who seems to have been a very scholarly king of Munster at the beginning of the ninth century, raided Clonmacnois: the fact was on record, though the circumstances were forgotten and were differently described in Munster and Leinster records. Munster scholars, who saw the situation as one of light comedy, maintained that in his early student days Feidilmid had been badly received by the contemporary equivalent of the provost, the provost's wife, the butler, and the dog, and later took his revenge by making them perform an obscene ring-a-rosy:

> In matra,
>   Cia beith do gairbe a gotha,
> Curthar fírchenn a sróna
> I fírchenn tóna in tsrotha. . . .

However rough his voice, stick the tip of the dog's nose up the extreme end of the master's rear.

Clonmacnois scholars, feeling that the incident was in the realm of high tragedy, recorded that their patron saint, Cíarán, pursued Feidilmid relentlessly until he finally disposed of him with 'a poke in his belly with his bachall' — stabbed to death with a crozier, that is. The professional poet who sang Feidilmid's praises wisely said nothing but that he was 'the king to whom it was a day's work to unking Connacht without a battle and subjugate Meath'.

The two anecdotes are a very simple illustration of the weakness of history as seen from a tribal monastery. Some time towards the end of the seventh century the secular sagas had become so popular that word went about that they must be countered by other stories in which the virtues of the Irish saints were proclaimed. These stories I prefer to call 'pseudo-sagas'. Their heroes, the saints, were required to have conceptions and births superior to those of the saga heroes, and to destroy more people with their prayers and curses than the saga heroes could destroy with their swords. In the matter of conception those saints who got off with an incestuous one may be said to have been born in the odour of sanctity.

The simplest way of summarizing the usual type of pseudo-saga is to say it deals with a king who provokes some saint; the saint curses him and the king comes to a sticky end. They are frequently anachronistic and deal with a sixth-century saint and a seventh-century king, but the principal feature is that the churchman always wins. At their basest — and I know nothing baser in literature — one can see the process at work in the late seventh-century accounts of the life of St. Patrick, who like a true druid curses and blasts everyone and everything. In another story Aed mac Ainmire, King of Tara, asks his half-brother, the Abbot of Glendalough, to swear in the heathen way by his genitals, and the abbot prophesies that a she-wolf will soon eat the king's own genitals, which she duly does. (Meyer's translation of the queen's epigram on this in *Bruchstücke der älteren Lyrik Irlands* misses the point.)

In another story an Ulster king called Suibne quarrels with a really horrible saint named Rónán and is driven mad and dies a miserable death.

But the curious thing is that it is the pseudo-sagas that seem to have attracted the poets. On the whole the poetry of the sagas, if we exclude 'Rónán's Kin-slaying' and 'The Sick-bed of Cú Chulainn', is not very good, while some of the finest poetry in Irish is contained in one group of pseudo-sagas from West Munster.

This may have originated in the monastery of Clonfert, which, having been founded by a Kerryman, St. Brendan, continued for centuries as a West Munster monastery. One of its abbots was Cummíne the Tall, another Kerryman, who was the author of a famous penitential that deals very firmly with all sorts of peculiar sexual practices. He is one of the principal characters in this cycle of stories, along with his friend Guaire, King of Aidne, whose capital was Gort in South Galway; Guaire's brother, Mongán, a hermit; his daughter Créd, and her West Limerick lover, Dínertach; his friend, Mac Dá Cherda ('Son of the Two Musicians'?), who is a sort of Parsifal figure — a holy fool; Liadan, the Cork poet, and her poet lover from Connacht, Cuirithir; and last, and most important, the Nun of Beare, subject of the greatest of Irish poems.

Some of these characters are probably historical. Cummíne did probably write the famous penitential, but since he turns up in Munster stories as the child of an incestuous union it would seem that he was already beginning to turn into folk-lore. Liadan, I suspect, is a real person and may be the St. Liadan who gave her name to a County Limerick church. Guaire, too, may be historical; his brother is probably a fiction; and his daughter, Créd, was originally probably intended to represent his wife. Mac Dá Cherda is pure folk-lore, and I feel sure that the Nun of Beare is the goddess of Munster.

I cannot discuss 'King and Hermit', the beautiful poem in which his brother expounds to King Guaire the charm of a hermit's life, because I find the text too difficult. But this still leaves us with three poems or poem groups — Créd's lament for the death of Dínertach; the story poem, 'Liadan and Cuirithir', in which St. Cummíne intervenes disastrously in a love affair between the two poets; and 'The Nun of Beare', in which he also appears as spiritual director of an ex-mistress of the kings of Munster. His authorship of the penitential made him seem to the story-tellers a proper person to deal with lovers.

These poems have all been dated very differently by different scholars. My difficulty is that from the same cycle of stories, all confined in space to the little kingdom of West Munster and to an extreme limit of 150 years during which they could have been written, we have three remarkable poems, all supposed to be spoken by passionate women, and all echoing one another. If this means I have to assume the existence of three major poets, the law of limitation of effort comes into effect, and I suggest if not a single author, at least one poet outstanding enough to form a school.

The first, 'Créd's Lament', is the simplest of the three.

> *It é saigthi gona súain*
> *Cech trátha i n-aidchi adúair*
> *Sercgoí lia gnása iar ndé*
> *Fir a toeb thíre Roigne.*
>
> *Rográd fir ala thíre*
> *Ro-shíacht sech a chomdíne*
> *Ruc mo lí, ní lour dath,*
> *Ním léici do thindabrath. . . .*
>
> *Binniu laídib a labrad*
> *Acht Ríg nime noebadrad;*
> *Án bréo cen bréithir mbraisse,*
> *Céile tanae toebthaisse.*
>
> *Imsa noídiu robsa nár*
> *Ní bínn fri dula dodál;*
> *Ó do-lod i n-inderb n-aís*
> *Rom gab mo théite togaís.*
>
> *Táthum cech maith la Gúaire*
> *La ríg nAidne adúaire;*
> *Tocair mo menmae óm thúathaib*
> *Isin íath i nIrlúachair. . . .*[2]

These are the attacks that wound sleep at every hour of the bitter night, spears of love, slingstones of passion at day's end for the man from the side of Royny's country.

Extreme love for a man from another country who reached above his contemporaries has taken my complexion — there is little colour left; it does not let me sleep.

Except for praise of the King of Heaven his speech was sweeter

[2] Gerard Murphy, *Early Irish Lyrics* (Oxford, 1956), 86-88. (*GT*, 78.)

than all songs; a splendid lover without a boasting word, a soft-skinned slender bedmate.

When I was a child I was shy; I did not go on the evil trysts of passion; since I reached the instability of age my wantonness has begun to deceive me.

I have every good with Guaire, the king of cold Aidne, but my mind seeks to go away from my tribes into the country of Irluachair. . . .

Nevertheless there are difficulties. One, as I have said, is that it shows Créd as the wife of Guaire, not his daughter: no unmarried girl in an Irish story would describe herself as being 'in the instability of age', nor would she say of her father, 'I have every good with Guaire, the king of cold Aidne . . .' Two of the twenty-four lines of the original echo lines from 'The Nun of Beare': 'my mind seeks to go' echoes 'my body seeks to go'; and 'my wantonness has begun to deceive me', 'my sense has begun to deceive me'. The curious line, 'Except for praise of the King of Heaven' is also strongly reminiscent of a line in 'Liadan and Cuirithir', 'except for fear of the King of Heaven', though this could be a poetic cliché.

But if there is anything in my guess at a common authorship of the three poems, the poet was interested only in mature women and in serious moral problems. These three poems are unique in Irish because of their psychological maturity. I can plead only a vague suspicion that 'Créd' is a single lyric from a romance that described the moral problem of a passionate woman married to a kind and generous husband, which in the original story may well have involved the husband's friend, St. Cummíne, as the other stories do.

The trouble is that in 'Créd' and 'The Nun of Beare' the prose context is missing. We have the prose context of 'Liadan and Cuirithir', but only in the form of notes, which often maddeningly skirt the essential scenes. When the story opens Liadan is on a professional tour in Connacht. The fact that she is a member of the poetic corporation, a purely male organization at nearly all periods, suggests that she was the daughter of one of the ecclesiastical families. She meets the poet Cuirithir, who makes her a proposition couched in unforgettable terms. 'Liadan, why should you and I not sleep together? A son of ours should be splendid.'

Though the story implies that they did become lovers, Liadan formally declines, because it would interrupt her round of professional engagements, but invites him to visit her in Cork. Cuirithir sets off in a way that suggests we are watching how the professional classes functioned in the early Middle Ages. He removes the heads of his spears and packs his poet's gown with them; that is to say, he travels in ordinary dress and unarmed. Outside Liadan's house he resumes his gown, fixes his spearheads again, and asks the Holy Fool, Mac Dá Cherda, to deliver a message in privacy to Liadan. As Mac Dá Cherda does not know which of the girls she is, he shows off the fearful ingenuity of the Irish professional poets by addressing her in a poem, composed in a code based on a number of false etymologies, like *Liadam* ('stone church') and *Liathdoim* ('grey bird-flocks').

Being a professional poet herself, Liadan gets the point, which is more than I do; but by this time she has apparently decided to become a nun; and the two lovers enter Clonfert under the spiritual guidance of St. Cummíne. He separates them, and Liadan sings her first song in which she uses the word *athéces*, 'ex-poet'. The common word for 'monk' was *athlaoch*, 'ex-laic', and she twists it to suit Cuirithir's position. The word for 'church' is the same as we find in 'The Nun of Beare' — *derthach*, meaning 'oak-house', the one big wooden building in the older sort of monastery, mainly constructed with reed or wattle and daub.

> *Carsam — ním ráinic a less —*
> *Cuirithir int athéces:*
> *Inmain fíadu dá coss nglass;*
> *Bid dirsan a bithingnas.*
>
> *In lecc fri derthach an-dess*
> *Forsa mbíd int athéces,*
> *Meinic tíagar di im cach ndé*
> *Fescor íar mbúaid ernaigde.*
>
> *Nícon bia aice bó*
> *Ná dáir inna dartado,*
> *Nícon bia cnáim do leiss*
> *For láim deiss ind athécis.*[3]

[3] Kuno Meyer (ed. and tr.), *Liadain and Curithir* (London, 1902), 17. (*GT*, 75.)

Once the ex-poet Cuirithir
And I were lovers; there's no cure,
And I am left to bear the pain
Knowing we shall not meet again.

South of the church there stands a stone
Where the ex-poet sat alone;
I sit there too at close of day
At twilight when I come to pray.

No girl will ever be his mate,
No son or daughter share his fate,
No thigh beside his thigh repose —
Solitary the ex-poet goes.

To test their virtue Cummíne suggests that they sleep together,
separated only by an acolyte, and both protest that this would be
highly unsafe. Cuirithir says:

Masu oenadaig as-bir
Feisse dam-sa la Líadain,
Méiti la laech nod fiad
Ind adaig ní archríad.

So I and my love, Liadan,
Should sleep together without sin,
While any layman on the earth
Would boast of what that chance was worth!

Liadan says:

Masu oendadaig as-bir
Feisse dam la Cuirithir,
Cid blíadain do-bermais fris
Boíthiunn imma-rordamais.[4]

Though I and my love, Cuirithir,
Had practised virtue for a year,
Left together for one night
Our thoughts would stray before daylight.

[4] Meyer, *Liadain and Curithir*, 21. (GT, 77.)

They prove that they know their own passion better than Cummíne, and Cuirithir leaves Clonfert in anger and remorse. Liadan then sings the most beautiful love song of the Middle Ages —a sort of eighth- or ninth-century *Liebestod*, and once more I can only beg my readers to consider the emotional maturity of these poems.

Cen áinius
  In gním hí do-rigénus;
An ro charus ro cráidius.

Ba mire
  Nád dernad a airersom
Mainbed omun Ríg nime.

Níbu amlos
  Dósom in dál dúthracar,
Ascnam sech phéin i Pardos.

Bec mbríge
  Ro chráidi frimm Cuirithir:
Frissium ba mór mo míne.

Mé Líadan;
  Ro carussa Cuirithir;
Is fírithir ad-fíadar.

Gair bása
  I comaiteacht Chuirithir;
Frissium ba maith mo gnássa.

Céol caille
  Fom-chanad la Cuirithir,
La fogur fairrge flainne.

Do-ménainn
  Ní cráidfed frimm Cuirithir
Do dálaib cacha dénainn.

Ní chela:
  Ba hésium mo chridesherc,
Cia no carainn cách cena.

Deilm ndega
  Ro thethainn mo chridese;
  Ro-fess nicon bía cena.[5]

Sadness
  Is in the bargain I have struck;
One that I loved I wrought to madness.

Mad beyond measure
  But for God's fear that numbed her heart
She who would not do his pleasure.

My desire
  Was that we two should keep our tryst
And meet in Heaven beyond the fire.

Was it so great,
  My treason? Was I not always kind?
Why should it turn his love to hate?

Liadan,
  That is my name, and Cuirithir
The man I loved — you know my sin.

Too fleet
  The joys I knew when by his side;
With him the passionate hours were sweet.

Woods woke
  About us for a lullaby
And the blue waves in music broke.

Too late
  More than for all my sins I grieve
That I turned his love to hate.

Why hide
  That he is still my heart's desire
More than all the world beside?

A furnace blast
  Of love has melted down my heart;
Without his love it cannot last.

[5] Meyer, *Liadain and Curithir*, 23. (GT, 72.)

But with 'The Nun of Beare' we are back to textual problems because we have no prose context, and the brief prose introduction we have is worse than useless. St. Cummíne we know from 'Liadan and Cuirithir' as the universal sexual expert. The Nun is probably a tutelary goddess like Medb or Macha. Like Medb, her relations with so many kings had given her the reputation of being very flighty as well as being very old. The story-teller cast her as an Irish Mary Magdalene and changed her name to Dígdiu, the Penitent.

The first verse runs:

> *Aithbe dam cen bés mora*
> *Sentu fom-dera croan;*
> *Toirsi oca cia do-gneo,*
> *Sona do-tét a loan.*[6]

> Ebbtide is all my grief,
> Old age has sucked my blood,
> But, though I get no relief,
> Merrily returns its flood.

It needs no great scholarship to see that this verse has been misplaced to provide a first word that can be echoed as last, or that its real place is immediately before a verse that runs:

> *Céinmair insi mora máir,*
> *Dosn-ic tuile íarna tráig;*
> *Os mé, ní frescu dom-í*
> *Tuile tar ési n-aithbi.*

> Happy island of the main,
> To you the tide returns again,
> But to me it comes no more
> Over the deserted shore.

This alone would be sufficient to indicate that a dotty eleventh-century editor had been at work, obliterating the prose framework and making a single poem out of what in effect were probably

[6] Gerard Murphy, *Proceedings of the Royal Irish Academy*, LV., C. 83-109. (*GT*, 48.)

half a dozen. The first verse requires a setting by the sea with the Nun old and poor, but the third, fourth, and fifth show her in a midland plain — almost certainly Cashel — riding in a chariot and speaking to a group of young men whom we have not met before and shall not meet again, and describing them as useless lovers.

These three verses are certainly an independent lyric from a point in the story at which St. Cummíne had not yet appeared, and I believe the whole poem is a group of lyrics from a lost pseudo-saga that dealt with the Nun and St. Cummíne. At the end I believe that the Nun challenged Christ to spend the night with her (or fill her empty larder, I am not sure which), was converted by the miracle, and at the end of the poem praised old age, which she had begun by denouncing. There is nothing greater in Irish than the verses in which she denounces it. From beginning to end they are magic.

Is mó láu
Nád muir n-oíted imma-ráu;
Testa már mblíadnae dom chruth
Dáig fo-rroimled mo chétluth.

Is mó dé
Damsa in-diu cen buith té;
Gaibthi m'étach cid fri gréin
Do-fil aes dom aithgin féin. . . .

Am minecán, mon-úar dam,
    Cach derc caín is erchraide,
Iar feis fri caindlea sorchai
    Bíthum dorchae derthaige. . . .

Céinmair insi mora máir,
Dosn-ic tuile íarna tráig;
Os mé, ní frescu dom-í
Tuile tar ési n-aithbi.

Is súaill mo mennat in-diu
    Ara taibrinnse aithgniu:
An-í ro boí for tuiliu
    A-tá uile for aithbiu.

'Tis many a day
Since I sailed on youth's bay
   Year on year has scored my flesh
Since my fresh sweet strength went grey.

Many a day
I have been as cold as they;
   Even in the sun I wear my shawl;
Age has put me too away. . . .

A poor old woman, let me be;
   The eyes are dark that were so fair;
The glittering ones I slept with pass
   And leave me to the dark and prayer. . . .

Happy island of the main,
To you the tide returns again,
But to me it comes no more
Over the deserted shore.

Seeing, I can scarcely say
'Here is such a place'; today
What was water far and wide
Changes with the ebbing tide.

CHAPTER SIX

The Norse and After

About the year 800, on the very eve of the first Viking raids, a fine poet, Óengus of Clonenagh, celebrated the triumph of the Irish Church in verses that deserve to be classical — my own translation is a very limping affair beside the gorgeous rhetoric of the Irish.

> *Senchathraig na ngennti*
> *Imma rérad rudrad*
> *It fássa cen adrad*
> *Amail láthrach Lugdach.*

> *Ind locáin ro gabtha*
> *Dessaib ocus trírib,*
> *It rúama co ndálaib*
> *Co cétaib, co mílib.*

> *Ro milled in genntlecht*
> *Ciarbo lígdae lethan;*
> *Ro lín flaith Dé Athar*
> *Nem, talam la trethan.*[1]

> Old haunts of the heathen
>   Filled from ancient days
> Are but deserts now
>   Where no pilgrim prays.

> Little places taken
>   First by twos and threes
> Are like Rome reborn,
>   Peopled sanctuaries.

> Heathendom has gone down
>   Though it spread everywhere;
> God the Father's kingdom
>   Fills heaven and earth and air.

[1] Stokes (ed.), *Félire Óengusso Céli Dé.* (GT, 61.)

Óengus believed that he was writing of a state of affairs that would last forever, but within a few years all the great monasteries were in ashes. It was fully a hundred years before they could be reconstructed, and then they were rebuilt in stone — stone churches, stone towers, and stone crosses, which are the first indication of a native resurgence. At the same time there is a vast increase in the influence of the professional poets. Though this had begun before the invasions its strength must be due to a certain decline in the monastic schools, which were now being attacked and plundered by Irishmen as well as Norse and offered only doubtful shelter to humanists. We gather as much from a bitter little fragment of a poem on the plundering of Clonmacnois, the metre of which is tenth or eleventh century.

> '*Can as tic mac légind?*'
> '*Ticim o Chluain chélbind;*
> *Iar légad mo légind*
>   *Tégim sis co Sord.*'
> '*Indis scéla Cluana.*'
> '*Indisfet 'na cuala:*
> *Sinnaig imm a huaga*
>   *Ethait bruana bolg.*'[2]

> 'Whence are you, learning's son?'
> 'From Clonmacnois I come;
> My course of studies done
>   I am off to Swords again.'
> 'How are things shaping there?'
> 'Oh, things are keeping fair;
> Foxes round churchyards bare
>   Gnawing the guts of men.'

Stylistically — judging by the many fragments that remain — the court poetry of this period was very good, probably because the poets were still under the influence of Latin rhetoric learned in the monastery schools, but the pretentiousness is sometimes a little exhausting, as in the verse about an eleventh-century King of Derry.

[2] Gerard Murphy, *Early Irish Metrics* (Dublin, 1961), 70.

Ní mó grád Gallbraite
Ri Ua Céin Conchobhar
Do chor 'na innarad —
*   Is é so a fhír —*
Indá nodíbuirged
Lán glaicce glasubull
I roimse romessa
I medón ardchaille
*   Ó Ríg na ríg.*[3]

Conor the king
As little heeds
His wagons packed
    With Danish loot
As in the woods
In autumn, God
Heeds how he drops
    The golden fruit.

With the older type of poet came a new type of scribe, who clearly was well paid for his efforts to restore the cultural past. Unfortunately the restorers had almost forgotten what they were trying to restore; they had little or no critical spirit and do not seem even to have been aware that the language they were writing had changed and that they often had only the vaguest notion of what they were transcribing. Most of the early manuscripts must have perished, and of those that remained many must have been in a dilapidated condition, consisting perhaps of no more than a few leaves. This did not deter the scribes at all, and the figure Thurneysen has identified as First Murderer of 'The Cattle Raid' text, and whom he calls the 'Compiler', can stand for scores of others without his (literally) diabolical energy. He tackled every job of editing in the spirit of a small boy trying to make a bicycle from the wreck of a perambulator; we can see him travelling from monastery to monastery, copying like mad from the scraps he found, injudiciously blending two or three or even five redactions of a story, duplicating passages from variant readings and interrupting himself to add cheerfully : . . . 'alii libri dicunt . . .' It is the

³ K. Meyer, *Bruchstücke der älteren Lyrik Irlands* (Berlin, 1919), 25. (*GT*, 201.)

'other books' that break one's heart, because we know that the industrious idiot is knocking together the remains of five hundred years of a manuscript tradition that is lost to us; and in the absence of an Irish manuscript from before 1100 we can only guess at the devastation he is wreaking.

It is impossible to write with restraint of the damage done by those well-meaning, unscholarly men. I doubt if ten or even five per cent of the literature has come down to us in anything like its original form. 'The Cattle Raid' has been rendered practically un-intelligible, and the beautiful 'Sick-bed of Cú Chulainn' has been compiled from two entirely different versions with a bit of an-other, unrelated story thrown in. Though this may well represent the chaos of odd leaves the Compiler had before him, we must still regret that he was unable to use them with more discretion.

The tragedy is that the old spirit of the literature was very much alive and renewing itself in all sorts of odd ways. One of the mani-festations of the demented antiquarianism was the attention professional poets were devoting to metres. We have three hand-books of prosody still unedited; one from the ninth, another from the tenth, and a third from the late eleventh century, and though the metres are becoming progressively more complicated, new metres like those of the two verses I have just quoted are being introduced from Latin. Besides, there seems to have been a revival of interest in the old alliterative metres, and in two scenes in 'Bricriu's Feast' and 'The Sick-bed of Cú Chulainn' some poet tried to revive the old dramatic form of story telling as we find it in the earliest stratum of 'The Cattle Raid'. Another metrist, as skil-ful as Robert Bridges, wrote a group of poems on the seasons to show his students how the alliterative metres could be used in a contemporary way.

> *Ráithe fó foiss fogamar,*
> *Feidm and for ech oenduini*
> *Fri oíb na llá lángairit.*
> *Loíg brecca i ndiaid deisseilte,*
> *Dínit rúadgaiss raithnige.*
> *Rethait daim a dumachaib*
> *Fri dordán na damgaire.*
> *Dercain, subai i síthchailltib,*

Slatta etha imm ithgurtu
Ós íath domuin duinn.
Draigin, drissi delgnacha
Fri duai in láir lethshlissi,
Lán do mess tromm teinnithir,
Do-tuittet cnoí cainmessa
Cuill, robili ráth.[4]

Fall is no man's travelling time;
Tasks are heavy; husbandmen
Need horses as the light grows less;
Lightly their young drop from the deer,
Dandled in the faded fern;
Fiercely the stag stalks from the hill,
Hearing the herd in clamorous call.
Cobbled the mast in windless woods,
Weary the corn upon its canes,
    Colouring the brown earth.
Endless the thorns that foul the fence
That frames the hollow of some house;
The heavy ground is filled with fruit,
And by the fort, hard from their height,
    Hazelnuts break and fall.

Nature poetry, as we can see from this, was very much alive, and nature poetry is the most extraordinary feature of early Irish literature. It is also very difficult to trace its origin. That it was of native origin we are compelled to believe if we accept Gerard Murphy's theory that it originated with the Irish hermits of the sixth and seventh centuries or Kenneth Jackson's that it originated in the pagan songs of the seasons. For me the overwhelming argument against either of these theories is that about the year 1200 it disappeared completely, and I find it impossible to believe that this could have occurred to any form which was not an exotic.

Besides, a number of the poems and fragments are quite demonstrably of a late date and I know of none that would suggest the sort of early date assumed for them by Professors Murphy and Jackson. One of the best known is a fragment from a poem about the sea in flood.

[4] *Eriu*, VII. (*GT*, 140.)

Fégaid úaib
Sair fo-thúaid
In muir múaid
   Mílach;
Adba rón
Rebach rán
Ro gab lán
   Línad.[5]

Look, wild and wide,
North-east the tide
Beneath which bide
   The dragon's brood;
The seals' delight,
All foam and light,
Mounts to full height —
   The sea's in flood.

The metre of the original eight lines, which I have not been able
to follow, is practically that of a twelfth-century song in Old
French about a jealous husband.

Le jalous
Envious
De cor rous
   Morra;
Et li dous
Savourous
Amourous
   M'aura.[6]

Though it can be called syllabic verse, it is actually stressed, and
it differs from the French merely in the fact that the Irish poet
begins the third and seventh lines with an unstressed syllable so as
to get a dance beat of three long syllables in succession. Both because of the eight-line verse and the stressing of certain syllables
this fragment cannot possibly be older than the eleventh century,

[5] Murphy, *Early Irish Metrics*, 73. (*GT*, 205.)
[6] C. C. Abbott, *Early Medieval French Lyrics* (London, 1932), xxi.

nor can the equally admired fragment about the blackbird by Belfast Lough.

> *Int én bec*
> *Ro léic feit*
> *Do rind guip*
> *   Glanbuidi;*
> *Fo-ceird faíd*
> *Ós Loch Laíg*
> *Lon do chraíb*
> *   Charrbuidi.*[1]

> What little throat
> Has framed that note?
> What gold beak shot
>   It far away?
> A blackbird on
> A leafy throne
> Tossed it alone
>   Across the bay.

Also of the eleventh, if not of the twelfth, is the lovely poem on winter, because when we worked on it together David Greene found it perfectly easy to transcribe as Modern Irish.

> *Is mairg do mheanbhaig na n-éan*
> *   An ghaoth ghéar is an t-oighreadh fuar;*
> *Ní fhaghbhann lon droma daoil*
> *   Díon a thaoibh i gCoilltibh Cuan.*

> *Sádhail ar gcoire dá dhrol,*
> *   Aistreach lon ar Leitir Cró;*
> *Do mhínigh sneachta Coill Ché,*
> *   Deacair dréim ré Beanna Bó.*

> *Cubhar Glinne Ridhe an fhraoigh*
> *   Ón ngaoith aichir do-gheibh léan;*
> *Mór a thruaighe agus a phian,*
> *   An t-oighreadh do shiad 'na bhéal.*

[1] Murphy, *Early Irish Metrics*, 73. (GT, 206.)

Éirghe do cholcaidh is do chlúimh —
Tug dot úidh! — nochan ciall duit;
Iomad n-oighridh ar gach n-áth;
Is é fáth fá n-abraim 'Fuit!'[8]

God help young birds who cannot last
In the cold snow and icy blast,
    For the blackbird of Cuan Wood
Finds no shelter that holds fast.

Nothing's cosy but our pot;
The blackbird of Letter Cro is not,
    And in woodlands crushed with snow
On Ben Bo the trail's forgot.

The old eagle of Glen Rye,
Even he neglects to fly;
    With the ice blown in his beak
He is now too weak to cry.

Best lie still
In wool and feathers take your fill;
    Ice is thick on every ford
And the word I used was 'Chill'.

The oldest of the poems, so far as I understand them, is the
magnificent 'Tempest', and this I should say is tenth century. The
nearest thing to it in English is probably Hopkins' 'The Wreck of
the *Deutschland*'; the 'rocking metre', as the metrists call it, almost
lets us feel the lurch of the boat and hear the straining of
timbers.

Anbthine mór ar muig Lir,
Dána tar a hardimlib;
    At-racht gáeth, ran goin gaim garg
    Co tét tar muir mórgelgarb;
Do-s-árraid ga garggemrid.[9]

[8] Kuno Meyer, *Revue celtique*, XI, 125. (*GT*, 134.)
[9] Kuno Meyer, *Otia Merseiana*, II, 76-83. (*GT*, 126.)

Tempest on the plain of Lir
Bursts its barriers far and near
And upon the rising tide
Wind and noisy winter ride —
Winter throws a shining spear.

On the other hand the two poems 'Summer' and 'May Day' both seem to me to be the work of the same hand, and that not a very late one. They are the last word in wit and sophistication. All the verses of 'Summer' except the fifth and last are in a five-syllable metre, which seems to have three strong beats at the end of each line, and — unless the text is worse than I think — the other two are in a six-syllable metre that resembles a waltz. Translated into English, the two poems always read like something from the Japanese, but they are really more like Gilbert and Sullivan in a happy moment. In Irish they sparkle with sheer fun.

Fúam ngáeth mbáeth i mbruig
    Dairi duib Druim Daill;
Rethid graig máel múad
    Dia mbí dín Cúan Caill.

Maidid glass for cach lus,
    Bilech doss daire glais;
Tánic sam, ro faith gam,
    Goinit dam cuilinn chais.

Canaid lon dron dord
    Diambi forbb caill cherb;
Súanaid ler lonn líach,
    Fo-ling ıach brec bedc.

Tibid grían dar cach tír —
    Dedlaid lim fri sín sal —
Garit coin, dáilit daim,
    Forbrit brain, tánic sam![10]

[10] K. Meyer (ed. and tr.), *Four Old Irish Songs of Summer and Winter* (London, 1903), 20. (*GT*, 137.)

Wanton winds blow shrill
   In the Drumdell trees;
Bald herds skip about
   In the woods with ease.

Green bursts out everywhere;
   Oakwoods are full of leaf;
Summer's come, winter's gone;
   Stags find the briers' grief.

And the woods' wise lord,
   The bold blackbird sings;
Weary, wild, water sleeps,
   And the salmon springs.

Sunlight all round proclaims
   Good-bye to seasons drear:
Hounds call and deer in pack;
   Ravens thrive, summer's here!

'May Day', so lovely that we have all tried our hand at translating it, exists only in one obscenely inaccurate transcript of which
Kuno Meyer and Gerard Murphy have tried vainly to make linguistic sense. In spite of the fact that Meyer ascribed it to the
ninth or early tenth century and Murphy to the eighth or ninth, I
feel certain it was written by the author of the previous poem,
scarcely earlier than the eleventh century, and that what Kenneth
Jackson calls its 'curious style' is the deliberate archaism of an
excellent scholar, who not only played with new metres, but
omitted definite articles and the conjunction *ocus*. I give my own
text, which bears little relation to that of Meyer or Murphy, and
a simple prose translation.

> *Gairit cuí cruaid den*
>   *'Is fochen sam saír!'*
> *Suidid síne serb*
>   *I mbí cerb caill chraíb.*
>
> *Cerbaid sam sruth snuad;*
>   *Saigid graig luath linn;*
> *Lethaid fat fraích folt;*
>   *For-beir gort fann finn.*

Fuabair os scéith sciach;
Im-reith réid rian rith;
Cuirithir suan sál;
Tuigithir bláth bith.

Berait beich bec nert
Bert bonn bochtai bláth
Berid slabrai sliab,
Feraid seng sian sáith.

Seinm crot, caille ceol
Co ngrenn seol síd slán;
Sethair denn do dinn;
Dethaid loch linn lán.[11]

The harsh, sturdy cuckoo calls, 'Welcome, beautiful summer.'
The expanse of the heather's hair spreads and the pale weak
corn thrives.
    The budding of the hawthorn threatens the deer; the sea tide
runs smoothly; the sea goes to sleep and blossom covers the
earth.
    Bees of small strength carry a load of plucked blossom; the
mountain sustains the cattle; the lean one sings a song of plenty.
    The music of the wood is like harp-playing, a perfect peace of
melody. The house is cleared of garbage, the flooded pool drops.

My own view of nature poetry, which I admit is little more
than a guess, is that it developed about the ninth or tenth century
as the result of a hint from some contemporary Latin verse, and
was fostered by scholars who enjoyed the metrical games it enabled
them to play. In 'Suibne Geilt', a twelfth-century romance, it
begins to fade into metrical virtuosity. That sort of literary scholarship would eventually result in the arid correctness of later professional poetry, but in the work of the eleventh and twelfth
centuries it is fascinating to watch the way in which poets escape
the pitfalls their children and grandchildren fell into.
    In her charming little anthology of late bardic verse from 1200
to 1600 Miss Knott prints one poem in which a father who has

[11] Meyer, *Four Old Irish Songs*, 8.

lost his family listens to the sad song of a blackbird, and notes that 'it is a little earlier than our period'. This is one period where 'a little earlier' might just as well be four hundred years earlier because it belongs to a period when the individual voice is still the important thing. 'The Blackbird' is as much an Early Irish poem as the poem on the cat.

> *Cumhthach labhras an lonsa,*
> *An t-olc do fhuair dfheadursa:*
> *Cidh bé do théalaigh a theagh*
> *Is fa éanaibh do hairgeadh.*[12]

> The blackbird sings his song in tears;
> I know the grief he suffers:
> Whoever ravaged his small nest,
> Of birds he is the saddest.

This note one can find even in the poems of Mael Ísu O Brolchán, the most famous religious poet of the eleventh century. In the year 1086 he earned the 'white martyrdom' by dying in the monastery of Lismore. Except for a rather fine hymn to St. Michael I find most of his religious poetry pretty dull, but, if Professor Carney's ascription of the poem is right, when he entered Lismore he found there a Psalm-book he had owned when he was a boy of seven with the names of four later owners entered on the fly-leaf. Conventionalizing his find as the discovery of an old mistress, he begins a poem in the language of courtly love and then soars gradually into a great frenzy of religious passion. One could scarcely imagine a more scholarly poem, because almost every word either alliterates or rhymes, and yet if ever there was such a thing as personal utterance, it is here.

> *Do-beire do thimna toí*
> *Do chách co imda ar bith ché;*
> *Síthlai dúin uile in cech ló*
> *Ní gó guide díchra Dé.*

---

[12] Eleanor Knott, *An Introduction to Irish Syllabic Poetry of the Period 1200-1600* (Cork, 1924), 22. (*GT*, 154.)

> *Do-rata Día Debraid dúin*
> *Ar ré rit ar menmain mín;*
> *Rop rolainn rinn gnúis Ríg réil*
> *Íar n-ar léim ór colainn chrín.*[13]

> You give your silent testimony
> To men of what we all must heed;
> Each day your lovers learn anew
> God's grace is all the skill they need.

> So may He grant me by your grace
> A quiet end, an easy mind;
> And light my pathway with His face
> When the dead flesh is left behind.

(Later, having endured six months of torture, the same man wrote a 'Grace before Death', which I find difficult to read because in it the grace and scholarship clash with naked human suffering. But it too is intensely personal poetry.)

At the same time scholarship killed even the nature poetry. One of the most beautiful of twelfth-century poems is Grania's 'Lullaby' for her lover, Díarmait, which Yeats turned into a lovely lullaby of his own. Grania has eloped with Díarmait; they are being pursued by her husband, Fionn, when Díarmait falls asleep. Grania sings him a lullaby, describing the storm outside, which drives even the little birds from their nests, and bids him sleep soundly like the other great lovers of Irish history. Nature poetry here, as in another famous poem of the period, 'A Winter Night', is merely a background, but it is the historical litany that indicates to us that we are dealing with a tradition that is near its end. In another twelfth-century poem, Cormac mac Cuileannáin, the scholarly king of Munster, is supposed to defend his chastity against his wife by meditating on great saints — John, Finnbarr, Cíarán, Scuithín, Colum Cille, Mo Laise, and Patrick — who came safe from their encounters with women; and in a still sillier one a girl is comforted for the loss of her pet goose by a list of great Irish heroes who had also died — a characteristic and fatuous theme of professional poetry up to its end in poems like 'The Woman of Three Cows'.

[13] Kuno Meyer, *Zeitschrift für celtische Philologie*, VI, 266. (GT, 167.)

Ní chodail an lacha lán;
Maith a láthar re deaghshnámh;
Ní dhéan súan ná sáimhe ann,
Ina hadhbhaidh ní codlann.

A-nocht ní chodail an ghearg
Ós fhraochaibh anfaidh iomard;
Binn foghar a gotha glain
Eidir shrotha ní chodail.

Rob ionann is codladh teas
DeighFhiodhaigh na n-airdéigeas,
Dá dtug inghin Morainn bhuain
Tar ceann Conaill ón Chraobhruaidh.

Rob ionann is codladh tuaidh
Fionnchaidh Fhionnchaoimh Easa Ruaidh,
Dá dtug Sláinghe, séaghdha rainn,
Tar ceann Fáilbhe Chotatchinn.[14]

The duck that bears her brood tonight
  By many a sheltering bank must creep,
And furrow the wild waters bright,
  Among the reeds she will not sleep.

The curlew cannot sleep at all;
  His voice is clear above the deep
Reverberations of the storm;
  Among the streams he will not sleep.

You must sleep as in the south
  He who from Conall long ago
With all the arts of speech and song
  Made Morann's daughter rise and go.

And sleep the sleep that Finncha found
  In Ulster with his stolen bride
When Slaney went from home with him
  And slept no more at Falvey's side.

[14] E. MacNeill, *Duanaire Finn* (London, 1908), i, 84. (*GT*, 184.)

'We do it wrong, being so majestical, to offer it the show of violence', but it is obviously Irish poetry tottering on the edge of Augustan elegance. Four lines are all that remain of a ninth-century version of the same story, and again it is Grania speaking:

> *Fil duine*
> *Frismbad buide lemm díuterc*
> *Ara tabrainn in mbith mbuide*
> *Uile, uile, cid díupert.*[15]

> There is one
> I would wish to see again,
> And give the golden world to win —
> All, all, though all were vain.

Down to the final word, *díupert*, the legal term for the bad bargain, the contract that cannot be remedied, this seems to me to have the very accent of early Irish poetry; the voice of a woman speaking from the heart of the situation, rather than of one standing aside and admiring herself in it, like some Jacobean heroine.

[15] Murphy, *Early Irish Lyrics*, 160. (*GT*, 112.)

CHAPTER SEVEN

Romanesque and Gothic

As I have said, the earliest existing Irish manuscript written in Ireland was produced by a scribe named Mael Muire who was killed in Clonmacnois in 1106. Everything before that date exists in a sort of prehistoric twilight where the historian, the linguist and the critic must watch his step carefully.

About the year 1100 the lighting gradually begins to improve. This is largely due to a reform party within the Church, which tried to reimpose the episcopal type of organization on the tribal monastic one. The reformers began their work through the Norse-Gaelic towns where the tribal influence was weakest, and we hear of a bishop in Dublin, then of one in Waterford, then of bishops in Cork and Limerick. Finally the Munster group, with the aid of individual clerics and rulers throughout the country, set out to organize the Irish Church on the model of the English one, with Armagh as the Irish York and Cashel as the Irish Canterbury. Unfortunately, their influence is principally perceptible in architecture. Its first monument — indeed, the first major monument we have after the Neolithic tombs in the Boyne Valley — is Cormac's Chapel in Cashel; a miniature cathedral which is a fine example of pure European Romanesque. After this, Romanesque decoration becomes the hallmark of the reformers, and the style spreads rapidly throughout the whole country.

Cormac MacCarthy, the builder of the chapel, was one of the leaders of the reform movement, and probably built a great deal more. It is certain that he built two churches in his favourite haunt, Lismore, though nothing remains of these but the effigy of a bishop, and some fine arch-stones of a Romanesque cathedral in Cork suggest that he built one there. To do this he must have imported masons, because no Irish mason of the time could have solved some of the complicated problems of Cormac's Chapel. Within twenty years his friend St. Malachy imported a French master-builder to train his monks in the building of the first abbey at Mellifont. This was too elaborate for native builders to cope with — indeed, too elaborate for the much more highly skilled English builders — and later Irish buildings are simpler, though infinitely complex compared with the little dolls' houses they replaced.

The emphasis was switching from the spiritual to the material. In the eighth century Ireland had the greatest literature in western Europe and no architecture worth speaking of. In the twelfth century literature was collapsing imperceptibly into provincialism, but the country was being filled with the most exquisite little buildings, decorated with lovely carvings and paintings. Ireland, in fact, was becoming a part of medieval Europe.

The smaller monasteries could not compete. Though St. Laurence built the beautiful little church of St. Saviour in Glendalough, he retired to Dublin to build Christ Church cathedral, and though that pious and much-traduced lady, Dervorgilla, built a charming little Romanesque chapel for the nuns of Clonmacnois, she retired herself to the great monastery of Mellifont, where you could go to the lavatory or attend Vespers on a wet night without being soaked to the skin. Yet none of the great twelfth-century monasteries produced a school like that of Clonmacnois or a manuscript like the lost 'Cín Dromma Snechta'; none of the poetry that follows their erection fires our imagination as do a few lines like 'Sweet little bell, struck in the windy night', written in some monastery that had no lavatory at all.

With the building of Mellifont the Irish had begun to live on a different level of politics and economics. To support such an abbey the tribal laws about land tenure had to be swept aside. To establish the primacy the old ecclesiastical family that owned Armagh had to be overthrown by force.

Then, with the Norman invasion, all this intellectual ferment stops. The visibility improves though. We have unexceptionable evidence — English state documents, papal documents, Irish Court poetry and English and Irish architecture. We can watch what is happening. There is the swift advance of the Anglo-Norman invaders in province after province until half the historic Irish kingdoms are eliminated. By about 1200 there are three surviving monarchies recognized by Rome: the kingdom of 'Cork', the kingdom of 'Limerick' and the kingdom of 'Connacht'. Then there is a slow-down that turns to a stalemate — the real disaster of Irish history, for the Normans could not rule the country themselves, but they were strong enough to prevent anyone else's ruling it, so that it was more disunited than it had ever been under tribal rule. It was a country without a centre; a people without a head.

As some enlightened Englishmen (for example, King John) realized, the stalemate could have been ended by the extension of English law to the Irish who remained in the rest of the Irish kingdoms, but this would also have stopped the further extension of the invasion, which from the invaders' point of view was unthinkable. That they themselves could be exploited in the same way by later waves of invaders of course did not occur to them. It is the tragedy of colonialism that it is self-perpetuating, and that each generation of exploiters considers the previous one fair game.

It is all very regrettable, of course, but in spite of the endemic warfare occasioned by an incomplete conquest, Ireland of the later Middle Ages cannot have been such an unpleasant country as it became in later times. Architecture shows us clearly how the Normans, with their immense military superiority, dug themselves in, pushed back the Irish, and established their fine castles and beautiful churches. The Irish themselves, now with some skill in church architecture, were building their own beautiful abbeys and churches where the Normans could not penetrate, and the results, whether in a Norman settlement like Gowran, or an Irish one like Cong, were equally satisfying.

Nor does the literature, such as it is, suggest that anything very tragic had happened. If it had, the Irish at least were not aware of it. To be sure, there was the emergence of a real type of folk literature in the stories and ballads of Fionn mac Cumhaill and the Fianna, but these have nothing much to do with my subject of the moment, nor has what passed for literature in the townships of the English Pale. We know from an ordinance of the Bishop of Ossory in the middle of the fourteenth century that his Kilkenny clerics sang love songs in Old English and Norman-French like 'Alas, How Shold Y Syng?' and 'Heu, helas, paramour, qui me mist en tant doulour!' But so far as the written evidence goes, the majority of literate people were among the Norman marchers and the remaining Irish lords, and the culture they shared was that of the Irish professional classes hammered into shape in the eleventh and twelfth centuries.

As I may have made clear, this is not a culture that appeals to me, but it was a real culture, and, like the fine architecture on which its way of life was based, deserves more attention than has been paid to it. To begin a criticism that, in the peculiar ignorance of our time, must also be a defence, it is a purely aristocratic culture with no popular element whatever. In this way it represents a reversion to pre-Christian culture, because I doubt if an Irish cleric of the eighth or ninth century would have stood for very much of it. It has no real prose, and consequently no intellectual content. It is purely poetic, and hinges on the concept of the king as a sacred person, whoever the king might be, Irish or English, and whatever his real rank in the feudal system. Like the poet himself, the king is not so much a person as a function. To a professional Irish poet the Norman earl filled the function as well as any Irish king, and Norman earls seemed to have shared this view. The poet's purpose was to praise the king and so increase the harvest, and if it was necessary he was required to admonish and even satirize him. This function made the poet expect a quasi-equality with the king, not unlike that which Thomas Becket expected with Henry II, and naturally this sometimes led to bad blood. We have seen Murrough O'Daly shocked at the behaviour of the King of Tyrconnell when he had merely cut down an impudent tax-collector.

Ever since John O'Donovan made the extraordinary statement that the Irish professional poet 'fulfilled many of the functions of a modern journalist', it has been repeated by every scholar and writer until the whole subject has become fogged. O'Donovan's remark is mere nonsense: there was nothing of the journalist, ancient or modern, about the Irish court poet. There *was* a great deal of the magician and the priest, and Irish court poetry can be studied only as a ritual.

The Irish aristocracy had a nervous breakdown unless it received sufficient praise; the Normans could apparently take a great deal of it without noticing anything wrong. Neither liked criticism or satire, which brought bad luck, just as praise brought good luck; and the magical dispensers of both were people whose arrogance was fed by the peculiarly ambiguous situation in which they found themselves. For the first time since the fifth century they had no serious opposition from the Church. They frequently offended their masters and had to eat humble pie. For this, also, there was a recognized ritual: if the king did not accept the first friendly poem, one wrote another to an intermediary; to his wife requesting her not to go to bed with him or to his son requesting him not to play with his father till the situation was regularized. And then the fun began again.

I know no religious poetry of the period that was not written by professional poets, so it is perhaps natural that it should be an echo of Court poetry. God was regarded as an Irish ruler, Gaelic or Norman, to whom the poet had certain duties and from whom he expected certain rewards. The poet might approach God directly, but in case of any little difficulty he had recourse to God's mother, or — failing Her — to any saint that he thought might be sufficiently influential.

A good example of what I mean occurs in a beautiful thirteenth-century poem by Giolla Bríde Mac Conmhidhe, who found himself without a son to carry on his name. To any Irishman or Norman of the time this would have been serious enough, but for a poet in a society where poetry was a hereditary profession it was a tragedy. In the poem he asks God for a son, but he does so as though he were addressing a local prince and asking for a horse.

> *Déan oram trócaire, a Thríonóid,*
> *Tug radharc i rosg an doill;*
> *Féar tres an gcreig, a Dhé, is doilghe;*
> *Ná leig mhé, a Choimdhe, gan chloinn.*

> *Cuire bláth tre bharr an fheadha,*
> *A Athair Mhóir (mairg nach tuig!);*
> *Bláth tre bharr na gcrann-sa, a Choimdhe,*
> *Clann damhsa gár dhoilghe dhuid?*[1]

[1] T. F. O'Rahilly (ed.), *Measgra Dánta* (Cork, 1927), 163.

Blessed Trinity, have pity!
    You can give the blind man sight;
Fill the rocks with waving grasses;
    Give my house a child tonight.

You can bend the woods with blossom —
    What is there you cannot do? —
All the branches burst with leafage —
    What's a little child to you?

Then comes the part which is less poetic but much more characteristic.

Mo dhá itche, a Airdrí nimhe —
    Neamh an chéidní chuingheas mé;
Madh áil lat is lór a rádha,
    Mac i lógh mo dhána, a Dhé.

Faghaidh dhamh, a Mhuire Mháthair,
    Mac ré ndul don domhan ché;
Im chrú nochar fhuirigh aonarc,
    A bhrú ar dhuinigh daonnacht Dé.

Guidh liom clann do bheith 'na mbeathaidh,
    A Bhrighid ór baisteadh mé;
Ná léig t'fhear dána fá dhímheas,
    A bhean ghrádha dhíleas Dé.

God, I ask for two things only;
    Heaven when my life is done;
Payment as befits a poet;
    For my poem pay a son.

Plead with Him, O Mother Mary,
    Let Him grant the child I crave —
Womb that spun God's human tissue
    I no human issue leave.

Brigid after whom they named me,
    Beg a son for my reward;
Let not your poet empty-handed
    Leave the dwelling of his Lord.

So far as modern taste goes the best of these poems are the most personal, like Giolla Bríde's, or Murrough O'Daly's beautiful poem on the death of his wife, Geoffrey O'Daly's on the death of his son, and Tadhg O'Higgins' on the death of his brother; but even in such an apparently unexceptionable opinion I suspect we may be all completely wrong. I doubt very much if any of the poets would have understood our view that a poem on the death of a wife or son took precedence of one on the death of a king. The poet of the poem 'Cumhthach labhras an lonsa' — 'The blackbird sings his song in tears' — which I quoted in a previous chapter, would have understood us perfectly. Death was death to him as to the blackbird, and the question of whether the death was that of a real aristocrat or not would simply not have occurred to him, but as Miss Knott reminded us the poem was 'a little earlier than our period'. In classical Irish poetry one might almost say that there is no such thing as a personal poem. Son or wife or brother was commemorated as part of a system of which the king was the earthly and God the heavenly head. God, whose man the poet is, has deprived him of one of his privileges, and as a loyal servant the poet must accept this, but always the complaint is against the king, not against life itself as in the poem on the blackbird's nest. Or as Murrough O'Daly puts it in his own beautiful elegy on his wife:

> Is é rug uaim í 'na ghrúg,
> Rí na sluagh is Rí na ród;
> Beag an cion do chúl na ngéag
> A héag ó a fior go húr óg.

> It was the king of hosts and roads
> Who snatched her from me in her prime;
> Little she wished to leave alone
> The man she loved before her time.[2]

I cannot help feeling that this extraordinary feudal conception of the relationship between God and man is at the bottom of the curious melancholia that underlies so much of the Irish religious

[2] 'Unpublished Irish Poems, XXVII.' *Studies*, Sept. 1924.

poetry of the time. It is the melancholy of people who have made a feudal compact with a lord whose behaviour is ultimately irrational but against whom they cannot rebel. Life itself never seems to become detached in their minds from its individual and slightly peculiar Author. Once more, their minds are too concrete, too incapable of abstraction.

I think too that it is at the bottom of an attitude by which every commentator has been outraged — the poets' acceptance of the Norman invaders and their readiness to write poetry for them exactly like the poetry they wrote for native chiefs. 'Ireland is swordland', wrote one, and another, addressing Richard de Burgo, says, 'Richard's charter to Ireland is the charter of the sword — what better is there?' Our greatest authority, Miss Knott, tells us that Geoffrey O'Daly 'sums up the matter frankly in some cynical lines addressed to the Earl of Desmond'.

> A sovranty they never got we promise the Irish in our poems; you need take no notice of this, it is our custom. . . . There are two races for whom poetry is composed in Ireland of the cool springs — the Irish, eager for fame, and the English of Britain's dewy isle. In poetry for the English we promise that the Irish shall be banished from Ireland; in poetry for the Irish we promise that the English shall be routed oversea.[3]

'To frown deeply at such sentiments would perhaps be to miss the perspective of history', she adds wisely, but surely 'the perspective of history' was lost sight of long ago when scholars adopted O'Donovan's dotty view that poets like O'Daly were fulfilling 'the functions of a modern journalist'. But is O'Daly expressing any such sentiments as Miss Knott imputes to him? I think not; I believe the word 'cynical' applied to these lines is completely meaningless because it is based on a meaningless analogy.

I have already discussed the extraordinary capacity of those tribal poets for absorbing alien elements — something which may, as I have suggested, have to do with the fact that they themselves had to move among conflicting tribes. It was not only English

[3] Eleanor Knott, *Irish Classical Poetry* (Dublin, 1957), 60.

observers who objected to this peculiar literature of praise and blame, nor was the objection merely to the fact that it fomented tribal jealousies. There was always a certain amount of resentment against it by religious men. 'It is a wicked thing to distort all that Christ died for on the cross, all he created of His mere will and all that the Judge of Doomsday fashioned', wrote Tadhg MacEgan in a poem against professional poetry. One friar came back from a pilgrimage to Rome with what he declared to be a papal denunciation of professional poetry, but unfortunately all we know of it is a noble reply by Giolla Bríde Mac Conmhidhe, whose poem on his childlessness I have already quoted.

> The Son of Mary will give me a reward that no human being could give me; for one of my excellent poems I shall get Heaven as O'Heffernan got it.
> All praise of men is praise of Him who created them all; no man on earth has any praise that is not also praise of His wonder.

Once more Giolla Bríde links the concept of the earthly and heavenly king. When Geoffrey O'Daly explains to the Earl of Desmond that there are two sorts of poetry, one intended for the Irish, the other for the English, and says, 'You need take no notice of this, it is our custom', he is no more being cynical than a priest would be who explained to two belligerents that he was compelled to pray for the welfare of both. 'It is our custom'; contradictory, but not in the least cynical. What makes it seem cynical is O'Donovan's assumption that a religious function is a journalistic one.

From the point of view of the literary man it is both too religious and too professional. There is a contemporary Welsh Court poetry of much the same kind and perhaps the greatest living poet was the professional Dafydd Ap Gwilym, but Welsh poetry has been strongly affected by Norman-French poetry (I can find no such influence in Irish), and the poet is at the same time a magician and an entertainer. Many of Dafydd's best poems are comic turns that chronicle his disasters in pursuit of the imaginary Morfydd.

The only poet we in Ireland have who can be classed with

Dafydd — and that, I am afraid, a long way behind — is Gerald, Earl of Desmond, at the end of the fourteenth century. He was the small boy whom Geoffrey O'Daly requested not to play with his father till the old man forgave Geoffrey's insolence, and Geoffrey was probably his tutor. He represents the collapse of the Norman cultural empire during the twelfth and thirteenth centuries, because when French ceased to be the common tongue of the invaders they could revert only to English, Irish and Welsh, and themselves became Englishmen, Irishmen and Welshmen.

Gerald grew up not only to be the English justiciar, but an Irish poet more famous than Geoffrey O'Daly. He is a strange, romantic figure, typical of the fourteenth century. He was sufficiently of his time to have a genuine devotion to the Blessed Virgin and ended every poem with a verse addressed to her. For some reason — possibly because he posed as a great lover — he was also attracted by the Fenian hero, Díarmait O Duibne, Grania's lover in the romance, and addressed the second last verse of each poem to him. But as well as that he had a passionate friendship with Diarmuid Mac-Carthy, the Irish lord of Muskerry, and addressed the *third* last verse of each poem to him. When Diarmuid MacCarthy died in 1381 he continued the practice, which is not to be recommended.

In the year 1370 Brian O'Brien of Thomond crossed the Shannon, defeated Gerald at Monasternenagh in Limerick and took him prisoner. For more than a year, until the lord deputy ransomed him, Gerald was detained first in Killaloe, then in Ennis, and wrote a remarkable group of poems about his experience. Gerald's poems have only recently appeared, and the text is very bad. This was obviously written when he was in Ennis.

> Gá lá fhúigfead Innse an Laoigh —
> Tosach bhios ar laoidh dom dhán;
> Is mithid liom dul amach
> Anois, má tá damh i ndán.

> I nInnse an Laoigh ar lár cuain
> I gCluain Ramhfhada na ríogh
> Ag eisteacht re nuall na sreabh
> Atá mé re feadh dhá mhíos.

Cruit í Bhriain fa sirim beoir
Fa hiad mo thrí ceoil do gnáith;
Faoidh chluig Innse don taobh thiar,
Nuall na lice ag triall sa sál. . . .[4]

When shall I leave Ennis behind?
That's how my poem should begin.
Indeed it's time that I got out,
Considering all the time I'm in.

In Ennis at the river's mouth
O'Brien's prisoner I have been,
And listened here for two long months
To the murmur of the stream.

O'Brien's harp at drinking time,
The water lapping on the stone,
The sound of the Ennis abbey bell
Are all the music I have known. . . .

This is what I really mean by amateur poetry. It is not too finished; it is in aid of nothing in particular except getting out of prison, and when it comes to cynicism, it seems to me that Gerald can beat Geoffrey O'Daly hands down. I assume that the poem from which I shall quote was written at the same time. It is a remarkable document because it describes perfectly the tragedy of colonialism, particularly at the moment when the common language of the colonists breaks down and they are thrown on the mercy of a vernacular.

Do lidhfidis Saxanaigh
Orainn i dteirtibh falaigh
Nach romhó do thargamair
Ar Ghaoidhealaibh ná ar Ghallaibh

Fuilngim tír na nÉireannach
Nach rachainn i gceann Ghaoidheal
Mina tíosadh éigeantas
Ó ríogh Shaxan dom laoidheadh. . . .

Fearr liom bheith 'gam bráithreachaibh
Gidh créd a n-intinn umainn
Ná beith a gcoir bhraighdeanais
Ag ríogh Shaxan i Lunainn. . . .[4]

The English with their perjured tricks
  Would drag me through their courts and then
Say I had rarely raised my hand
  To Irish more than Englishmen.

I call on every Irish friend
  To bear me witness in this thing
I never fought with Irishmen
  Except for fear of England's king. . . .

And I had sooner fight again,
  However they revile and prate
Than rot in London in the tower
  For England's king to choose my fate. . .

Cynicism? Yes, but cynicism we can understand as we cannot
understand the supposed cynicism of Gerald's tutor. In another
poem, which begins 'Mór idir anocht 's aréir' ('It is a long time
from last night until tonight'), I am inclined to think that 'Mór' is
a punning reference to Mór, the daughter of Brian O'Brien, who
later married O'Carroll of Ely and was the mother of Margaret
O'Carroll, the Ottoline Morrell of the fifteenth century. In other
words Gerald, having failed to get round the king, was trying to
get round the king's daughter, who admired his poetry, in the best
professional manner inculcated by Geoffrey O'Daly.

This was in 1371 and Gerald had not long to wait for his release.
Ten years later the man he loved, Diarmuid MacCarthy, died, and
no doubt the professional poets wrote elegies on him that I should
admire if they had been preserved. Gerald's poem on his death, if
my reading of it is correct, is like no professional poetry ever written. It is amateur poetry and not the best amateur poetry either,
but it moves me because Gerald was not thinking of the king or
God or of anything else but his own personal loss, which he sym-

---

[4] G. Mac Niocaill, *Studia Hibernica*, III, 1963.

bolized in terms of a cattle raid, much as any hero of 'The Cattle
Raid of Cooley' might have done. It begins with an invocation to
some of the rivers of Munster.

> Ach, a Dhaoil,
> Gidh iomdha deaghlaoch red taoibh,
>> Do-bheirim briathar gan bhréig
> A bhfuil idir Fhéil is Daoil —
>
> Ach, a Mháigh!
> Dar an leabhar bhíos im' láimh
>> Dá mbeath ar cumas dam féin
> A bhfuil idir Fhéil is Máigh —
>
> Ach, a Shiúir!
> Gibé ní re bhfuil mo shúil
>> Ó ghlansruth Mhaighe go Daoil
> A bhfuil ó Dhún Chaoin go Siúir —
>
> Dámadh liom th'airgead is th'or
>> Ach, a Mhumha mhór mhic Con,
> A bhfuil idir tuaith is cill
>> Idir caladh is linn is loch.
>
> Ach, a Dhiarmaid mac an ríogh
>> A ua Charrthaigh o shíodh Bhreagh,
> Atá anocht i n-iomdhaidh fhuair,
>> Is ionnat do-chuaidh mo chreach.[5]
>
> Ah, Deel!
> Though much you may have to steal,
>> I give you my word without lie
> That all between Feale and Deel —
>
> And you, Maigue,
> Though robbers may pillage and plague,
>> If I owned everything
> That lies between Feale and Maigue.

[5] Ibid.

And Suir, Suir!
Whatever may rest secure
    From the banks of Maigue to Deel
And all from Dunquin to the Suir. —

Munster, all silver and gold
    That raiding bands could take,
Plunder of people and priest,
    Harbour, river, and lake.

All, Diarmuid MacCarthy, my friend,
    The King of Muskerry's son,
Asleep in your cold bed —
    All went when you were gone!

I am not saying that this is great poetry. I feel sure that Geoffrey O'Daly would have had a few words to say of it. But I should prefer to be the author of that poem — that is to say, assuming that I am not — than of anything that Geoffrey O'Daly wrote.

CHAPTER EIGHT

The Renaissance in Ireland

The last great outburst of literature in Irish is best represented by the love poetry collected by T. F. O'Rahilly in *Dánta Grádha*. We may add a few occasional poems in the same editor's *Measgra Dánta* and a handful of Bergin's editions of Court poetry.

As its technical excellence shows that it was widely admired and practised, there was clearly a great deal more that has perished — personal poetry always stood a bad chance of preservation beside professional; but even the hundred and odd poems that remain form a remarkable group. They have not been studied with any great critical attention, and vague suggestions of influence from Provençal and Norman-French strike me as far-fetched. There is no hint of French influence in the poems of the Earl of Desmond, and if French influence had not made itself felt by the end of the fourteenth century, when it was strongest in Wales, it is most unlikely that it made itself felt at all.

These poems are part of the sort of development one might expect — the mingling of English and Irish strains. One can see this very clearly in architecture, particularly in the Franciscan abbeys built during the fifteenth century. The English had lost much of the elegance of their thirteenth-century architecture, the Irish much of the charm of theirs. There is no Graiguenamanagh or Gowran on the one side, no Jerpoint or Cong on the other. Both shared a practical functional style, rather standardized, very dignified, but a little forbidding. There is little of the lovely tracery of English windows of the Perpendicular style, and what there is is rather simple-minded. The love poetry has something of the same quality. So far as I can date the poems, they are Tudor, Jacobean and one at least Restoration.

In searching for origins I doubt if we need go much farther than English. By the sixteenth century it was beginning to play the same part as Latin had played in the literature of the early Middle Ages; it was expanding the whole conception of literature and bringing

the practice of it back where it belonged, to the amateurs, though
the amateurs were now noblemen rather than churchmen. What
Desmond did because he wanted to do it, people like Pierce Ferriter,
Richard Burke, the Earl of Clancarty, and the Countess of Argyll
in Scotland did because it was the thing to do, and the professional
poets joined in the game and made the rules a bit harder.

What mainly distinguishes it from English poetry of the period
is that it had to be grafted onto the technique of professional
poetry, and naturally, this is particularly true of poems written by
professional poets, like Cú Chonnacht O'Clery, who occasionally
seem uncertain whether they are writing for God, the king, or a
lady. One of the conventions of courtly love was, of course, that
you were dying on the woman's account, like Romeo, 'stabbed
with a white wench's black eye'. But Cú Chonnacht will blow this
up into an elaborate piece of professionalism like the poem I quote.
(Bergin calls it 'mysterious', and there is a fine romantic translation
by James Stephens, which may be consulted by way of comparison.)

> Ní mé bhar n-aithne, a aos gráidh,
> Ná sginnidh le sgáth seachráin;
> Fuar dár seise im ionad ionn,
> Spiorad mheise nach maireann.
>
> An dóigh libh, a lucht m'fhéaghtha,
> Nach taidhbhse i dtruaill aieurtha
> Nó spiorad anma fhallsa
> Tarla im ionad agamsa?
>
> A aithne is éidir damhsa
> Sibh gan fhiacha oramsa;
> Dá mbeth cás fám eág oraibh
> Mo bhás créad nach gcualabhair? . . .[1]
>
> My comrades, I am not your friend!
> No, pray do not be frightened!
> It is difficult enough to bear
> Being but a lifeless spectre.

[1] O'Rahilly (ed.), Dánta Grádha, 66.

But you need have no doubt of it,
Indeed I am a spirit;
Or else some ghost 'midst living men
From me my place has taken.

Easy to tell by you at least
That I in life was honest;
For if I had owed you anything
You would know of my undoing. . . .

It is all great fun, and very beautiful, but it is as queer as a coot, and anyhow has more Donne than Wyatt in it. It is even stranger when we find courtly love in what I take to be one of those formal odes in which some local lord is solemnly invited to accept the throne of Ireland: 'A sovranty they never got we promise to the Irish in our poems; you need take no notice of it; it is our custom.' All the same, I think even Geoffrey O'Daly would have been astonished by one such poem, written by another member of the O'Higgins family, and, if we accept Professor Carney's view, nearly forty years after Cromwell. In this Ireland is depicted as the wife of O'Rourke of Breany, torn between her true husband and a pretender, Tomás Costello. Costello is supposed to be the speaker in the greatest of Irish folk-songs, 'Uná Bhán', which deals with a tragic love-affair between himself and Una MacDermott.

> *B'fhearr liom bheith im luighe léi ar leaba dhá pógadh*
> *Ná im shuidhe insna flaithis i gcathaoir na Tríonóide.*

I had sooner be lying in bed kissing her than sitting in Heaven in the chair of the Blessed Trinity.

This is a popular song metre, but there is nothing popular about 'O'Rourke's Wife'. The curious thing is that with all the conventional clichés and chevilles of the professional poet — 'O gold hair! O sweet voice!' and so on — the poem analyses the mind of a married woman in love as delicately as Stendhal might have done it.

Ná creid cách, ní meirdreach mé;
Óg fuaras fios mo chéile;
Fada ó tharla Aodh ormsa;
T'fhabhra ná claon chugamsa.

Bhar bhfé fia ni feirrde dhuit;
Aithnim thu d'aimhdheoin h'iomlait;
A bhradaire, ná mill mé;
Fill, a ghadaighe an gháire.

Cosg th'álghais uaim ní bhfuighe,
A bhraidín, a bhréagaire;
Let uaisle ná mearaigh mé;
Buail-se um cheanaibh gach críche.[2]

Forget the things the neighbours say;
    I am no harlot as you think;
I was a girl when first I loved;
    I have not strayed; you must not wink.

The enchantment of desire is vain;
    I see through every mask you don;
You rascal, pity my good name!
    You thief of laughter, get you gone.

You bandit of my heart, away!
    I shall not give your lust release;
Smother the frontier posts in flame
    But let my foolish heart have peace.

Here it seems to me we are dealing with Baroque poetry, but
Baroque of a peculiar kind, grafted on to an Indo-European ritual
such as Geoffrey O'Daly described, and it was not unique, nor was
it confined to love poetry. At the beginning of the seventeenth
century Hugh Maguire, one of Tyrone's lieutenants, was on a winter campaign in Munster, and his professional poet, Eochy O'Hussey,
wrote one of the standard complimentary poems to him. In its own
way it is almost as unusual as the poem to Tomás Costello, and it

[2] O'Rahilly (ed.), *Dánta Grádha*, 55.

is scarcely a matter for wonder that James Clarence Mangan translated it into a torrent of nineteenth-century romantic eloquence.

> Where is my Chief, my Master, this bleak night, *mavrone?*
> O, cold, cold, miserably cold is this bleak night for Hugh,
> Its showery, arrowy, speary sleet pierceth one through
>   and through
> Pierceth one to the very bone.

In Irish the poem is rather more functional than that, but even if you translate it into pseudo-Horatian, as I prefer to do, it remains quite different from earlier professional poetry. It has been given a strong injection of the concreteness of the love poetry.

> *Saoth linn, do loit ar meanmain,*
> *Learg thais a thaoibh míndealbhaigh*
> *'Gá meilt a ngruamoidhche ghairbh*
> *A mbeirt fhuarfhoirfe iairn.*

> *Bos tláith na dtachar n-édtláth,*
> *Síon oighridh dá fhuaighéaltáth*
> *Re crann rionnfhuar gcaol gceise*
> *Ionnfhuar dh'Aodh san oidhchese. . . .*

> *Líonaid re hucht na n-ánrath*
> *Bruaigh ísle na n-uaránshroth;*
> *Cluana sgor fa sgingbheirt reoáidh*
> *Da gcor tar ingheilt d'aimhdheoin. . . .*[3]

> I can scarce bear to conjure up
> The contour of his body crushed
>   This rough and gloomy night
>   In its cold iron suit.

> The generous and war-mastering hand
> To the slim shaft of his cold spear
>   By icy weather pinned —
>   Cold is this night for Hugh. . . .

[3] Osborn Bergin, 'Unpublished Irish Poems, xv.' *Studies*, Sept. 1921.

The low banks of the swollen streams
Are flooded where the soldiers pass;
Meadows are stiff with ice;
The horses cannot graze. . . .

O'Hussey himself was aware of the difference in atmosphere, and
writes about it most amusingly in another formal poem to Rory
O'Donnell, Earl of Tyrconnell, who was in London in 1603. The
compliment is in the implication that O'Donnell found no difficulty
in reading classical Irish and it is probably exaggerated.

Ionmholta malairt bhisigh:
Tárraidh sinne 'sa amsa
Iomlaoid go suarrach sona,
Do chuaidh a sochar dhamssa.

Do thréig sinn sreatha caola
Foirceadal bhfaobhrach ffrithir
Ar shórt gnáthach grés robhog
As mó as a moltar sinne.

Le dorchacht na ngrés snoighthe
Do bhínnse ag tuilliodh gráine:
Fa hí ughachta mhórain
Nár dhíol róghráidh ar ndáinne.

Maithim, giodh mor an t-easba
Énbhonn feasda dá thoradh
Má theid énrann gan tuigse
Dom dhánsa ó dhuine as domhan.

Dán bog ar bhéal na slighiodh
Ós é anois sirthior orainn,
Cuirfeadsa dhíom na fiacha
Go gcead d'Iarla Chlann gConaill. . . .[4]

I like the simple ways
That modern poetry goes,
Fatuous but worthy praise,
And lucrative, God knows.

[4] Osborn Bergin, 'Unpublished Irish Poems, IV.' *Studies*, Dec. 1918.

I have left the manly skill
　Of academic art
For a sort of easy thrill
　That makes men take my part.

At poetry I drudged
　And earned contempt and wrong,
For many a patron grudged
　A sixpence for my song.

I waive, though great my loss,
　One farthing of my fee
If now my verse surpass
　Man's mediocrity.

Limp verse for travelling fit
　Being everyone's intent
All royalties I remit
　With the earl's kind consent. . . .

　Most of the love poems are less elaborate than those I have been quoting, but they are all based on this technique. They never seem to me to catch the romantic overflow of Elizabethan poetry, which sometimes fails either through technical clumsiness or through sheer excess of genius to keep the precise distance that the convention of courtly love requires. Irish, for instance, never becomes so intensely personal that it blows the convention to blazes as happens in some of Shakespeare's sonnets. The English poetry has magic — 'Fair house of joy and bliss where truest pleasure is' — the Irish has a concreteness that one might almost call meanness; a certain commonness of material eked out by strict technical control. The poet tends to stress the drama : O'Clery does not say, 'Your eyen two will slee me sodenly'; he says, 'I am dead', and then proceeds to act out the scene. O'Higgins does not say, 'Ireland calls to you'; he says, 'I am Ireland and though married to someone else, I love you.' In one very funny poem Laoiseach Mac An Bhaird (Lewis Ward), adopting a tone of intense complacency, meets a girl in tears, dismisses the notion that one of her family is dead, presumes she is in love, presumes that, of course, she is in love with himself, and ends up by hinting that if only she will be reasonable her dreams may come true this very night. Another favourite poem of mine seems to be about a girl in love with a married man who is still devoted to his unpleasant wife — not an unfamiliar situation. The poet dramatizes it very sharply: the girl affects to have roused her lover's jealousy by flirting with another man, and in a series of paradoxes shows us the whole unreasonable love affair as if it were turned inside out before us.

> *Abair leis ná déanadh éad,*
> *'S gur bréag an sgéal do cuireadh faoi;*
> *Is aige féin atá mo ghrádh,*
> *Is m'fhuath do ghnáth aga mhnaoi.*

> *Má mharbhann sé mé tré éad*
> *Rachaidh a bhean d'éag dom dhíth;*
> *Éagfaidh féin do chumha na mná,*
> *Is tiocfaidh mar sin bás an trír.*

> *Gach maith ó neamh go lár*
> *Chum na mna agá bhfuil m'fhuath,*
> *'S an fear agá bhfuil mo ghrádh,*
> *Go bhfagha sé bás go luath!*[5]

> Tell him it's all a lie!
>   I love him as much as my life;
> He needn't be jealous of me;
>   I love him and loathe his wife.

> If he kills me through jealousy now
>   His wife will perish of spite,
> He'll die of grief for his wife —
>   Three of us dead in a night!

> All blessings from heaven to earth
>   On the head of the woman I hate!
> And the man I love as my life,
>   Sudden death be his fate!

⁵ O'Rahilly (ed.), *Dánta Grádha*, 103.

The merits of this sort of poetry, I should say, are different from those of Elizabethan poetry. There is in it a cold, practical quality that, refusing to accept the convention, forces it just a little in the direction of comedy, and then suddenly falls on an entirely new conception of the situation. The odd, startling verses that stick in one's mind are not invocations like 'Fair house of joy and bliss', but poignant little human comments like 'A danger to my soul is all my body has dreamed' or 'She is but a serving maid to love and no longer mistress of herself'. Catullus' 'I love and hate' is part of the convention, but even this is more sharply dramatized:

> *Thugas grádh don fhuath,*
> *Cuirim suas don ghrádh . . .*[6]

> Hate alone I love,
> Love I set aside. . . .

This was a poem that Yeats thought a great deal about, as we see from the way he transmutes it in the late 'Supernatural Songs':

> Why should I seek for Love or study it?
> It is of God and passes human wit.
> I study hatred with great diligence
> For that's a passion in my own control. . . .

The last two lines are almost a direct translation of the Irish, and it is interesting that they come so late in Yeats' career, because it seems to me that the difference I am trying to define is that between an old civilization and a young one. The Elizabethans adopt courtly love with all the enthusiasm that young people in the twenties showed over free love, but it seems to me that the Irish adopt it with the feeling of having been there before. It may be significant that one of the finest poems of the period is about a man so old and physically exhausted that he can no longer have sexual relations with the woman he loves. I doubt if an English Elizabethan would not have considered the subject comic rather than moving.

[6] O'Rahilly (ed.), *Dánta Grádha*, 123.

A bhean lán do stuaim,
  Cuinnibh uaim do lámh;
Ní fear gníomha sinn,
  Cé taoi tinn dár ngrádh.

Féach ar liath dom fholt!
  Féach mo chorp gan lúth!
Féach ar thraoch dom fhuil —
  Créad re bhfuil do thnúth?

Ná saoil mé go saobh,
  Is ná claon do cheann;
Bíodh ar ngrádh gan gníomh
  Go bráth, a shíodh sheang.

Druid do bhéal óm bhéal —
  Doiligh an scéal do chor;
Ná bíom cneas re cneas,
  Tig ón dteas an tol.

Do chúl craobhach cas,
  Do rosg glas mar dhrúcht,
Do chíoch chruinngheal bhláith
  Thairngeas mian gach súl.

Gach gníomh ach gníomh cuirp
  Is luighe id chuilt shuain,
Do-dhéanainn tred ghrádh,
  A bhean lán do stuaim.[7]

Woman full of wile,
  Take your hand away!
Nothing tempts me now;
  Sick for love you pray.

But my hair is grey
  And my flesh is weak,
All my blood gone cold —
  What is it you seek?

[7] O'Rahilly (ed.), Dánta Grádha, 133.

Do not think me mad;
  Do not hang your head;
Slender witch, let love
  Live in thought, not deed.

Take your mouth from mine,
  Kissing's bitterer still;
Flesh from flesh must part
  Lest of warmth come will.

Your twined branching hair,
  Your grey eye dew-bright,
Your rich rounded breast
  Turn to lust the sight.

But for the wild bed
  And the body's flame,
Woman full of wile,
  My love is still the same.

Ireland at the turn of that terrible seventeenth century was changing rapidly and violently, and much of the change must be attributed to the extension of the knowledge of English — not because it was a superior language, but because, like medieval Latin, it was acting as a sort of lingua franca. Some of the changes were scarcely for the better. In the old verse I have quoted the syllables are counted as in French without regard to the tonic accent, which in Irish was very strong. Now the harpers were playing foreign airs with a metronomic beat, and poetry was being written not according to the number of syllables, but according to the number of accented words in the line, more or less in the manner of English verse but with the musical beat accentuated by assonantal rhyming. Every peasant poet was hammering it out with hobnailed boots like an ignorant audience listening to a Mozart minuet. It is no wonder if it offended O'Hussey's delicate ear; it often offends mine. Here is a rather charming epigram by a Franciscan priest called Hackett to a girl named Ellen Carew :

Oilléan Carrún, laglúb líomhtha léir,
Foiléim ainiúl teacht dúinn sínte léi,
Bruithshéis taighiúir fhrais-chiúin chaoin a téad
Thug mé ag machtnú feadh cúig n-oíche ndéag.

Ellen Carew, a soft, versatile, sharp-witted girl; it was great folly for me to compete with her, for the magic, streamy, quiet cadence of her harp strings has kept me dreaming for fifteen nights.

Practically every syllable in this rhymes assonantally — U e, A u, A u, I a, E. It goes very nicely to the tune of the 'Rakes of Mallow' but any tune you can fit it to turns out like a sixteenth-century dance. All the poet has really done is to take a country dance and use a pattern of assonance to illustrate it; and this soon becomes wearying to the ear.

But at any rate the end of this extraordinary culture was now in sight, as even that little verse can teach us; for the poet's name is Hackett, an Anglo-Norman name, and the girl's Carew, which is as English as they come, but from the point of view of the new wave of Englishmen who were pouring in — the Cromwellians — both were merely Irish papists.

CHAPTER NINE

Anglo-Irish Literature

With the seventeenth century we come to the heart of our problem — the point at which Irish literature becomes Anglo-Irish literature proper. The literature of the late Middle Ages and the Tudor period is also Anglo-Irish, but with a difference: that the main element is Irish. By the time we reach the eighteenth century the dominant, indeed, the only significant element is English.

To understand this change we must make a clear distinction between cultural and political nationality. What the Old English (as they were called) and the Irish shared was a cultural nationality that did not impinge upon their political identity. They remained clearly distinguished up to Cromwellian times and probably later; but when they wrote, when they sang and when they built they were practically indistinguishable. The cultural nationality was partly destroyed during the Cromwellian wars because the Cromwellians were the English lower and middle classes; towns-folk who could not understand a cultural nationality that belonged to a landed gentry with feudal and royalist ideas. (A similar movement of the Irish lower and middle class seems to have occurred of which we know very little.)

Its destruction was completed by the Whig revolution, which clamped on the majority of the population a set of laws intended to exterminate them. The Penal Laws sent thousands of young noblemen to Austria, France and Spain, where their genealogy was still respected and where they could rise to a position appropriate to their birth. One of the moving things I remember was living in the home of Sir Desmond MacCarthy outside London with a genealogical tree of the MacCarthys in my bedroom that some ancestor had brought abroad to prove that his family was noble. Somewhere in the reminiscences of Mozart's friend Michael Kelly there is a description of how some Irish officers in South Germany addressed him in Irish, and he, to the king's question as to why an Irishman like himself did not speak Irish, replied, 'Sire, in Ireland only the lower classes speak Irish.'

By the end of the seventeenth century the position of such families as the MacCarthys was desperate. One of the most beautiful of Irish folk-songs dates from that time. It is called 'John O'Dwyer of the Glen' and is a lament for the English clearance of the old woodlands. In fact, it is not a folk-song at all but a poem written by a professional poet in one of the new song metres; but since it was not recorded until after it had passed into the folk memory it cannot be restored. Its spirit is entirely feudal: the local lord regrets the cutting down of the woods as an interference with his sport, and then — and only then — as a hardship on his tenants.

> Ar m'éirghe dham ar maidin,
> Grian an tsamhraidh'g taithneamh,
> Chuala an uaill d'á casadh
>   Agus ceol binn na n-éan;
> Bruic is míolta gearra,
> Creabhair na ngoba bhfada,
> Fuaim ag an macalla
>   Is lámhach gunnaí dtréan.
> An sionnach ruadh ar an gCarraig,
> Míle liúgh ag marcaigh,
> Is bean go dubhach 'san mbealach
>   Ag áireamh a cuid géadh.
> Anois tá an choill d'á gearradh;
> Triallfaimid tar caladh,
> 'S a Sheáin Uí Dhuibhir an Ghleanna,
>   Tá tú gan géim.[1]

> When once I rose at morning
> The summer sun was shining;
> I heard the young wind crying
>   And the birds' merry songs;
> There were badger and weasel,
> Woodcock and plover,
> And echo repeating
>   The music of the guns;

[1] Róis ní Ógáin, Duanaire Gaedhilge (Dublin, 1921), 1, 75.

The weary fox was flagging,
The horsemen followed shouting;
Counting her geese on the highway
Some woman's heart was sore;
But now the woods are falling,
We must go over the water;
John O'Dwyer of the Valley,
Your pleasure is no more.

By the end of the century people like John O'Dwyer had been forced to leave for France in their hundreds, and the laments that were written for them were also in popular metres, though these no longer represented an interesting literary exercise.

Annsúd atá siad, barr-uaisle Éireann,
Diúici, Búrcaigh is mac Ríogh Shéamais,
Caiptín Talbóid, croidhe na féile,
Is Pádraic Sairséal, grádh ban nÉireann.

Oversea they all are, Ireland's best;
The Dukes and the Burkes, Prince Charlie and the rest;
And Captain Talbot their ranks adorning,
And Patrick Sarsfield, Ireland's darling.

Irish literature in the late seventeenth and the eighteenth centuries was dying in its sleep. It was linked to a semi-feudal aristocracy and could either disappear with it or linger on with that small element of the aristocracy that remained, and was gradually, by denial of education and advancement, being forced down into the ranks of the peasantry, themselves condemned to an existence resembling that of Russian serfs or Negro slaves.

In the seventeenth century small remnants of the aristocracy remained, but as outlaws. We have seen John O'Dwyer. The hero of another famous seventeenth-century song was also a Tipperary gentleman, Edmund O'Ryan. The genuine fragment of this exists only as part of a later folk-song, but we can see that it consisted of a dialogue between O'Ryan and his sweetheart.

'Cé hé sin amuigh
A bhfuil faobhar ar a ghuth
    Ag réabadh mo dhorais dúnta?'
'Mise Eámonn an Chnuic
Atá báidhte fuar fliuch
    Ó shíor-shiubhal sléibhte is gleannta.'
'A laogh ghil 's a chuid,
Cad a dhéanfainn-se dhuit,
    Muna gcuirfinn ort beinn dem' ghúna?
Mar tá púdar go tiugh
D'á shíor-shéideadh riut,
    'S go mbeimís araon múchta.'

'Is fada mise amuigh
Fé shneachta is fé shioc
    'S gan dánacht agam ar aoinne;
Mo sheisreach gan scur,
Mo bhranar gan cur,
    Is gan iad agam ar aon chor.
Níl caraid agam,
Is danaid liom san,
    Do ghlacfadh mé moch ná déidheanach,
Is go gcaithfidh me dul
Tar fairrge soir,
    Ó's ann nach bhfuil mo ghaolta.'

'Who's out there in the night,
His voice sharp with fright,
    Beating on my locked door?'
'I'm Ned of the Hill,
Half drowned and chill
    With walking the mountain and moor.'
'My love and delight,
How can I ease your plight
    Only shelter you under my gown?
For powder and shot
Are forever your lot,
    And together we both may go down.'

'It is long I am lost
In the snow and the frost

And none who will give me a hand;
My plough-team is gone,
And my sowing's not done,
    And I've small claim enough to the land.
It's a sorrowful end
Without even a friend
    Who will shelter me late or soon;
And so I must flee
To the east, oversea,
    Where none of my kindred is gone.'

We can catch scores of glimpses of them, these Irish aristocrats, but perhaps none more moving than that of the Butlers of Kilcash in a song of the early eighteenth century. We are still in Tipperary, among the O'Ryans and O'Dwyers, though now the name is a Norman one.

Cad a dhéanfaimid feasta gan adhmad?
    Tá deire na gcoillte ar lár;
Ní'l trácht ar Chill Chais ná a teaghlach
    'S ní cluinfear a cling go bráth.
An áit úd 'na gcomhnuigheadh an deigh-bhean
    Fuair gradam is meidhir tar mnáibh,
Bhíodh iarlaí ag tarraingt tar tuinn ann
    'S an t-Aifrionn doimhinn dá rádh.

What shall we do without timber?
    The last of the woods is down;
Kilcash and the house of its glory
    And the bell of the house are gone,
The spot where that lady waited
    Who shamed all women for grace
When earls came sailing to meet her
    And Mass was said in the place.

By the eighteenth century that old aristocracy hardly existed at all, even as outlaws, and professional poetry did not exist except as a peasant imitation. Very odd it is too, when the publican, the priest or the village blacksmith is addressed in epithets stolen from the old incantatory ones of court poetry. Egan O'Rahilly was the best of these peasant imitators, and his heavy-handed verse occasionally blazes out in lines that influenced Yeats' later work.

> Mo ghlam is minic is silim-se síor-dheora,
> Is trom mo thubaist is is duine me ar míchóthrom;
> Fonn ní thigeann im ghoire is me ag caí ar bhóithribh
> Ach foghar na muice ná gointear le saigheadóireacht. . . .

> Stadfad feasta, is gairid dom éag gan moill
> Ó treascradh dreagain Leamhain, is Léin is Laoi;
> Rachad a haithle searc na laoch don chill,
> Na flatha fá raibh mo shean roimh éag do Chríost.[2]

> I can never cease, weeping these useless tears;
>   I am a man oppressed, afflicted and undone,
> Who where he wanders mourning no companion hears
>   Only some waterfall that has no cause to mourn.

> Now I shall cease, death comes and I must not delay
>   By Laune and Laine and Lee diminished of their pride;
> I shall go after the heroes, ay, into the clay;
>   My fathers followed theirs before Christ was crucified.

Unlike Daniel Corkery, who wrote a very lyrical and wrong-headed book on it, I can see nothing to admire in Irish eighteenth-century poetry. (Naturally, I exclude the very beautiful folk-songs, whatever their date may be or wherever they originated.) This is a poetry that, like the people who wrote it, was being steadily degraded socially. There is a curious and moving counterpoint between it and the literature in English that was developing at the same time and in the same places, completely uninfluenced by it. Uninfluenced, because after the Cromwellian invasion of the mid-seventeenth century the old cultural attraction between the Irish and the invaders had completely broken down. There was no necessity for the Government to warn the new class of Englishman against having 'bards and rhymers' in his home. He had no such tendency. All that the Irish and English now shared

[2] Egan O'Rahilly, *Poems of Egan O'Rahilly*, 2nd ed. (ITS, III), Dublin, 1911.

of the old culture was a little harp-playing and musical composition, and that only in a sporadic and tenuous way. That is why
the only name we recognize from Irish literature that is even
vaguely associated with the names of Swift and Goldsmith is that
of the harper Turlough O'Carolan, and what a trifling link it is!

I have mentioned why this violent dislocation of cultural life
took place. It was caused first by the Cromwellians, a type of
Englishman the Irish had scarcely met before: lower or lower
middle class, urbanized, anti-Royalist and anti-Catholic. This
tyranny was welded on to the country by the Whig revolution at
the end of the seventeenth century.

And here, if we are to understand the development of Irish
literature in English, we must make a clear distinction which no
English or American student of Swift has ever made. In Ireland
Whig and Tory do not mean what they mean in England; in fact
it would be safer to say that they mean precisely the opposite. In
the history of England, after the fanatical emergence of the party,
Whig came to represent constitutional government as opposed to
absolutism, religious toleration as opposed to sectarianism, liberal-
ism as opposed to conservatism, but in Ireland it never represented
any of these things. Indeed by the nature of things it could not
do so since the vast majority of the population was kept in
subjection by the Whigs.

I had always assumed, wrongly as it turns out, that Swift himself
began with this knowledge, which would ultimately drive him
into the arms of the English Tories, but in a letter of 1713 you can
find Archbishop King of Dublin spelling it out for him. King is
replying with mock humility to a snub from Swift, who preferred
to believe that Ireland and England must move step by step.

As to the first thing, that it is impossible for the two Kingdoms
to proceed long upon a different scheme of politicks I believe it
is true, but withall I think it impossible to set the two parties
on the same foot in Ireland as in England, for our division is
founded on the right of our Estates which are all claimed by
the forfeiters and nothing can restore them but the Pretender
nor any thing take them from us but bringing him in, whereas
all your contests so farr as I understand them have no other
foundation, but who shall have the ministry and employments

the gaining these has no connexion with the Pretender, you may have them without him or under him. But you see the case is widely different with us and here is the true source of the zeal and violence of the Protestants of Ireld. Remove the fear of the Pretender, and you may lead them like a dog in a string.[3]

Nine years later, when Swift is the leader of a nationalist opposition, he explains it all over again to Pope, almost in King's words, but with a description of the Cromwellian element in the Irish population of which King would scarcely have approved.

> I ought to let you know, that the Thing we called a Whig in England is a creature altogether different from those of the same denomination here . . .
> I was discoursing some years ago with a certain Minister about that whiggish or fanatical Genius so prevalent among the English of this kingdom: his Lordship accounted for it by that number of Cromwell's soldiers, adventurers establish'd here, who were all of the sourest Leven, and the meanest birth, and whose posterity are now in possession of their lands and their principles.[4]

I am not sure that his lordship was not being a little impertinent, for Swift himself had nothing much to boast of in the way of ancestry; his family might easily be described as adventurers, and there was a sour leaven in himself. He was part of that extra-ordinary adventure of colonial England, which tried to establish a bit of home everywhere among people of different races, creeds, and languages, and went about it without charity, intellectual curiosity or imagination. King, who disliked Swift personally and had neither his genius nor integrity, was Scottish by ancestry, and he had real imagination. He saw that the colonists simply could not continue to ignore the subjugated mass of the native Irish; he wished to assimilate them to Protestantism, and he saw that the only way to do this was through the Irish language. What he did *not* realize was that the adoption of Protestantism by the native

[3] Harold Williams, *The Correspondence of Jonathan Swift* (Oxford, 1963), II, 3.
[4] Ibid. II, 371.

Irish would raise precisely the same problems that would be raised by the coming of the Pretender. Once Protestantism ceased to be a minority religion, the Protestant ascendancy ceased. But if King did not realize it, Convocation did, and it had no intention of permitting the native Irish to become Protestants.

> We shall, I believe, have some considerations of methods to convert the natives; [King wrote to Swift] but I do not find, that it is desired by all, that they should be converted. There is a party amongst us, that have little sense of religion, and heartily hate the Church : these would have the natives made Protestants; but such as themselves are deadly afraid they should come into the Church, because, say they, this would strengthen the Church too much. Others would have them come in, but can't approve of the methods proposed, which are to preach to them in their own language, and have the service in *Irish*, as our own canons require.[5]

King, of course, was knocking his head against a wall. An Anglican Ireland and an Irish-speaking Ireland were both intolerable in the eyes of people who belonged to the so-called 'English interest'. (Nevertheless, King can have heard few sillier objections to the adoption of Irish than that of Swift himself, who argued that Irish-speaking clergymen would necessarily have strong Irish accents and be ridiculed when they preached in England!)

Cultural nationality, which was what King was really proposing, was impossible, but there was another sort of nationality that was highly possible — a nationality of common interests. With his deadly cold eye for the political facts King had seen this long before Swift did. There was no way of stopping a conquest once begun except by 'breaking the connection with England' as Wolfe Tone put it later in the century. An Englishman who came to live in Ireland as Swift's father had done was safe for a generation, but, no matter how loyal he was, his children became possible enemies of 'the English interest', the people whose interest it was to go on milking the colonial cow indefinitely. They could attend Trinity College and become ripe scholars, but when a bishopric

[5] Ibid. I, 244.

or any other state appointment was vacant, they were liable to be overlooked in favour of some obscure chaplain or lawyer, imported by the latest viceroy. Again, long before it had occurred to Swift, King was spelling it out for him.

> I reckon, that every chief governor who is sent here comes with a design to serve first those who sent him; and that our good only must be so far considered, as it is subservient to the main design. The only difference between governors, as to us, is to have a good-natured man, that has some interest in our prosperity, and that will not oppress us unnecessarily; and such is his Grace. But I doubt, whether even that will not be an objection against him on your side of the water: for I have found, that those governors, that gained most on the liberties of the kingdom, are reckoned the best; and therefore it concerns us to be on our guard against all governors, and to provoke as little as we can. For he, that cannot revenge himself, acts the wise part, when he dissembles, and passes over injuries.[6]

In other words the Irish colonists could only grin and bear it. But there was also a nationality of common interests which King himself was incapable of exploiting, and Swift was the very man to encourage it because, though his cultural interests were limited, he had a very fine head for the economics of a moneyed society. Here the Irish, with their feudal attitudes, were lost. John O'Dwyer's poet had little sympathy for the poor farmer's wife whose geese were killed by the huntsmen, though he sympathized with the tenants on his own demesne lands when the English clearance of the woodlands left them without the means of existence.

> *Táid fearainn Chum a tSrotha*
> *Gan ceann ná stuagh ar a lochtaibh;*
> *I Sráid na gcuach ní moltar*
> *A sláinte ná a saol.*

> The homes of Coomasrohy
> Have neither roof nor gable;
> In Strade where birds are silent
> No one recites their praise.

[6] Ibid. I, 243.

Swift was equally concerned for the clearances but for a quite different reason.

> As to shipping of its own, this kingdom is so utterly un-provided that of all the excellent timber cut down within these fifty or sixty years, it can hardly be said that the nation hath received the benefit of one valuable house to dwell in, or one ship to trade with.[7]

This was the sort of language that the smallest Protestant shop-keeper could understand; and indeed, Swift made quite certain that he did, for he did not hesitate to write as a Protestant shopkeeper with all the shopkeeper's fantasies about papists, the Pretender and contemporary economics. Swift was one of the great character actors of all time, and he delighted — usually in high good spirits but often in arrogance and malice — in acting a part out to the last extravagance. 'He walked straight to the curate's house, de-manded his name, and announced himself his master. . . . The curate's wife was ordered to lay aside the Doctor's only clean shirt and stockings, which he carried in his pocket, nor did Swift relax his airs of domination until he had excited much alarm.' This was exactly how he took up a part when he was in the company of his friends as well.

One night Pope and Gay called on him and he invited them to dinner. They had already dined, so Swift went off into a long calculation of how much it would have cost him if they had not. 'Let me see, what should I have had? A couple of lobsters; ay, that would have done very well; two shillings, tarts a shilling. . . . A bottle of wine, two shillings — two and two is four and one is five. There, Pope, there's half a crown for you, and there's another for you, sir; for I won't save anything by you, I am determined.' And Pope and Gay took the money because they dared not cross him while he was playing out a part.

This is the tone people heard when they read his reply to Wal-pole's threat to make the Irish colonists swallow Wood's halfpence in fire-balls; the mocking voice taking off a brisk, outraged, Protestant shopkeeper affronted by wild romantic statements.

[7] Swift, *Short View of the State of Ireland.*

As to swallowing these halfpence in fireballs, it is a story equally improbable. For to execute this operation the whole stock of Mr. Wood's coin and metal must be melted down and moulded into hollow balls with wildfire, no bigger than a reasonable throat can be able to swallow. Now the metal he hath prepared and already coined will amount to at least fifty millions of halfpence to be swallowed by a million and a half of people; so that, allowing two halfpence to each ball, there will be about seventeen balls of wildfire apiece to be swallowed by every person in this kingdom, and to administer this dose there cannot be conveniently fewer than fifty thousand operators, allowing one operator to every thirty, which, considering the squeamishness of some stomachs and the peevishness of young children, is but reasonable.[8]

Less than forty years after Swift's death Henry Grattan, having completed a bloodless revolution and set the colony free, could say in the Irish House of Commons: 'Spirit of Swift, spirit of Molyneux, your genius has prevailed. Ireland is now a nation; in that new character I hail her, and bowing to her august presence I say Esto Perpetua.' Grattan, whose speeches have a tendency to resemble Gaev's speech to the bookcase in The Cherry Orchard, was a little bit previous because eighteen years later he had to pronounce the funeral oration of an independent Ireland. This new Irish nation of his oscillated violently between two extremes, self-interest and fear, but Grattan was right to hail Swift as its real founder because that tremendous irony could lash the hysterical colonists until they almost forgot their fear of the submerged native population. It could indeed make fun of their fear while it led them, in King's words, 'like a dog in a string'.

For first, as I have already observed [he writes in A Modest Proposal] it would greatly lessen the number of papists, with whom we are yearly over-run, being the principal breeders of the nation as well as our most dangerous enemies, and who stay at home on purpose with a design to deliver the Kingdom to the Pretender, hoping to take their advantage by the absence of so many good Protestants, who have chosen rather to leave

[8] Swift, The Drapier's Letters, no. iv.

their country, than stay at home and pay tithes against their conscience to an episcopal curate.

The first great masterpiece of literature written in English in this country is *A Modest Proposal*, and I would ask you to remember that it is a political tract. That political note, I would suggest, is characteristic of all Anglo-Irish literature. I know no other literature so closely linked to the immediate reality of politics.

CHAPTER TEN

Eighteenth-century Literature in English

Irish literature in English during the eighteenth century is a pretty problem in classification. Russell Alspach says flatly that the poetry 'has even less distinction than the poetry from the invasion to 1700',[1] but then, he excludes Goldsmith as not being Irish at all. So does Thomas Flanagan.

> The Irish held Goldsmith in high regard not so much because he was himself Irish as because his *Deserted Village* had created, though in a somewhat inappropriate idiom, an image of their countryside and a sense of the sadness of their situation. As a child Gerald [Griffin] copied out the poem and wrote beneath it, 'The Deserted Village, an invaluable treasure.' 'Irish' poetry, of course, it was not, although Goldsmith's casual account of Carolan suggests that he could respond to the native traditions.[2]

This seems to me a critical judgement of Solomon. I am inclined to attach more significance to what a family like the Griffins felt than Professor Flanagan is, because I see no other standard by which to judge the nationality of a writer and his work than that of relevance. That relevance is itself largely irrelevant to questions of value, and becomes of importance only when you consider the audience as an essential part of the work. When you do it becomes very important indeed. Taking it at its simplest, one can say that the only architecture the average Irishman sees for the greater part of his life is Irish architecture. It is not the best form of architecture and most of it is in a deplorable state of preservation, but if he does not see it he does not see architecture at all. Relevance plays an analogous part in literature. Whatever you choose

---

[1] Russell Alspach, *Irish Poetry from the English Invasion to 1798*, London, 1943.
[2] Thomas Flanagan, *The Irish Novelists, 1800-50*, London, 1958.

to call Swift, he is part of the air we breathe. His verse is perhaps less relevant, because there was so much of himself that he did not put into it, but his prose is not only relevant, it is essential to the understanding of Irish literature after him.

When in 1735 Berkeley asks 'whether if there was a wall of brass a thousand cubits high' round Ireland the people would not be better off he is certainly thinking of Swift: when Maria Edgeworth calls her two best novels *Castle Rackrent* and *The Absentee* she is thinking of Swift's denunciation of exacting landlords and absentee landlords; and when Goldsmith wrote 'The Deserted Village' it must surely be with a conscious recollection of Swift. At times he seems to translate him. Swift writes: 'Where the plough has no work one family can do the business of fifty, and you may send away the other forty-nine. An admirable piece of husbandry, never known or practised by the wisest nations, who erroneously thought people to be the riches of a country.'

Goldsmith takes it up in noble verse.

> Ill fares the land, to hastening ills a prey,
> Where wealth accumulates, and men decay;
> Princes or lords may flourish, or may fade;
> A breath can make them, as a breath has made;
> But a bold peasantry, their country's pride,
> When once destroyed, can never be supplied.

I think we can now see the real difficulty of professors Alspach and Flanagan, which becomes our own the moment we ask whether 'The Deserted Village' is Irish or English. After all, Goldsmith himself was not thinking of an English village when he wrote 'There is something so seducing in that spot in which we first had existence that nothing but it can please; whatever vicissitudes we experience in life, however we toil or wheresoever we wander, our fatigued wishes still recur to home for tranquillity, we long to die in that spot which gave us birth, and in that pleasing experience opiate every calamity.' Clearly he was thinking of Lissoy, here, as in 'The Deserted Village':

> I still had hopes, my long vexations past,
> Here to return — and die at home at last.

But we have to recognize too that what he is describing in fact
is not Lissoy, but an English village, for where on earth in Ireland
did peace and plenty ever cheer 'the labouring swain'? Goldsmith
himself realized the anomaly when he described the village ale-
house, which is in fact the ale-house of Lissoy, but rendered in
terms of an English ale-house.

> The white-washed wall, the nicely sanded floor,
> The varnished clock that clicked behind the door,
>
> . . . .
>
> The pictures placed for ornament and use,
> The twelve good rules, the royal game of goose;
> The hearth, except when winter chilled the day,
> With aspen boughs and flowers and fennel gay;
> While broken tea-cups, wisely kept for show,
> Ranged o'er the chimney, glistened in a row.

To his brother Henry, in Ireland, he sent another set of lines,
but this time, as he says himself 'taken from Nature'; that is to
say, describing the ale-house of home as it really was.

> The sandy floor that grits beneath the tread;
> The humid wall with paltry pictures spread;
> The game of goose was there exposed to view
> And the twelve rules the royal martyr drew.
>
> . . . .
>
> The morn was cold; he views with keen desire
> A rusty grate unconscious of a fire.
> An unpaid reckoning on the frieze was scored
> And five cracked tea-cups dressed the chimney board.

These two passages seem to me a fantastically clear illustration
of the problem of the Irish writer in England. To make his experience relevant to his English readers he has to alter it to fit their
experience, but to make his poem relevant to his brother, Goldsmith
has to translate himself back into Irish poetry. I am sure that both
Mr. Alspach and Mr. Flanagan would agree that the second set of
lines *are* Irish poetry, because in fact they might occur in Bryan
Merryman's *The Midnight Court*, which itself is clearly influenced
by Goldsmith. It is all very confusing, but I should not be too ready

to dismiss the reaction of the Griffin family to 'The Deserted Village'. If we must make distinctions, they cannot be merely in terms of the author's religion, race, or language : they must be in terms of the reader's frame of reference. Compare with Goldsmith's beautiful poem another on a later series of evictions which is obviously much more Irish, being as it is so much closer to our frame of reference.

> The answer to Joyce's murder was swift. Two strokes of the
>   pen,
>   Set by Miss Blake's fair hand on parchment white as her face
> Gave what remained of the parish, lands, tenements, chapel,
>   and mill,
> All to a Scotch stock farmer to hold on a single lease.
>
> Here stands the story written. The parchment itself could
>   show
>   Hardly more of their death than this great desolate plain.
> The poor potato trenches they dug, how greenly they grow,
>   Grass, all grass for ever, the graves of our women and
>   men ![3]

There *is* Irish poetry, Irish as Goldsmith's is not. Ah, yes, but whereas the author of 'The Deserted Village' was a Roscommon lad, the author of 'The Canon of Aughrim' was an English land-owner, Wilfrid Scawen Blunt. You will not find it in any English anthology, nor have I ever met an English man of letters who had heard of it. To them it was simply not relevant, but to me it is as relevant as Swift. What we may call it does not really matter; it remains part of the story.

What was really wrong with Anglo-Irish poetry in the eighteenth century was, as Goldsmith saw, Anglo-Irish society, people 'who spend their whole lives in running after a hare, drinking to be drunk, and getting every girl who will let them with child'. Subtly, and without a solitary word of explanation, the American scholar Alspach entitles his work *Irish Poetry from the English Invasion to 1798*, as who should say, 'Ninety-nine shillings and elevenpence'. I shall try to suggest what I think Mr. Alspach means.

---

[3] W. S. Blunt, 'The Canon of Aughrim' in *The Land War in Ireland*, London, 1912.

Irish society of the eighteenth century was, as one of its historians describes it, 'a moral anomaly'. It was held together by self-interest and fear. When self-interest was uppermost it was very patriotic; when fear was uppermost it was capable of any baseness. In 1801 it abandoned its very existence for cash down.

There are two ways of looking at this society : from outside, as Maria Edgeworth looked at it in her first and most important novel, *Castle Rackrent*, or from inside in its own occasional memoirs and verse. Because she looked at it from outside Maria Edgeworth looked at it in Swift's way. The four masters of Castle Rackrent she describes are four aspects of Swift's denunciation of Irish landlords. Sir Patrick is a drunkard; Sir Murtagh a litigious maniac who sweats his tenants and ruins himself; Sir Kit is a money-mad duellist who dies as he has made so many others die; and Sir Condy an amiable half-wit who squanders what little remains on his silly wife's pleasures. Miss Edgeworth not only uses Swift's approach; she uses Swift's method. Thady McQuirk, the old steward who tells the tale, is the average, reasonable man of Swift's satire, who disgusts us with everything he praises.

> Now, Sir Condy, being tender of the consciences of them that had not been on the ground, and so could not swear to a freehold when cross-examined by them lawyers, sent out for a couple of cleavefulls of the sods of his farm of Gulteeshinnagh; and as soon as the sods came into town, he set each man upon his sod, and so then, ever after, you know, they could fairly swear they had been upon the ground. We gained the day by this piece of honesty.

Here we have the origin of the disgusting casuistry that still disfigures Irish public life. But in spite of it Sir Condy is harshly served by his English paymasters in the House of Commons.

> . . . every post-day I looked in the newspaper, but no news of my master in the House; he never spoke good or bad, but, as the butler wrote down word to my son Jason, was very ill-used by the Government about a place that was promised him and never given, after his supporting them against his conscience very honourably, and being greatly abused for it, which hurt

him greatly, he having the name of a great patriot in the country before.

According to my friend Professor Flanagan : '*Castle Rackrent* is that rare event, an almost perfect work of fiction.' Here I find it impossible to follow him : no great work of fiction could be so utterly didactic and censorious as *Castle Rackrent*, and what virtue it has is in its satire, not its story-telling. We do not care for any of its characters because none of them belongs to civilized society, and the novel presupposes a civilized society.

Nor can we care much for this society when we find it described with nostalgia from inside by an old ruffian like Sir Jonah Barrington. Barrington was a lawyer, and his *Personal Sketches* is the forerunner of many similar books, of which the best is Maurice Healy's *Old Munster Circuit*. Of course, law as we understand it was not the strong point of the Irish bench and bar. One of its most distinguished figures, John Edward Walsh, writing in 1847, describes how a few years earlier a law student consulted the vice-provost of this college, who at the time was old and doddering. 'My young friend,' said Hodgkinson, 'practise four hours a day at Rigby's pistol gallery, and it will advance you to the woolsack faster than all the Fearnes and Chittys in the library.'

All the same the lawyers did form a sort of society within a society; venal but inquisitive, brutal but witty, drunken but literate. It is only when you examine what they produced in the way of literature that you discover that it was a purely masculine society, with its drinking songs, squibs, and hangman's ballads. Its drinking songs are better than Professor Alspach is prepared to admit, like Dawson's 'Bumpers, Squire Jones!', which is a very good song, and Curran's 'Let Us Be Merry'.

> If sadly thinking with spirits sinking
>   Could more than drinking my cares compose
> A cure for sorrow from sighs I'd borrow
>   And hope tomorrow would end my woes.
> But since in wailing there's no availing
>   And death unfailing will strike a blow,
> Then for that reason and for a season
>   Let us be merry before we go.

This ranks with 'The Night before Larry was Stretched', one of the best poems in thieves' cant ever written. It has been ascribed to Curran but was certainly written by some member of the bar. Like another poem of the same kind called 'The Kilmainham Minuet', it ends in a curious anticlimax, which gives it a certain ghostly quality, as though the poet's voice were fading in the distance.

> When he came to the nubbing cheat
>   He was tucked up so neat and so pretty,
> The rumbler jogged off from his feet,
>   And he died with his face to the city;
> He kicked too, but that was all pride
>   And soon you might see 'twas all over;
> Soon after the noose was untied,
>   And at darkee we waked him in clover,
>   And sent him to take a ground sweat.

And yet we do not even have to invoke Villon to show that this poem is part of the 'moral anomaly' that John Edward Walsh wrote of, and that the author was at heart a barbarian. The first four lines of a contemporary song from the West of Ireland show us that clearly enough.

> *Is ar an mbaile seo chonnaic sibh an t-iongnadh,*
> *Donnchadh Bán agus é dá dhaoradh;*
> *Bhí caipín bán air i náit a hata,*
> *Is róipin cnáibe i náit a charabhata.*

> Ye have seen a marvel in this town,
> Yellow-haired Donagh and he put down,
> In place of his hat a little white cap,
> In place of his neck-cloth a hempen rope.

In such a society the only people with whom one can feel sympathetic are the United Irishmen, believers in the French Revolution, who were tired of an absentee monarchy, tired of the Protestant ascendancy, and sick to death of the so-called 'Patriot Parliament'. Their policy was simple: in the words of their greatest figure, Theobald Wolfe Tone, 'to unite the whole people of Ireland, to abolish the memory of all past dissensions, and to substitute the common name of Irishman in place of the denominations of Protestant, Catholic and Dissenter'. It is only when one studies each alternative party to theirs — the fierce Whig ascendancy, the weak Liberal opposition, and the knock-kneed Tory element represented by the Irish Catholic gentry and bishops — that one recognizes them as the only force capable of projecting Ireland into the nineteenth century. Alone in their time they stand for the modern world. Now perhaps we can understand why Professor Alspach stops two years short of the century's end. Those two years are what counted; the Belfast song that ran:

> For was I not oft telling thee
> The French could fight right heartily
> That carmagnoles would set you free
> But you would never mind me?

That, and another poem, also from the North of Ireland.

> There our murdered brother lies;
> Wake him not with woman's cries;
> Mourn the way that manhood ought —
> Sit in silent trance of thought.[4]

But meanwhile something was happening that was to form a real second front of the political movement, and was to become more powerful in the following century. In 1760 James Macpherson published his supposed translations from a poet he called 'Ossian', which became part of the romantic movement and had an immense success all over Europe. They did not take in old Samuel Johnson, who pronounced them forgeries for all the wrong reasons: because he did not like Scotsmen, and did not believe that Irish and Gaelic were the same language or that there were any Irish manuscripts in existence. They also failed to take in Irishmen who knew there were scores of 'Ossianic' manuscripts, but that none of them resembled Macpherson's 'Ossian'. The truth of the Macpherson mystery is probably what Skene suggested a hundred years ago — Macpherson *did* have Gaelic originals, but they were

---

[4] William Drennan, 'The Wake of William Orr'.

contemporary poems written by a namesake of his in imitation of the English poetry of the time.

Naturally the Irish did not wish to be left behind. In 1789 Charlotte Brooke of County Cavan published her *Reliques of Ancient Irish Poetry*, and lest anyone might accuse her of forgery she published her originals as well. Some were genuine Ossianic ballads that were still popular in my youth, some were well-known folk-songs, one was a genuine Renaissance love poem by a professional poet; but her principal showpiece — a poem on Cú Chulainn's killing of his son, which Yeats would later choose as subject for a play — is certainly an eighteenth-century forgery in the manner of Macpherson's lost originals.

Miss Brooke's translations are about as bad as they could be, but historically they are of great importance, because they represent the beginning of a new cultural nationalism to replace that which was lost in the Cromwellian invasions. By this time literature in the Irish language had been effectively destroyed. The last of the important poets wrote *The Midnight Court* about the year 1790. Bryan Merryman was a fine poet — as good as Swift, Goldsmith, or Burns, all of whom he seems to have studied closely — and, writing in Irish, he had the advantage, which only the writer in Irish had, of not worrying whether what he wrote was Irish or not. Accordingly he wrote of the simple things that mattered in his own neighbourhood — the unmarried girls, the illegitimate children and the priests who had love affairs on the side.

> Many a girl filled byre and stall
> And furnished her house through a clerical call;
> Everyone's heard of priests extolled
> For the lonesome women that they consoled.

But Irish was dead, and Merryman was to have even less influence than Wolfe Tone. Charlotte Brooke's was to be more enduring. The classical civilization of the Renaissance was breaking up all over Europe, and people were taking more interest in the older cultures it had obscured. Side by side in Goethe's works you will find translations 'from the Irish' as well as 'from the Serbian'. The Anglo-Irish were not a highly literate people, but even they began to look with some curiosity at the old ruins on their estates, and landowners who could not read or write Irish employed drunken schoolmasters to copy what were supposed to be venerable Irish manuscripts to grace their libraries. These went well with the mock machicolation on their homes.

It was to be a long haul, but Miss Brooke had opened a way that Ferguson, Mangan and Yeats would follow. Certain names had been uttered that would not remain forgotten and that would crop up with greater and greater frequency. They were names few of the population could pronounce (most of us cannot pronounce them properly yet) but they were repeated like a spell — Conor, Cú Chulainn, Emain Machae, Deirdre, Tara, Finn. We can see Thomas Moore trying them out in

> By the red cloud that hung over Conor's dark dwelling
> When Usna's three champions lay sleeping in gore. . . .

Ireland had begun to look backward again!

CHAPTER ELEVEN

The Background
of Modern Irish Literature

In 1801 the Act of Union put an end to the independent parliament of Ireland and made the country part of the United Kingdom. This produced such a profound change in the whole life of the community that it makes the literature that followed it seem more like a new subject than a new phase. Naturally one has to consider whether, as some writers believe, such a change occurred after the Flight of the Earls in 1607 or after the Battle of the Boyne in 1690; but the only period that seems to me as though it might be considered a real solution of continuity is that from 1801 to 1850: that is to say, from the Act of Union to what is called the 'Great Famine'. If Irish literature can be said to have continued after this period, it can have done so only in a very different way.

Up to 1801, in spite of the country's having been ravaged by two middle- and lower-class invasions from England, the people were still largely feudal in attitude. What happened to them happened mainly from above. The Irish parliamentary tree under which they sat was not a satisfactory one and conducted more lightning than it produced fruits, but, for good or ill, things dropped unexpectedly from it. It might be a minor concession to Catholics or a new reign of terror, but they could observe it and speculate on it. At any time it might drop something really worth while, such as Catholic Emancipation or some qualified recognition of the Irish language.

Now the tree had been cut down, and what dropped under the greater tree in London, hundreds of miles away, they could not observe; nor could they anticipate much of it. In other words, the people were left to their own devices, and their devices were unbelievably inadequate. Since the vast majority of them could not really possess either homes or land, they had lost all their traditional skills. Outside of Ulster they had lost even the two skills without which civilization cannot exist — carpentry and cookery.

When they went abroad they could neither build nor cook, so they made bad settlers. They were merely a few million unskilled rustics, speaking a half-dead language they could neither read nor write, thrown in with well-educated populations who were highly skilled in industrial techniques. Neither abroad nor at home could they compete; their only hope was to survive, and even this they were in no position to do well. The culminating point of the period is the Famine. 'Famine' is a useful word when you do not wish to use words like 'genocide' or 'extermination'.

This is the first great difference that the Act of Union made. The Cromwellian and Whig settlers were frequently maddened by fear and indulged in atrocities that make one sick, but it is hard to imagine an Irish Parliament's assenting to the cold, deliberate ferocity and cant of the 1840s. This required cooler heads and colder hearts, and it found them in people like Sir Charles Trevelyan.

Besides, the problems of Ireland had grown since the days of Grattan's Parliament. There were three distinct waves of Irish emigration to the United States. The first, up to 1801, was satisfactory enough from the American point of view; and this was not, as historians would have us believe, because the emigrants were all clean-living, hard-working Scottish Presbyterians, temporarily domiciled in Ulster. The second wave, up to 1845, was quite different. The best observer of pre-Famine Ireland, the evangelist Asenath Nicholson, asked what she was doing in Ireland, replied: 'To learn the true condition of the poor Irish at home, and ascertain why so many moneyless, half-clad, illiterate emigrants are daily landed on our shores.' The third wave of emigrants, after the Famine, was practically hopeless — illiterate, drunken, and despairing.

The population had been mounting at a phenomenal rate. The increase probably began with the seventeenth-century clearance of the woodlands and the change-over to an agricultural economy, but we need more than this to explain what was happening in the late eighteenth and early nineteenth centuries. In 1725 Swift calculated the population at a million and a half; at the end of the century Fitzgibbon gave it as four and a half millions, and by 1825 it was eight millions. But for the drain of emigration it would probably have been nearer ten. There is only one possible

explanation : the vast majority of the people were living well below
the minimum subsistence level.

Not that the expansion of the population was the only significant
factor. With a population of about four millions Ireland is still
under-populated. What made it worse was that this starving,
illiterate, hysterical mass had no guidance from above. The Act
of Union not only ruined Dublin; it scattered the Irish landlords.
Not until Charles Stewart Parnell in the 1870s took up the reins
that Grattan had dropped during the 1790s did the ordinary people
get effective leadership from a superior class, and Parnell's tragedy
was that he had no party among his own class. The colleagues who
overthrew him were only one generation removed from the
peasantry themselves. The only leadership the people could get was
that of O'Connell, the Catholic Church and the secret societies,
also struggling for survival. Survival being the only possible aim,
it is useless blaming these for the mistakes they made. The most
disastrous was to connive at the extirpation of the Irish language,
the one mark of cultural identity left to the people and the loss of
which left the way open for the synthetic nationality that still
afflicts us.

The best descriptions of this depressing period that I know are in
Asenath Nicholson's *Ireland's Welcome to the Stranger*[1] and
William Carleton's unfinished 'Autobiography', which was printed
in D. J. O'Donoghue's *Life of Carleton*. The latter book is little
known; the former is almost entirely unknown, though in its own
right it is one of the really remarkable travel books, like Huc's
Travels in Tartary and Thibet. Like Huc's book, which describes
the experiences of two Catholic missionaries on their way to Lhasa,
it has also a certain comic charm, because it is the story of an
American Protestant missionary who trudged through Ireland dis-
tributing tracts, slept in country cabins, and lived, like the natives,
on a few potatoes. What makes the situation funnier is that this
stout Protestant seems to have fallen madly in love with the
Capuchin priest and temperance advocate Father Matthew. We
may even suspect that he fell a little in love with her, because she
admits rather coyly that he gave her a gold brooch. Her book is
a love song; a Protestant love song to a Catholic people, and it is

[1] London, 1847.

significant that the preface to the only edition is dated from Dublin on 10 June, 1847. Mrs. Nicholson had come back to run a soup kitchen and rescue what poor human fragments she could from the ruin that she had foreseen.

What gives the book its historical importance is that she was a genuine missionary. Unlike the great George Petrie, who was tramping the country at the same time, recording music, poetry and old buildings, she was not in the least interested in culture, and what she reveals of it she reveals unconsciously and without prejudice. The Nicholson family had had nine servant girls all from the one village of Johnstown, County Kilkenny, and she went there to see their relatives and reassure them. There was nothing these poor people could do for her but invite her to join their Sunday dance. This, as a good missionary, she had to refuse, so she went to church instead. But on her return, she tells us, 'a crowd of all ages walked in, decently attired for the day, and without the usual welcomes or any apology, the hero who first introduced me seated himself by my side, took out his flute, wet his fingers, saying, "This is for you, Mrs. N. and what will you have?" '
Then she goes on:

The cabin was too small to contain the three score and ten who had assembled, and with one simultaneous movement, without speaking, all rushed out, bearing me along, and placed me upon a cart before the door, the player at my right hand. And then a dance began, which, to say nothing of the day, was to me of no ordinary kind. Not a laugh — not a loud word was heard; no affected airs, which the young are prone to assume; but as soberly as though they were in a funeral procession, they danced for an hour, wholly for my amusement, and for my welcome. Then each approached, gave me the hand, bade me God speed, leaped over the stile, and in stillness walked away. It was a true and hearty Irish welcome in which the aged as well as the young participated. A matron of sixty, of the Protestant faith, was holding by the hand a grandchild of seven years, and standing by the cart where I stood; and she asked when they had retired, if I did not enjoy it? 'What are these wonderful people?' was my reply. I had never seen the like.[2]

[2] Nicholson, 74-75.

This is something you do not get at all from English descriptions of Irish life at the time and even have to deduce from the work of a native cultural enthusiast like Petrie. The moment the paragraph begins we are right into the score of *Don Giovanni* : this is a dance of the peasants to welcome the lady of the castle; and we realize that debased, hungry and ragged as they were, the Irish were still a race of artists, 'But thrown upon this filthy modern tide and by its formless spawning fury wrecked.'

What keeps Mrs. Nicholson's book from depressing us with its suffering and polemic is that, quite unintentionally, it is filled with music and dancing.

> I sat down to enjoy [the morning] upon a moss-hillock, and commenced singing, for the Kerry mountains are the best conductors of sound of any I have ever met . . . I had sung but a passage, when, from over a widestretched valley, a mountain boy, with a herd of cattle, struck up a lively piper's song, so clear and shrill that I gladly exchanged my psalmody for morning notes like these. . . . I listened till a pause ensued, and again commenced; instantly he responded, and though the distance was a mile at least, yet alternately we kept up the song till his was lost in the distance.[3]

It was not that the people were too simple to realize the Dachau-like nightmare of their circumstances, or that Mrs. Nicholson, the Puritan Yankee, did not understand the reasons for them, but as she says herself, 'So fond are the Irish of music, that in some form or other, they must and will have it.' After the description of her curmudgeonly reception by the O'Connells of Derrynane, she gives us a characteristic picture of the country folk gathering seaweed on the strand below. 'And all you have for your labour is the potato?' she says bitterly to one middle-aged woman.

> 'That's all, ma'am, that's all; and it's many of us that can't get the sup of milk with 'em, no, nor the salt; but we can't help it, we must be content with what the good God sends us.'
>
> She hitched her basket over her shoulder, and in company with one older than herself, skipped upon the sand made wet with rain, and turning suddenly about, gave me a pretty specimen of

[3] Nicholson, 337-8.

Kerry dancing, as practised by the peasantry. 'The sand is too wet, ma'am, to dance right well on,' and again, shouldering her basket, with a 'God speed ye on ye'r journey,' leaped away.

Here, as in so many other passages, the evangelist and reformer almost drops away in sheer delight.

> I looked after them among the rocks, more with admiration for the moment, than with pity; for what hearts, amid splendour and ease, lighter than these? And what heads and stomachs, faring sumptuously every day, freer from aches than theirs, with the potato and the sup of milk? This woman, who danced before me, was more than fifty, and I do not believe that the daughter of Herodias herself, was more graceful in her movements, more beautiful in complexion or symmetry, than was this 'dark-haired' matron of the mountains of Kerry.[4]

I have, perhaps, stressed such passages unduly, but I feel that if we are to understand the real awfulness of post-Famine Ireland, we need a clearer idea of what the people were like before it. When George Petrie in a passage that should be famous tries to tell us what the effect of the Famine really was, he does not speak of the shrunken population, the hundreds of gutted villages, the Famine pits or the emigration boats. In the Introduction to his collection of Irish music he says:

> The green pastoral plains, the fruitful valleys, as well as the wild hillsides and the dreary bogs had equally ceased to be animate with human life. 'The land of song' was no longer tuneful; or, if a human sound met the traveller's ear, it was only that of the feeble and despairing wail for the dead. This awful, unwonted silence, which, during the famine and subsequent years, almost everywhere prevailed, struck more fearfully upon their imaginations, as many Irish gentlemen informed me, and gave them a deeper feeling of the desolation with which the country had been visited, than any other circumstance which had forced itself upon their attention . . .[5]

Carleton's 'Autobiography' is profoundly interesting because in

[4] Nicholson, 332.
[5] *The Petrie Collection of the Ancient Music of Ireland* (Dublin, 1855), xii.

it we see one of this people of artists trying to come to terms with the contemporary world. Of Carleton's talent there is no doubt, and we may believe him when he tells us that his mother was a famous singer in their part of Tyrone. Indeed we should have guessed as much from a remark of hers when she was asked to sing 'The Red-Haired Man's Wife' in English: 'I will sing it for you, but the English words and the air are like a man and his wife quarrelling.'

But Carleton himself could not accept that anonymous folk artistry. He wanted to be an equal of the parish priest and the gentleman, and his life story is fascinating because from it we see an extraordinary natural genius being first directed, then diverted and finally frustrated by outside circumstances. His position for achieving his ambition was comparatively favourable: he lived in Ulster, where the land laws were mild by comparison with those in the other provinces, and he could make a character tell his mother to 'boil the mutton and roast the beef', which means that there was both meat and the skill to cook it.

Carleton's ambition to be a classical scholar can only be understood fully in terms of his environment. The learned languages were the key to the professions from which Catholics were practically excluded, and to them education meant first and foremost Latin and Greek. This obsession continued among all classes almost up would glibly quote Crashaw in Latin to me during a fitting, and would glibly quote Crashaw in Latin to me during a fitting, and, as Rose Macaulay once said to me, he was probably the last tailor in these islands who could.) Protestant schools were of little interest or use to Catholics, because, as Asenath Nicholson was told when she inspected Lady Wicklow's school: 'They are educated according to their rank; they belong to the lower order, and reading, writing, arithmetic and a little knowledge of the maps is all the education they will ever need.'

It was the same all over Ireland, and by the time she reached Kerry Mrs. Nicholson was getting very impatient with it.

'But have they not talents to be cultivated and is this not a professedly Christian school, instituted by missionaries?' 'It is,' she answered; 'but I must do as I am bidden. They are poor, and

must be educated according to their station.' Again I enforced
the obligation imposed on us by Christ to 'occupy till he come'.
She did not understand me; and though she belonged to the
Protestant Church, I could not see that her dark understanding
had ever been enlightened by the Spirit of God, or that she was
any more capable of teaching spiritual things than the Catholics
about her whom she viewed as being so dark.[6]

Because they did not wish to be educated according to what
Protestants thought their station in life, the people had to turn for
education to the hedge-schools — those nurseries of the secret
societies — and the very few Church schools, in both of which
Latin was taught.

But there was still a linguistic difficulty. If the people were to
survive they had to speak English, and any little knowledge they
had was based upon Latin. Accordingly they tended to avoid Anglo-
Saxon words, the connotations of which they were not familiar
with; were chary of Norman-French words, and as often as possible
opted for Latin. A Cork folk-song of my youth, 'Cnocáinin Aerach
Chill Mhuire' ('The Little Breezy Hill of Kilmurray'), became in
popular translation 'The Flourishing States of Kilmurray'. That sort
of Babu English was common all over Ireland in the nineteenth
century, and when Gerald Griffin wished to introduce a comic
Irishman he had only to make him sing in Babu.

> And are you Aurora, or the goddess Flora,
>   Or Eutherpasia, or fair Vanus bright?
> Or Halen fair, beyond compare
>   Whoam Paris stole from the Grecian's sight?
> Thou fairest creature, how you've inslaved me!
>   I'm intoxicated by Cupid's clue,
> Whoase golden notes and infatuations
>   Have deranged my ideas for you, Colleen rue.[7]

Carleton himself must have used Babu with his unfortunate
father if, as I suppose, he is the real hero of 'Denis O'Shaughnessey
Going to Maynooth'.

[6] Nicholson, 335-6.
[7] G. Griffin, *The Collegians* (Dublin, 1918), chap. xxiii.

I think, father, that upon considering the consequence to
which I am now entitled, and the degree of respectability which,
in my own person — *in propria persona* — I communicate to the
vulgarians with whom I am connected — I call them vulgarians
from no derogatory motive; but you will concede yourself, that
they are ignorant of the larned languages, an' consequently,
though dacent enough, still, in reference to Latin an' Greek, but
vulgarians! — Well! *Quid multis?* — I say, that taking all these
things into speculation, looking at them — *veluti in speculum* —
it is neither dacent nor becoming that I should ate in the manner I have done, as vulgarly as themselves — that I should ate,
I say, any longer without knife and fork.[8]

There was also a religious difficulty. Carleton became a Protestant, for whatever reason, and found himself a small job as a
teacher. The real tragedy of this was that it involved him in a life-
long faction-fight between Protestants who wanted his work to be
a denunciation of Catholicism and Catholics who wanted to read
nothing about themselves that was not treacle. The loss of the Irish
language had resulted in a synthetic nationalism that was accompanied by a synthetic religiosity. Because he wrote in Irish, Merryman could still describe the Catholic priesthood with urbane
humour :

> People I've known throughout the county
> Have nothing but praise for the curate's bounty,
> Or uphold the canon to lasting fame
> For the children he reared in another man's name . . .

But by Carleton's time the synthetic priest, the Soggarth Aroon,
was taking his place with the Colleen Bawn and the Boatman of
Kinsale in the minds of the Catholic Irish, and Carleton's giant
talent was being rent asunder by faction-fighters who wished him
to write from one distorted standpoint or the other.

This period of Irish literature — and in spite of the terrible con-
ditions in which the people existed some fragments of real literature were written — came to a dead halt with the Famine, and

[8] In William Carleton (ed. D. J. O'Donoghue), *Traits and Stories of the
Irish Peasantry* (London, 1896), IV.

after this nothing was the same again. Having reviewed Miss Woodham-Smith's *The Great Hunger* I realize that it is a subject one cannot discuss without bringing down an old house on one's head. The word 'famine' itself is question-begging for it means 'an extreme and general scarcity of food', and to use it of a country with a vast surplus of food — cows, sheep, pigs, poultry, eggs and corn — is simply to debase language. Irish historians, who are firmly convinced that the Famine was all a mistake in the office, explain it in terms of an economic theory called *laissez-faire*. This is another cock that won't fight, for the *Shorter Oxford Dictionary* defines it as 'a phrase expressive of the principle of the non-interference of government with the action of individuals, especially in trade and in industrial affairs'. Anyone who can believe that the British maintained a garrison of 100,000 men in Ireland for the purpose of *not* interfering in trade and industrial affairs attaches some meaning to the word 'history' that escapes me. The *Oxford History of England* sums up the Famine adequately in a single sentence: 'It was the misfortune of Ireland that the fate of Governments was decided at Westminster.'

But behind Irish history for the last fifty years of the nineteenth century looms the shadow of the Famine — not the Famine as historians see it but as ordinary people saw it. In a passage from the autobiography of Father Peter O'Leary he describes a single small family he and his parents were friendly with — Paddy Buckley, his wife, Kate, and their two young children, Sheela and Little Diarmuid.

Then came the Famine, and Sheela, her father, mother and Little Diarmuid had to go down to Macroom and enter the Workhouse. As soon as they were inside they were separated. The father was put among the men, the mother among the women. Sheela was put with the little girls and Little Diarmuid with the infants. The whole workhouse and all the poor people in it were swamped with every sort of serious illness: the people almost as fast as they came in, falling with hunger — God between us and all harm! — dying as soon as the disease struck them. There was no room for half of them. Those who could not get in merely lay out on the river bank below the bridge. You saw them there every morning after the night out, stretched in rows, some moving and some very still, with no stir from them. Later people came and lifted those who no longer moved, and heaved them into carts and carried them up to a place near Carrigastyra, where a big, wide, deep pit was open for them, and thrust them all together into the pit. The same was done with those who were dead in the Workhouse after the night.

The father and mother questioned as much as they could about Sheela and Little Diarmuid . . . When they found that the two children were already dead, they became so miserable and lonely that they would not stay in the place. They were separated, but they managed to communicate with one another. They agreed on escaping. Patrick slipped out of the house first. He stood waiting at the top of Bothar na Sop for Kate. After a time he saw her coming, but she walked very slowly. She had the disease. They continued up toward Carrigastyra and came to the place where the big pit was. They knew their two children were below in the pit with the hundreds of other bodies. They stayed by the pit and wept for a long time. Above in Derrylea, west of Cahireen, was the little hut where they had lived before they went into the poorhouse. They left the big pit and went north-westwards to Derrylea where the hut was. It was six miles away and night was coming but they kept on. They were hungry and Kate was ill. They had to walk very slowly. When they had gone a couple of miles Kate had to stop. She could go no further. They met neighbours. They were given a drink and a little food, but no one would let them in because they had come direct from the poorhouse, and the wife was ill. Paddy took his wife up on his back and continued towards the hut. . . .

Next day a neighbour came to the hut. He saw the two of them dead and his wife's feet clasped in Paddy's bosom as though he were trying to warm them. It would seem that he felt the death agony come on Kate and her legs grow cold, so he put them inside his own shirt to take the chill from them.[9]

From that passage more than from anything in the history books we can learn what Petrie meant in the passage I have quoted. For the first time in its recorded history a people who loved music had ceased to sing. It is scarcely to be wondered at.

[9] Peadar O Laoghaire, *Mo Sgéal Féin*, Dublin, 1915.

CHAPTER TWELVE

The Beginnings
of Modern Literature

Irish literature in the first, disastrous half of the nineteenth century is a tale of two cities — Dublin and London. There are two groups of writers, one writing for an establishment *de jure*, the other for an establishment *de facto*. As one would expect, the former is largely amateur, the latter professional. They can almost be exemplified by William Carleton and James Clarence Mangan on the one hand, and Gerald Griffin and Thomas Moore on the other. Neither group deserves the critical neglect it has suffered, though neither can be said to have produced a significant body of literature. Each in its own way was too divided in its allegiance. To have succeeded in London was almost to have forgotten Ireland: to have succeeded in Ireland was almost to have ignored Europe. With the rise of the Young Ireland movement in the late 1840s allegiance was doubly split, because a writer was expected to take a political as well as a religious side. This, in fact, is a literature crippled by the lack of a literate audience.

I suspect that Thomas Moore was the most deeply troubled by this dual allegiance, the most haunted by awareness of something he was not equipped to understand. In the *Irish Melodies* he tried to make up for this by using historic names as Shakespeare and Marlowe had used classical allusions, without realizing that, unlike them, he had not frequented the subject. All the same his use of them gave several generations of Irishmen a similar illusory sense of belonging to a tradition. L. A. G. Strong has quoted somewhere a remark I made to him one night we were discussing Moore, that my own first conscious realization of poetry came from two lines of a Moore song that my father used to sing:

> Though lost to Momonia and cold in the grave
> He returns to Kincora no more.

Possibly it is only when you hear them sung that you are conscious of the fine use of assonance, and the same may be true of 'Silent, O Moyle' with its steady rolling of 'R' sounds like the sea itself —

> Silent, O Moyle, be the roar of thy water;
> Break not, ye breezes, your chain of repose
> While murmuring mournfully Lir's lonely daughter
> Tells to the night-star her tale of woes.

Yet there is only one song of Moore that every critic recognizes as poetry, and the interesting thing about this is that it is written in a metre that is not English at all.

At the mid hour of night, when stars are weeping, I fly
To the lone vale we loved, when life shone warm in thine eyes . . .

Still more interesting, almost every anthology contains a fine translation by Jeremiah Joseph Callanan also written in this non-English metre.

> 'Tis down by the lake where the wild tree fringes its sides,
> The maid of my heart, the fair one of heaven resides . . .

Now, both Moore and Callanan got this metre from the Irish song that Carleton's mother did not like to sing to English words because 'the tune and the English words are like a man and his wife quarrelling' — 'The Red-Haired Man's Wife'.

> *Tá siad d'á rádh gur tú sáilin socair i mbróig,*
> *Tá siad d'á rádh gur tú béilin tana na bpóg;*
> *Tá siad d'á rádh, a mhíle grádh, go dtug tú dham cúl*
> *Cidh go bhfuil fear le fáil 's leis an dtáilliúr bean an fhir ruaidh.*[1]

> I hear them say that the heel in your shoe is neat;
> I hear them say that the kiss of your mouth is sweet;
> I hear them say, thousand loves, that you are gone
> And the tailor enjoys the wife of the red-haired man.

What makes these two poems important is that the metre itself seems to have brought out something original and striking in two

[1] Douglas Hyde, *Love Songs of Connacht*, Dublin, 1893.

different poets, one of whom was at best a minor poet, the other of whom can hardly be described as a poet at all. The meaning of this seems to be that what is most characteristic in poetry depends less upon the language and more upon the actual rhythm. (I realize that this could draw me into a discussion of the translation of classical poetry into English, which I am not qualified to sustain.) But how else are we to explain how a non-poet like John Philpot Curran came to write to another Irish air anything so beautiful as 'Let Us Be Merry', which Robert Frost would recite at the drop of a hat?

> If sadly thinking with spirits sinking
>   Could, more than drinking, my cares compose,
> A cure for sorrow from sighs I'd borrow,
>   And hope tomorrow would end my woes. . . .

How did an even greater non-poet, Sylvester Mahony — using the same metre but different tune — come to write 'The Bells of Shandon'?

> With deep affection and recollection
>   I often think of those Shandon bells,
> Whose sounds so wild would in days of childhood
>   Fling round my cradle their magic spells.

Neither of these metres existed at all in English poetry, and the use of them does seem to produce a quite perceptible effect on the writer's talent. This is not a minor coincidence that affects only Moore, Callanan, Curran and Mahony. It affects a much more exciting character, the painter and antiquarian George Petrie and his friend Sir Samuel Ferguson. Petrie's translation of 'Pearl of the White Breast' is the best version we have of an Irish song in English:

> There's a colleen fair as May,
> For a year and for a day
> I have sought by every way
>   Her heart to gain.
> There's no art of tongue or eye
> Fond youths with maidens try
> But I've tried with ceaseless sigh,
>   Yet tried in vain.

Ferguson's translation of 'Cashel of Munster' is almost as good, and again and again in modern Irish literature we realize that poets who make use of older material tend to rise above themselves. It is of course no guarantee of excellence, because Gerald Griffin also uses old tunes and verse forms while remaining completely flat-footed, but it would seem that Irish music preserves some of the rhythms of native speech and gives fairly ordinary verse a colouring of its own. But one cannot help feeling that it is even more than this. One of the most characteristic poems in Irish verse before Yeats is Mangan's translation of 'O'Hussey's Ode to the Maguire', and the metre of this is a sort of adaptation of French alexandrines. What is really important about verse forms is not so much that they should be Irish as that they should not be English. Merely because the similarity of language always threatens to suck the writer into the forms of the more highly evolved literature, he has to adopt every device to keep his distance from it. And this, of course, is the justification for Yeats, Synge and Lady Gregory in using what was little more than an artificial Anglo-Irish idiom. There was another justification, which I shall discuss when I am dealing with their work, but this alone would have been sufficient.

But the story-tellers of the early nineteenth century had no such method of keeping their distance. The best Irish story-teller of the time was probably Gerald Griffin, though this is not saying much. Characteristically, he arrived in London at the age of twenty with a blank-verse tragedy in his bag. When this failed, he followed it up with another called *Gisippus*. Judging by the one scene of it I have read, it might be the work of any stage-struck English parson. His best-known novel, *The Collegians*, is a different affair, and the first seventy or eighty pages is as good fiction as any Irishman has written. Though Griffin's only education had been in a hedge-school, he could, when he was working well, write excellent English, and compared with his contemporary, Carleton, he was a civilized and intelligent man.

The novel was inspired by a local murder. One of the Limerick gentry first seduced a girl and then had her killed by a hanger-on. Griffin shifts the emphasis: the 'Collegians' of his title are two young Trinity College men, one a man of sense, the other of sensibility. Being as opposed to sensibility as Jane Austen herself,

Griffin turns the emotional man into a murderer, which is an even greater *non sequitur* than Jane Austen's.

For close on a hundred pages Griffin describes his Ireland, and in these he is out on his own. Not only does he write excellent English; he shows that he is aware of a secret that few story-tellers master. No two human beings speak exactly alike, and each of Griffin's humbler characters speaks a language of his own. But the moment he approaches his real theme — the psychology of love and murder — Griffin simply collapses. As the old man in his novel *Tracy's Ambition* says, 'Faix, I never seen any love committed there, nor murthers aither.' Not only does he not know what a murderer is like; he has no idea what a lover is like or how a woman in a sexual relationship behaves. For a while I was tempted to believe that this was a class difference, and that Griffin, like Thomas Hardy, thought love-making an occupation better suited to the gentry since it had to be conducted in the most elegant style, but now I think that with Griffin it was more and worse than that. He is interested in men, and only in men, and the only sort of novel he could have done really well would have had to be based upon the psychology of friendship. Two fine scenes in the novel illustrate this. In one, Hardress Cregan, the man of sensibility, denounces the wickedness of duelling in a high-minded way, but a few minutes later when his friend, Kyrle Daly, has been insulted, he insists on fighting a duel with the man who had insulted him. In the second scene, Kyrle, realizing that Hardress has robbed him of his girl, is insane with rage, but later, at his mother's wake, he behaves with perfect friendliness to Hardress, and Hardress realizes that their friendship is at an end. If this were a novel about un-conscious homosexuality everyone would admire those scenes, but it isn't, and what Griffin gives us instead of a novel about love and murder is a five-act English melodrama in verse — English verse.

And not only that, but it is clear that he visualized it with English actors. 'What a deal I would give', he said himself, 'to see Edmund Kean in that scene of Hardress Cregan, at the party, just before his arrest, while he is endeavouring to do politeness to the ladies while the horrid, warning voice is in his ear.' All Hardress Cregan's tirades tend to turn into blank verse of the English type:

I would have saved her, but it is too late.
Now, my good angel, be at peace with me.
I would have saved her. I obeyed your call.
Amid the storm, the darkness and the rain
I flew to execute your gentle will.

No novel of Irish life could possibly have sustained an authentic note under those circumstances. More and more as the story goes on Griffin is sucked into the whirlpool of imitation.

Carleton is the very opposite of Griffin. His English is leaden, his judgement is dull, and he simply has no ear for speech. For Carleton there are not as many languages as there are people. There are only two languages — correct English and peasant English. Peasant English is further subdivided into honest peasant English and Babu — 'sesquipedalian and stilted nonsense', as he describes it himself in a rare flash of style. Peasant English, like correct English, is capable of what he would probably have called 'tender' passages, but Babu is purely comic in its effect. In this Carleton was wrong, as he was bound to be in any matter concerning language, because it is the stilted and artificial quality of Babu that most often gives us the poetic shock in the hymns and songs of the country people, in

O Holland is a wondrous place and in it grows much green,
'Tis a wild inhabitation for my love to be in.

Or

O my dear Jasus, too late have I known Thee;
My treasons bereaved me and reft me of sight;
I wandered through places most heinous, abjuring
The rules of salvation and maxims of light.

Because of this deafness to living speech, Carleton found it difficult to keep on one plane even for a page or two. I have quoted from 'Denis O'Shaughnessy Going to Maynooth' to show how he uses Babu with excellent comic effect. But when Denis has to separate forever from his beloved Susan, Babu is not enough. She must be made love to in 'correct' English. Susan faints, presumably at the shock of hearing it, and at this moment her father appears and hits Denis with his stick. Naturally, the father speaks 'peasant English', but what language is left for Denis to speak?

'Susan, my beloved, will you not hear me? [cries Denis] Oh, look upon me, my heart's dearest treasure, and tell me that you're living! Gracious God! Her heart is broken — she is dead. This — this is the severest blow of all! I have killed her.' . . .

'Your sowl to the divil, you larned vagabone,' said her father, for it was he; 'is this the way you're preparin' yourself for the Church? — comin' over that innocent colleen of a daughter o' mine before you set out . . . for Maynewth!'

'Why, you miserable vulgarian,' said Denis, 'I scorn you from the head to the heel. Desist, I say,' for the father was about to lay in another swinger upon his kidney — 'desist, I say, and don't approximate, or I will entangle the ribs of you.'

What was really wrong with Irish literature at the time was guessed by only a handful of people, and by an accident several of these were concentrated in (of all places!) the office of the British Ordnance Survey, which was then directed by an intelligent English officer named Larcom. Not only did Larcom choose George Petrie as his assistant; he learned Irish from one of the best of living scholars, John O'Donovan, and put him in charge of topographical detail. In this way the Ordnance Survey office became the headquarters of a conspiracy to give the people a real education. Everything was against them, for when the British authorities realized that a topographical survey must necessarily involve such details as the names of the original owners of confiscated properties, they clamped firmly down on the whole transaction, but even so, what those associated with it achieved was astonishing.

Its leader and inspirer was Petrie, whose works on Irish ecclesiastical architecture and Tara are still valuable, whose work on Irish music is indispensable, and who found time to knock off the best translation of an Irish song that we have.

One of Petrie's most intimate friends and a close associate of the whole group was Sir Samuel Ferguson, an Antrim lawyer and a man of remarkable character and ability. Nothing but a marriage into the Guinness family could have saved him from getting into serious trouble with somebody, because, though he was devoted to the English Crown, he had a sense of reality like a pile-driver. He studied Irish and anticipated Yeats in turning the old stories into verse narratives. He realized before anyone else and more clearly than anyone else that literature in Irish was an essential part of the education of any Irishman and tried to make it so. By his use of Irish subjects he kept his distance from English poets of his time, but he failed to keep his distance in matters of metre and diction. There was one ballad metre he used with some success in 'The Burial of King Cormac' and 'Aideen's Grave', but his best work is in the translations that reflect his debt to Petrie; and once again, it is extraordinary how the mere contact with the original metres produced a rhythmical freedom that simply is not in the longer poems.

> Put your head, darling, darling, darling,
>   Your darling black head my heart above;
> Oh, mouth of honey, with the thyme for fragrance,
>   Who, with heart in breast, could deny you love?

But his criticism of Irish literature is as true today as when he wrote it in 1840.

> In reviewing the whole progress and prospects of Irish litera-ture there is no event to which we would be disposed to attach so much importance as an effectual revival of that taste for *facts* which prevailed in the times of Ware, of Davies and of Ussher. It is a most prejudicial error to suppose that matter of fact, however the term may have been abused, is necessarily dry or uninteresting; on the contrary, there can be no true romance, no real poetry, nothing, in a word, that will effectually touch either the heart or the imagination, that has not its foundation in experience of existing facts, or in knowledge of facts that have existed in times past. . . .
> What we have to do with, and that to which these observa-tions properly point, is the recovery of the mislaid, but not lost, records of the acts and opinions and condition of our ancestors — the disinterring and bringing back to the light of intellectual day [of] the already recorded *facts*, by which the people of Ireland will be able to *live back* in the land they live *in*, with as ample and as interesting a field of retrospective enjoyment as any of the nations around us.[2]

[2] M. C. Ferguson, *Sir Samuel Ferguson in the Ireland of his Day*, London, 1896.

What Ferguson is actually discussing in this article is the *Dublin Penny Journal*, one of Petrie's most ambitious efforts, which in its day was probably as great an attempt at popular education as the world has seen. It was far too advanced for Ireland, though it was popular in England, and Southey is supposed to have described it as his favourite reading. What Ferguson is arguing is that the aim of any civilized nation must be cultural identity, and cultural identity can be achieved only by total acceptance of a common past. However much of this he owed to Walter Scott, Ferguson was clearly right. A hundred and twenty years later one can say without being contradicted that no nation in the world is so divorced from its own past as Ireland. One need only look at its monuments, so faithfully recorded by Petrie. Some of these have gone and many of the rest are disappearing rapidly. Native speakers of Irish are disappearing along with them — half a million in 1900, a quarter of a million twenty-five years later, seventy thousand today.

The one fine poet produced by what my friend Professor Flanagan calls the 'Ordnance Survey Gang' was James Clarence Mangan. Mangan is a shadowy figure. What he was like I have no idea except from John Mitchel's rather hysterical description of him as an assistant in the library of Trinity College. Inevitably we see him turning up as one of Petrie's protégés in the *Dublin Penny Journal* with translations from the German. Though Mangan's fame is necessarily associated with his translations, he was never a very good translator because to him the task was not one of catching the essential quality of a poem as it was to Petrie and Ferguson. Neither was he a very good original poet. The only time we do not believe in the misery of Mangan's existence is when we read something like 'The Nameless One'.

> Till, spent with toil, dreeing death for others,
>   And some whose hands should have wrought for him;
> (If children live not for sires and mothers),
>   His mind grew dim.
>
> And he fell far through that pit abysmal,
>   The gulf and grave of Maginn and Burns,
> And pawned his soul for the devil's dismal
>   Stock of returns.

His genius lives in a sort of mid-world between creation and interpretation; when he can take a hint from someone more forthright than himself and dress it up in all the panoply of an Arab chief or a German philosopher.

> I see thee ever in my dreams,
>   Karaman!
> Thy hundred hills, thy thousand streams,
>   Karaman, O Karaman!
> As when thy gold-bright morning gleams,
> As when the deepening sunset seams
> With lines of light thy hills and streams,
>   Karaman!
> So thou loomest in my dreams,
>   Karaman, O Karaman!

That (as you will have gathered) was from the Ottoman. This is straight from the Arabic.

> My eyes are filmed, my beard is grey;
>   I am bowed with the weight of years.
> I would I were stretched in my bed of clay
>   With my long-lost youth's compeers,
> For back to the past, though the thought brings woe,
>   My memory ever glides
> To the old, old time, long long ago,
>   The time of the Barmecides.

One may laugh at this (perhaps one should), but it is not English poetry. It has extraordinary rhythmical freedom; it has panache; and Mangan's greatest poem — one of the greatest in Irish poetry — delights us for the same reason, though this time the speaker is not an Arab chief but a German poet, the contemporary of Goethe and Schiller.

> Wifeless, friendless, flagonless, alone —
>   Not quite bookless though, unless I choose —
> Left with naught to do, except to groan,
>   Not a soul to woo except the Muse —

> Oh, but this is hard for me to bear,
>   Me, who whilom lived so much *en haut*,
> Me who broke all hearts like China ware
>   Twenty golden years ago!

If anything lucky can be said to have happened to that unfortunate man, he had one piece of good fortune when he came
into contact with the 'Ordnance Survey Gang', because they gave
him the one disguise that bore some relation to what Ferguson
called the 'facts' and made him write 'Dark Rosaleen', 'O Woman
of the Piercing Wail' and 'O'Hussey's Ode to the Maguire'. As I
have said, he was no translator, and Mangan being an Irish bard
could be quite as unreal as Mangan being Hafiz or Goethe, but
Ireland needed some image more vivid than the Minstrel Boy, and
the poor, drunken Dublin poet had the panache that no Irish poet
before him had. From the frosty elegance of O'Hussey's 'Too cold
this night for Hugh Maguire' he could extract 'Where is my Chief,
my Master, this bleak night, *mavrone?*'. From the inarticulate
maunderings of some popular seventeenth-century poet anticipating a Spanish invasion he could shape:

> O, my Dark Rosaleen,
>   Do not sigh, do not weep!
> The priests are on the ocean green,
>   They march along the Deep.
> There's wine from the royal Pope,
>   Upon the ocean green;
> And Spanish ale shall give you hope,
>   My Dark Rosaleen!
>   My own Rosaleen!
> Shall glad your heart, shall give you hope,
> Shall give you health, and help, and hope,
>   My Dark Rosaleen!

Not very great poetry, perhaps, but not English. Definitely not
English!

CHAPTER THIRTEEN

Death and Transfiguration

The year 1850 represents not only the end of that people of artists I have spoken of; it seemed to be the end of Irish nationalism itself. One of Gavan Duffy's correspondents knew that the end of Irish nationalism had come, at least in his time. When Gavan Duffy himself left for Australia in 1855, it was because he had come to believe it himself. Art — of a different sort — and nationalism would both revive, but it would have been impossible for Gavan Duffy to see how, for this depended on nothing within Ireland itself or the circumstances as he saw them.

Ireland looked dead, and to all intents and purposes it was dead. The population was falling precipitously as a result of emigration and the flight from the countryside. The Irish were becoming a nation of town-dwellers without even the excuse of industry and high wages. To this day you will still not find what you find in almost every European country — the town-dweller who pines for a little place where he can garden and keep hens. In Ireland the country represents poverty and ignorance — 'beyond the lamps' as they said in my youth. The Irish language, whose associations were all with the country, withered and died in the towns. In my youth an old Irish-speaker I knew was jeered at under the nickname of 'Irish'. Sean O'Casey was known in his Dublin slum as 'Irish Jack'. Irish was, as Arnold called it, 'the badge of the beaten race, the property of the vanquished'. Its place was taken by the horrible ersatz culture that Yeats fought and that is still with us, with its reach-me-down symbols — the Maid of Erin, the Harp and Shamrock, the Round Tower, the Soggarth Aroon and their stereotyped responses. Even those dreadful devices were discouraged in the so-called National Schools where children were taught that 'on the east of Ireland is England where the Queen lives; many people who live in Ireland were born in England, and we speak the same language and are called one nation'.

The principal cause of this was the Diaspora, the deliberate destruction and scattering of a whole people. But about 1850, when the spirit of the country was at its lowest, another factor entered into it. This was Vatican power politics. The Roman Catholic Church had begun to dream of the conversion of England. Ireland, if only it could be induced to discard its language and its sense of national identity, could be the perfect mission station. The British Government had also begun to believe that Irish nationalism could be finally suppressed with the aid of the Roman Catholic Church. Accordingly, from 1850 onward, the British Government and the Vatican worked hand in hand, and this was the change that Duffy's anonymous correspondent had noticed. 'Rome returns to her design of treating Ireland as an entrenched camp of Catholicity in the heart of the British Empire, capable of leavening the whole Empire — nay, the whole Anglo-Saxon race — and devotes every nerve to this end. But the first postulate of it is the pacification of Ireland. Ireland must be thoroughly imperialised, legalised, welded into England.'

This letter shows remarkable political insight, and it reveals very clearly the situation in which James Joyce found himself fifty years later. You accept our policemen, said the British, and we shall accept your priests; and the policeman and the priest become the twin objects of Joyce's hate.

— I am the servant of two masters, Stephen said, an English and an Italian.
— Italian? Haines said.
A crazy queen, old and jealous. Kneel down before me.
— And a third, Stephen said, there is who wants me for odd jobs.
— Italian? Haines said again. What do you mean?
— The imperial British state, Stephen answered, his colour rising, and the holy Roman catholic and apostolic church.

We cannot understand the full bitterness of Joyce's revolt unless we remember the degrading compact against which he was really revolting, and of which the downfall of his hero, Charles Stewart Parnell, was merely an incident.

What happened to a nation like Ireland, lying as someone described it, 'like a corpse on the dissecting table', was that all the essential decisions regarding its future were taken elsewhere. One essential decision had already been taken in Rome, but while the British Government and the Roman Catholic Church were conspiring to extirpate the Irish language forever, an obscure Bavarian schoolmaster called Johann Caspar Zeuss was contemplating a book that would change the attitude of educated people all over the world to the language they were destroying.

Zeuss, a poor and sickly man, wrote a book called *The Germans and their Neighbouring Tribes*, which roused his interest in the principal neighbours who were Celts. In Würzburg and elsewhere he found manuscripts in which Irish students abroad had translated difficult sentences from Latin, which gave him the key to their language and the languages of their fellow Celts in Wales and Brittany. After long, laborious years he managed to establish the grammar of their languages, and in 1853 — two years before Gavan Duffy gave up Irish politics — he published *Grammatica Celtica*, a tremendous work, which — since he was sure it would not interest his German colleagues — he wrote in Latin. In Ireland, where the language was still spoken over a large part of the country, *nobody* knew the grammar of the older language, nor had it been known for hundreds of years. For example, in O'Donovan's edition of the *Annals of the Four Masters*, published two years before *Grammatica Celtica*, the text is fairly accurately transcribed and translated, but the verse quotations from old sagas and histories were not understood by O'Donovan or the Four Masters themselves, who completed their work in 1636, and many of the verse quotations are rendered correctly for the first time in Kuno Meyer's *Bruchstücke der älteren Lyrik Irlands*, which appeared in 1919, during the last months of his life.

What Zeuss made plain was that Irish and Welsh were both part of the great Indo-European group of languages from which Latin and Greek came, and what this meant in terms of national prestige at the time is difficult for us to understand. The most astonishing claim of all was made for it by Matthew Arnold in 1867 when he argued that comparative philology had completely changed the attitude of educated Englishmen to Ireland.

I remember [he writes], when I was young, I was taught to

think of Celt as separated by an impassible barrier from Teuton;
my father, in particular, was never weary of contrasting them;
he insisted much oftener on the separation between us and them
than on the separation between us and any other race in the
world; in the same way Lord Lyndhurst, in words long famous,
called the Irish 'aliens in speech, in religion, in blood'.[1]

Knowing nothing of the Concordat, which was the real cause
of the change in attitude, he adds that 'the sense of antipathy to
the Irish people, of radical estrangement from them, has visibly
abated amongst all the better part of us; the remorse for past ill-
treatment of them, the wish to make amends, to do them justice,
to fairly unite, if possible in one people with them, has visibly
increased'. One does not need to take so exalted a view of the
healing power of linguistics, but that passage from Arnold does
show how respectable 'the badge of the beaten race, the property
of the vanquished' had suddenly begun to seem among European
scholars.

This was something Thomas Moore could not have achieved, or
even the 'Ordnance Survey Gang', who knew so much more than
he. You could afford to ignore Ferguson and Mangan, but you
could not afford to ignore scholars of international reputation. To
Germany in particular, from Zeuss himself to Siegfried, Ebel, Windisch, Zimmer, Stern, Meyer and Thurneysen, Ireland owes a debt
of gratitude which one can only contemplate with dismay.

There seems to be a curious reluctance even on the part of Irish
scholars to admit the importance of Arnold's *On the Study of
Celtic Literature*. It has been pointed out that Arnold did not know
any Celtic language — rather unnecessarily, I should say, since it
would have been remarkable if one of the greatest of English
nineteenth-century poets had been a fluent Irish speaker.

I have been rereading those famous lectures for forty-odd years,
and certain parts of them have naturally gone cold on me. Considering that of the many thousands of medieval statues, paintings,
stained-glass windows and tapestries only two or three survived
the Cromwellian period, it is rather wearisome to read that 'Ireland,

[1] M. Arnold, *On the Study of Celtic Literature* (Everyman ed., London,
1910), 23-24.

that has produced so many powerful spirits, has produced no great sculptors or painters', and considering that in Arnold's own lifetime the Irish often worshipped in the open air before little sheds that contained their altars, we can hardly take seriously a remark such as: 'The very soul of emotion breathes in the Scotch and Irish airs; but with all this power of musical feeling, what has the Celt, so eager for emotion that he has not patience for science, effected in music, to be compared with what the less emotional German, steadily developing his musical feeling with the science of a Sebastian Bach or a Beethoven, has effected.'

Arnold, I suspect, when he deals with the plastic arts is echoing a rather interesting criticism of Ruskin, who somewhere contrasts Irish illuminated manuscripts with Lombardic sculpture to the disadvantage of the former. Arnold Hauser in his great *Social History of Art* contrasts them much more effectively with Irish poetry of the period. 'In the old Irish poetry, the metaphorical power of the language produced images of natural life for which the art of painting, based on the ornamental style of the migration period, lacked the means of expression. In their poetry the Irish were dependent on quite a different tradition from that in their painting.' I do not know enough of art to say whether Hauser is right or not, but I do know that he opens one's mind to real distinctions.

Most of Arnold's weaknesses as a critic come from an absolute acceptance of a contemporary racialism, not so very different from that of his father. He quotes Chrétien de Troyes saying that 'all Welshmen are naturally stupider than grazing cows'. I think it was Tennyson who said that 'Kelts are all mad furious fools'; I know it was Hilaire Belloc who said that before the Normans 'England was a place of heavy, foolish men with random laws, pale eyes and a slow manner; their houses were of wood: sometimes they built (but how painfully and how childishly!) with stone. There was no height, there was no dignity, there was no sense of permanence.' (No dignity, no sense of permanence in Bede's *History of the English Church*, in the Northumbrian crosses, in Wing church, in the sculptures of Chichester?)

Mr. O'Faolain in his excellent *The Irish* comes up with the same sort of argument, if argument one can call it: the Irish never formulated a religion; they were incapable of creating an epic; they did not live in towns and owed to the Normans the benefits of abbeys and centralized ecclesiastical government. I am afraid I do not believe much in Normans, Anglo-Saxons or Celts: the civilization they all shared flowed from the one source round the Mediterranean basin, and the speed at which it flowed did not depend upon race. An idea or style may take twenty years to cross the English Channel, another ten to reach the West Country, and another twenty-five before it reaches the Irish east coast. In spite of the Norman invasion it was close on another fifty years before Gothic came to Ireland and then it appears almost simultaneously in Irish and Norman territory.

And yet 'we do it wrong, being so majestical'. When Arnold deals with the subject he knew better than anyone else — English poetry — he is not easy to contradict. His Celts, Teutons and Normans seem very shadowy figures to me, but when he derives the sense of style, the melancholy and the natural magic of English poetry from some Celtic source I find myself at a loss for a better explanation. When, for instance, he analyses 'I know a bank whereon the wild thyme blows' and shows it to be part of Shakespeare's classical heritage, and then goes on to prove that no classical heritage could have given us:

> Met we on hill, in dale, forest or mead,
> By paved fountain or by rushy brook
> Or in the bleached margent of the sea . . .

I can think of no better origin for it than some Welsh blood. That there is a strong Celtic strain in English literature is as likely as not, though I do not see how it can be proved or disproved. Arnold himself clearly believed that there was a real scientific basis to his criticism, but he was a fine poet and at his best only when he was thinking intuitively as he does here. Whether or not it is good science, it is excellent criticism because it makes clear distinctions. The rest is merely nomenclature.

It does not matter much whether or not we agree with Arnold, because *On the Study of Celtic Literature* is one of the really influential books of the nineteenth century, and we have to realize that it underlies a great deal of the early work of Yeats and his followers. A poem like 'The Wanderings of Oisin' would be almost unintelligible without it. It is true that Arnold was responsible for a good deal of bad work in the 'Celtic Twilight' manner, but he was also responsible for some good work — and in a quarter where it was no longer expected. It added greatly to the effect of German scholarship in making Ireland and things Irish dignified in the eyes of our own people. 'We work to add dignity to Ireland' was one of Lady Gregory's favourite sayings, but others had already worked upon that task.

One outside event that was also important was the American Civil War of 1861-5. By what, in effect, was the expulsion of millions of Irish people to the United States, Great Britain had raised up a considerable problem for herself abroad, and the more who were forced to emigrate, the greater that problem became. At first the immigrants were no trouble to anyone but the Americans, but after the Civil War they represented a considerable power, not so much because they were now trained soldiers as because they remained actively hostile to England. As revolutionaries they were childish, but they had funds, they had votes, they had a free Press. By themselves they could effect little, but as allies of anyone in a position to effect something, they were an enormous danger.

The real strength of Charles Stewart Parnell was that he was well aware of their value as allies, and he needed them all because of the power of the Concordat. In 1883 the Vatican announced to the Irish bishops 'it must be evident to your lordships that the collection called the "Parnell Testimonial Fund" cannot be approved by this sacred congregation, and consequently it cannot be tolerated that any ecclesiastic, much less a bishop, should take any part whatsoever in recommending or promoting it'. The only effect of this piece of impertinence was to double contributions to the fund. Other methods had to be used, and were in fact already being used, though circumstances — in this case a large personal fortune — made it impossible to take advantage of them. In 1882, when Parnell was a prisoner in Kilmainham Gaol, the intermediary who interviewed him on behalf of the British Government was the husband of his mistress, who had already had a child by him, but it was not until eight years later that O'Shea could strike at

Parnell through the divorce courts and the Irish bishops were in a position to proclaim: 'Without hesitation or doubt, and in the plainest possible terms, we give it as our unanimous judgment that whoever else is fitted to fill that highly responsible post (as Leader of the Irish Party) Mr. Parnell decidedly is not.' Within a couple of days Parnell's party dwindled into a disorganized, hysterical mob, and within a year he was dead.

What shows Parnell's real weakness is that, so far as literature was concerned, his revolution and his downfall had no immediate significance. He had not the support of members of his own class; his revolution was a middle-class revolution, and the Irish middle classes had no articulate voice. Yeats wrote a poem on his death, which is remarkable only for its triteness.

> Mourn — and then onward, there is no returning,
>   He guides ye from the tomb;
> His memory now is a tall pillar, burning
>   Before us in the gloom!

The real voice of the Irish middle classes was not heard for thirty years, until James Joyce wrote 'Ivy Day in the Committee Room' and the Christmas Day scene in *A Portrait of the Artist*.

— God and religion before everything! Dante cried. God and religion before the world!

Mr. Casey raised his clenched fist and brought it down on the table with a crash.

— Very well, then, he shouted hoarsely, if it comes to that, no God for Ireland!

— John! John! cried Mr. Dedalus, seizing his guest by the coat sleeve.

Dante stared across the table, her cheeks shaking. Mr. Casey struggled up from his chair and bent across the table towards her, scraping the air from before his eyes with one hand as though he were tearing aside a cobweb.

— No God for Ireland! he cried. We have had too much God in Ireland. Away with God!

— Blasphemer! Devil! screamed Dante, starting to her feet and almost spitting in his face.

Uncle Charles and Mr. Dedalus pulled Mr. Casey back into

his chair again, talking to him from both sides reasonably. He stared before him out of his dark flaming eyes, repeating:

— Away with God, I say!

Dante shoved her chair violently aside and left the table, upsetting her napkinring which rolled slowly along the carpet and came to rest against the foot of an easychair. Mr. Dedalus rose quickly and followed her towards the door. At the door Dante turned round violently and shouted down the room, her cheeks flushed and quivering with rage:

— Devil out of hell! We won! We crushed him to death! Fiend!

The door slammed behind her.

Mr. Casey, freeing his arms from his holders, suddenly bowed his head on his hands with a sob of pain.

— Poor Parnell! he cried loudly. My dead king!

It is a late response in literature to events of a previous generation, but it is also something more than that. It is part of an antithesis that was to develop in modern Irish literature between Yeats and Joyce, the idealist and the realist, the countryman and the townsman, the dead past and the unborn future. It is exemplified in the careers of the two men, Yeats abandoning what could have been a prosperous career in London to establish his little literary group in Ireland, Joyce setting off for exile in Trieste and Zürich because he will not defer either to the Roman Catholic Church or the British Government. Or in the noble words of the Second Synod:

One's own country is to be instructed first, after the example of Our Lord, and later, if this does not succeed, to be abandoned, after the example of the Apostle. But he who can succeed, even if he imperil himself, shall teach and show himself everywhere, and he who cannot, let him be silent and depart.

CHAPTER FOURTEEN

William Butler Yeats - I

It may, I hope, be accepted as common ground that no Irishman is of much interest until he has lost his faith.

The father of William Butler Yeats was the son of a Church of Ireland clergyman and became of interest only when he discovered himself to be an atheist, took up painting as a profession, and made immortal remarks such as 'The great difference between England and Ireland is that every Englishman has rich relations and every Irishman poor ones.'

He put his brilliant son into a difficulty because *he* had nothing to lose but his atheism, which is not the same thing at all. But, as the Christian who loses his faith always has a tenderness towards it — 'haunted by the mystery he flouts' as W. B. Yeats said of Shaw — so the ex-atheist has an unconquerable yearning for experiment and reasoning. His father took pleasure in rubbing it in that Willie hadn't a scrap of real religion in him. 'You can only pretend it — your interest is in mundane things and Heaven to you is the world made better — whether beyond the stars or not.'

W. B. Yeats, trying to remake the religion his father had shattered for him, was the ideal leader for the revival of anything, short of old music, for which his lack of ear disqualified him; though even this was something he felt needed his attention, and he argued that he had what he called a 'natural' ear. Natural it must have been because it was not acquired. To F. R. Higgins he told how George Sigerson, who had an old countrywoman in a hypnotic trance, made her put her hand on his face, and she said 'Poet', then 'Great poet', and finally 'Musician'. 'And then', Yeats added modestly, 'I knew she was genuine.'

Either he or George Russell told the twenty-year-old Joyce, 'I do not know whether you have enough chaos in you to make a world', but Yeats had enough chaos in him to make a whole cosmic system; and if you want to think of him as he was in life you must imagine a man who was for ever blundering about in search of the truth. When he was twenty he made a speech to the Dublin Theosophists in which he asked, 'Are there observed facts given that all the teachers and the schools of Europe can reduce to no law, facts which they try to reason out of existence as the professors of Genoa sought in the days of the telescope of Galileo to reason the stars out of heaven with the metaphysics of the schoolmen?'[1]

A couple of years before his death, when I told him over lunch some story I had heard in West Cork, he lost his temper with me and said, 'O'Connor, why do you close your eyes to these things when you know perfectly well that they were once the religion of the whole world?' Another night he told me that science had shot its bolt and that there were no major discoveries left to be made — this would have been ten or twelve years before the atom bomb.

And yet, far from being a fool, he had a first-rate intellect. Even in that speech to the Theosophists he said: 'On the road to truth lurks many a dragon and goblin of mischief in wait for the soul. Miracle hunger is one of them.' I know so well what his beloved Maud Gonne meant when she complained that 'Willy was so silly'. He was, but his was also a first-rate intellect, and I could not reconcile the two things. Once, in a fit of delighted exasperation, I said that he was the only man I ever knew who could deduce a universal truth from two fallacies and an error.

Finally I decided that he deliberately induced a sort of hypnotic suspension of the critical faculty to justify a blind indulgence in his intuition. D. H. Lawrence and Tolstoy did the same, though I doubt if either had so good a brain. As a man, the trouble in dealing with him was that you were never quite sure how long the intellect was going to be allowed to remain in abeyance. Unlike his friend George Russell, who took you to his bosom in the first five minutes, Yeats gave you the impression that he hadn't the faintest idea who you were, where you came from or what your business was. It was most unsafe to rely on that impression because he pounced on you like a hawk.

I think you can begin to see why this man was predestined to save

[1] Richard Ellmann, *Yeats: The Man and the Masks* (London, 1961), 43.

Irish literature. It took someone who was prepared to recreate 'the religion of the whole world' from a few folk-stories to recreate the literature of Ireland from a handful of translations, most of them inaccurate. Yet, but for an accidental meeting with the old Fenian leader John O'Leary, Yeats might easily have ended as a fine minor poet like Walter De La Mare. 1886 was a turning-point in his life because under O'Leary's influence he began to use Irish material in the way of Ferguson and Mangan, and after that he was dealing with a situation so explosive that he could not afford to trifle with it. He might be persecuted; he might even go in danger of his life; but he was always to be in the thick of things.

It seemed to have little effect on his silliness. In 1896 — ten years later — he was in correspondence with another brilliant young fathead, George Russell, about the possibility of restoring ancient Celtic religion, and Russell was writing to him in a guarded way.

(Private)   The Celtic adept whom I am inclined to regard as the genius of the renaissance in its literary and intellectual aspects lives in a little white-washed cottage. I feel convinced it is in Donegal or Sligo. There is a great log a tree with the bark still on it a few feet before the door. It is on a gentle slope. He is middle-aged has a grey golden beard and hair (more golden than grey) face very delicate and absorbed. Eyes have a curious golden fire in them, broad forehead. . . . *Don't spread this about.*[2]

In later years Russell told stories about Yeats' crystal-gazing. Once he saw the Golden Door and soon after the Guardian of the Golden Door, who turned out to be the doorman in the gilt public-house outside the window, but that peculiar letter would suggest that Russell himself was in the same line of business. As if it weren't enough, Yeats was also a member of a secret society called the Irish Republican Brotherhood. I was very curious to know how he got on with that group, and one night he replied : 'Oh, they were always sentencing one another to death. Once a man arrived at my house from London, raging because he'd been sentenced to death by the Dublin branch. I told him not to worry because there was no danger, but that only made him angrier. "Danger?" he

[2] Ellmann, *Yeats: The Man and the Masks*, 124.

said. "Do you think I'm afraid of what that crowd might do to me? It's the insult, man; the insult!"' I suppose it was in hope of making them more practical that Yeats thought up the scheme for stealing the Coronation Stone from Westminster Abbey and bringing it back to Ireland, but it seems that he got no support for that and had to leave it for the Scottish Nationalists to do.

He had also become involved with Maud Gonne, which was more serious than being involved with the Theosophical Society or the I.R.B. As a poet Yeats had been seeking a tragic heroine, and Maud filled the part beautifully. It was probably only in the last years of his life that it began to dawn on him that what she was was a really superb comedienne. She was an English society woman, the mistress of a French political journalist, and had two children, one of whom died in infancy while she continued to refer to the other delicately as 'my adopted daughter'. (Professor Ellmann makes her 'an adopted niece'.) She had no intention of marrying Yeats, but she realized that Lady Gregory — who disapproved of her — was in love with him, and she would not allow an enemy to make away with her victim. The youthful Yeats had no sense of comedy, and it was not only Lady Gregory who fretted over him. John O'Leary, who contributed the loan of an odd pound, knew Maud's tastes and asked Yeats who was paying for Maud's cabs. Yeats' reply is the last word in ingenuousness: 'She does not let me pay the whole fare, but stipulated a good while ago that she should pay her own share.'[3]

It is hard to imagine how any woman could fail to fall in love with a young man like that, but Maud Gonne failed, though she continued to play out the comedy with him as long as he lived. By the time he was sixty he had probably begun to see through her and enjoy her for what she was. One evening he told me that Maud had been to see him and in her beautiful tragic way asked him if he proposed to 'betray Ireland'. According to himself he replied: 'It's all very well for you, Maud. Your father was an English officer and it's not in your blood to betray Ireland. But my father betrayed Ireland, and my grandfather betrayed Ireland, and it's in my blood to betray Ireland too, Maud.'

All the same, something was beginning to take shape in the

[3] W. B. Yeats (ed. A. Wade), *Letters* (London, 1954), 186.

chaos of Yeats' mind, for in 1896, the year when Russell was revealing the existence of 'the Celtic adept', Yeats was collecting folk-stories with Lady Gregory and advising George Moore about the advantages of peasant speech. 'You don't mean the brogue, the ugliest dialect in the world?' Moore exclaimed, and Yeats replied, 'No dialect is ugly; the bypaths are all beautiful. It is the broad road of the journalist that is ugly.'[4]

In the following year he met John Synge in Paris and gave him some good advice as well. 'Give up Paris. You will never create anything by reading Racine, and Arthur Symons will always be a better critic of French literature. Go to the Aran Islands. Live there as if you were one of the people themselves; express a life that has never found expression.'[5] It shows how Yeats pushed everyone round that not only did he get George Moore writing 'the brogue'; in the following year he got Synge living on Aran.

Also in 1897 he was writing to that non-existent character, Fiona MacLeod: 'My own theory of poetical or legendary drama is that it should have no realistic, or elaborate, but only a symbolic and decorative setting. A forest, for instance, should be represented by a forest pattern and not a forest painting. . . . The acting should have an equivalent distance to that of the play from common realities. The plays might be almost, in some cases, modern mystery plays.'[6]

So by 1897, though there is no doubt about the chaos, there is also no doubt of a world beginning to emerge. From all his blunders Yeats has learned something, and he has made so many blunders in so many different fields of activity that what he has learned is beginning to assume the proportions of a universal scheme of religion, aesthetics and politics. What is more it is a scheme that can impress people so different as Russell, Moore, Synge, and Lady Gregory, all of remarkable intelligence. Like all universal systems it is basically simple: to escape the vulgarity of Victorian religion one returns to mythology and magic; to escape the commonplace of journalism one goes back to peasant speech; to break the tyranny of actor-managers one simplifies acting and stage design, and to

[4] George Moore, *Hail and Farewell! Ave*, London, 1911.
[5] W. B. Yeats, *Essays and Introductions* (London, 1961), 299.
[6] Ellmann, *Yeats: The Man and the Masks*, 132.

re-energize the theatre one brings back the miracle and mystery play. You will notice that though the problems are different, the answer is the same — a stream is purer nearer its source. This is characteristic of purely intuitive writers like Tolstoy and D. H. Lawrence: they, too, have one answer for every problem.

Anyhow, this is roughly the specification for Yeats' life-work, and so closely did he collaborate with his friends that it is often difficult to say who is responsible for what, except that the finished work usually bore a marked resemblance to his original idea. One small incident left me with the impression that he had a considerable share in the beautiful early plays of Lady Gregory. We were discussing the importance of having some piece of property on the stage that gave the action of a play visible concreteness. 'When we were rehearsing *The Rising of the Moon*,' he told me, 'I could not get the play to go right. I came back to the hotel and walked round and round the drawing-room, thinking. At last I got tired and collapsed onto the piano stool and it all became clear to me. "A barrel!" I said. "We must have a barrel!" '

I am not, of course, decrying the originality of Douglas Hyde, Moore, Synge, and Lady Gregory. Having myself collaborated with him, I know what they went through. Yeats had none of the shyness and secretiveness of the average writer; he tended to regard literature as a sort of co-operative activity, and was incensed by people who refused to join the co-operative and grumbled about 'barren pride'. I spent one enchanting evening rewriting a new Abbey Theatre play with him.

At the same time you were apt to find in collaboration with him that it was usually his ideas that came uppermost. As Oliver Gogarty put it to me one day: 'Yeats is writing a few little lyrics for me, so I'd better drop round and see how he's getting on.' Seeing how he was getting on was about as much as you could do once Yeats laid hands on your work. Once I had written a line that seemed to give him great pleasure for he kept rolling it round and round on his tongue: 'Has made me travel to seek you, Valentine Brown.' By the time I had heard him repeat it a score of times I was heartily sick of it, and I said, 'Oh, that's impossible; it's tautological. Let's say "Has made me a beggar before you, Valentine Brown."' At this he flew into a rage. 'No beggars! No beggars!' he shouted, and he actually had the audacity to print it as it stood.

Besides, the Yeats repair-and-maintenance service, though excellent, was not entirely free, and if he happened to compose a good line for you or even discovered a good line that you had written, it was quite liable to turn up in the poem he was writing himself at the time. 'Yeats has got off with the spoons,' said George Moore, but Yeats was always getting off with the spoons. Once when he asked me to dinner he could scarcely wait to tell me the good news. 'O'Connor, I've stolen another poem from you.' I said the only thing I could say under the circumstances, which was, 'Did you make a good job of it?' He preened himself and said, 'I made a *beautiful* job of it.'

As I have said, in all those works of his friends and collaborators it is hard to say what is the direct result of Yeats' influence. To take first the language question, the most important and the most difficult, in *Beside the Fire* (1890) Hyde for the first time successfully used the idiom of Anglo-Irish speech in the translation of folk-stories. I cannot help wondering whether this was entirely his own idea or whether Yeats had suggested it. It could easily have been an accidental discovery of Hyde himself, but it was a radical innovation for a rather conventional man, and it is to be noted that later, when Yeats was looking for mystery and miracle plays, Hyde obligingly wrote two, to scenarios by Yeats and Lady Gregory.

There is also some mystery about the style of acting that developed in the Abbey Theatre. We are always told that this was entirely the doing of Frank Fay, who had been impressed by the productions of Antoine, and no doubt this is true, but the style does turn out to be remarkably like that which Yeats had been arguing for. Its connection with French acting can only be accidental, because it is undoubtedly the style of acting that was common in European universities up to Shakespeare's day and associated with the production of Seneca's plays. It is an almost purely literary style, and one can summarize it by saying that no one speaks when moving and no one moves while someone else is speaking, so that attention is not distracted from the spoken word. It must have been out of date by Shakespeare's day, because in one of the *Parnassus Plays* there is a scene in which Burbage and Kemp give an audition to two young men from Cambridge who understand only the Senecan convention. Kemp says of it that it is like going for a walk with a man who only speaks to you when he is crossing a stile.

It is, of course, the antithesis of the modern English naturalistic style, in which, while the wife makes a long speech explaining why she has been unfaithful, the distracted husband picks up a match. Once Yeats and I were at the theatre during the performance of a play in which the visiting English actor was so overcome with emotion that he picked up a match, and later, in the foyer, Yeats disgraced me by caricaturing him. 'When he should have been calling down the thunderbolt' — he stood on tiptoe and reached towards the ceiling — 'he was picking up matches', and he grovelled on the floor at my feet, laughing his head off.

Whether or not he was responsible for the use of Anglo-Irish speech and Senecan acting, he was certainly responsible for the sort of play the theatre produced in its early days. He was an absolute master of his own sort of play, which was the one-act 'miracle', and so long as his colleagues wrote that they made no mistakes. They went wrong only when the construction had to be more complicated, as in the first act of Synge's *Playboy of the Western World*, where the author (through inadvertence, not guile) conceals from the audience that Christy Mahon's father is still alive and thus deprives them of the whole comedy of Christy's bragging. That particular error is curious because it is one that Yeats always looked out for. Once when a dramatization of a story of mine was performed he rushed up to me in a frenzy of excitement. 'O'Connor, you have made a terrible mistake! You should have let the audience know that the woman was the murderess. You must never, NEVER keep a secret from your audience.' He was perfectly right, but it interests me that he did not notice the same mistake in Synge's masterpiece or realize how much it accounted for the subsequent riots.

The influence of the miracle play is obvious in almost all the plays by himself and his friends. The only play — apart from his friends' work — that he accepted as part of the Abbey canon was Corkery's *The Yellow Bittern*, also a miracle. These plays are more

Victorian than critics generally recognize; what distinguishes them at the moment of revelation is that the drunken old tramp, instead of being revealed as the millionaire uncle, turns out to be a ghost, a saint, Christ, or the Blessed Virgin. Even when the revelation is not quite so obvious as it is in *The Countess Cathleen, Cathleen ni Houlihan, The Travelling Man,* or *The Yellow Bittern,* it results in a moral rather than a financial or psychological peripeteia, and becomes an acceptance of duty or punishment as in Lady Gregory's *The Rising of the Moon, The Gaol Gate,* and *Dervorgilla.* The idea of the acceptance of the tragic conclusion was one that Yeats was very fond of — 'Tragedy must be a joy to the man that dies' was how he put it.

Naturally, all those who came under Yeats' influence turn out with a strong bias against the middle classes. The latest 'safe period' for contact with the past is about the year 1600, just before the middle classes had begun to attain power. Something may be said in favour of Shakespeare, who did not like the middle classes either, but nothing for those who followed him. Synge saw on Aran precisely what he was supposed to see.

> Their way of life has never been acted on by anything much more artificial than the nests and burrows of the creatures that live round them, and they seem, in a certain sense, to approach more nearly to the finer types of our aristocracies — who are bred artificially to a natural ideal — than to the labourer or citizen, as the wild horse resembles the thoroughbred rather than the hack or cart-horse.

Naturally, since the middle classes, among their other faults, produced policemen. ('He is a policeman's son,' Yeats said blandly of a writer he did not like.)

> Yet these mechanical police, with the commonplace agents and sheriffs, and the rabble they had hired, represented aptly enough the civilization for which the homes of the island were to be desecrated.[7]

It is the most extraordinary feature of the literature of this

[7] J. M. Synge, *The Aran Islands,* London, 1907.

period and accounts for most of its obvious peculiarity. Leaving aside the question of whether policemen were really as 'mechanical' as Synge believed, there was in 1900 a peasantry of sorts in a few remote Irish-speaking communities, and poetry came as naturally as breathing to them, but there was no aristocracy, and this had to be supplied from history and saga. You limit your material in a most extraordinary way when you can only switch from Pegeen Mike in a Connemara shebeen to Deirdre in a Bronze Age fortress and Dervorgilla in a medieval monastery. It was an austere ideal, particularly for the Irish middle classes, who anyhow have a horror of the countryside and are never happy more than a mile from a water-closet, and it probably gave more offence than anything else in Yeats' system. The Irish middle classes took themselves very seriously; they had pianos and water-closets and read St. Thomas Aquinas. It was in revolt against it that Edward Martyn established a theatre of his own in which international ideas were discussed, though they failed to attract the attention they deserved. Joyce, the fine flower of the Catholic middle classes, resented it most of all. As he wrote in *A Portrait of the Artist*:

> John Alphonsus Mulrennan has just returned from the west of Ireland. European and Asiatic papers please copy. He told us he met an old man there in a mountain cabin. Old man had red eyes and short pipe. Old man spoke Irish. Mulrennan spoke Irish. Then old man and Mulrennan spoke English. Mulrennan spoke to him about universe and stars. Old man sat, listened, smoked, spat. Then said:
> — Ah, there must be terrible queer creatures at the latter end of the world.

The second sentence reveals the hurt feelings of the Irish middle classes. The unfortunate thing was that European and Asiatic papers *did* copy.

CHAPTER FIFTEEN

William Butler Yeats-II

In 1903 Yeats' heroine, Maud Gonne, married Major John Mac-
Bride, a decent County Mayo soldier whom Yeats was later to
describe, rather unnecessarily, as 'a drunken, vainglorious lout'.
The marriage broke up after two years, as all their friends had
been sure it would, and Yeats appealed to Lady Gregory for sympathy for the wronged wife. 'When you know the story you will
feel that if she were the uttermost stranger, or one's bitterest
enemy, one would have, even to the putting aside of all else, to
help her.'[1] His tone suggests that he suspected Lady Gregory would
see Mrs. MacBride damned first.

What happened to Yeats after the marriage is well described in
the Cú Chulainn plays into which he put a lot of himself that did
not go into the poetry. This, of course, is the real distinction
between him and his great predecessor, Ferguson. To Ferguson the
old stories were merely good subjects; to Yeats they were themes
for autobiography. 'Heart secrets there,' he says of *The Countess
Cathleen*. His poems and plays spring from a continuous soliloquy,
an unceasing interior monologue, interrupted only by voices from
outside. It is not always easy to detect whose the voices are or
what, precisely, they are saying, because they represent the un-
written part of Yeats' biography. This gives the poetry a certain
air of vagueness, which is ridiculed by Moore. 'Since *The Wind
Among the Reeds* he has written a sonnet that clearly referred to
a house. But to what house? A.E. inclined to the opinion that it
referred to the House of Lords, but the poet, being written to
from Ely Place, replied that the subject of his sonnet was Coole
Park. Mallarmé could not be darker than this.'[2]

But it is not a question of obscurity. As a rule it is the circumstances that are obscure, not the poem itself. One evening when
I was at his house with a friend I asked him to read us a poem

[1] Joseph Hone, *W. B. Yeats* (London, 1942), 210.
[2] George Moore, *Hail and Farewell!* III, *Vale* (London, 1914), chap. vii.

and he read 'Ribh denounces Patrick', which he had just written. He asked if we understood it. My friend said he did; I said I didn't understand a word of it, and Yeats explained. Later he turned it into a little anecdote: 'X and O'Connor were here, and I read them the last Ribh poem and asked if they understood. X said he did, and he didn't, and O'Connor said he didn't understand a word, and he understood it perfectly.' The next poem in the series begins 'What matter that you understood no word!' I doubt if it refers to my own impertinence, but someone said that phrase which started Yeats off again on his soliloquy, and as a result, the connection between the two poems is unnecessarily vague.

That vagueness of connection is much more obvious in another poem called 'Lapis Lazuli', the origin of which I remember. I went to see Yeats one night, very troubled by an unsatisfactory production of Lady Gregory's Dervorgilla, which had been spoiled for me because the heroine wept at the curtain. I put off speaking of it because I noticed on the mantelpiece a new acquisition; a beautiful piece of lapis carved with gay scenes of a Chinese pilgrimage. Yeats was very pleased with it and told me he was writing a poem to the man who had given it to him. Then he went on to tell me of a letter he had just received from Edmund Dulac, who was terrified of what was going to happen if London was bombed from the air. I told him of my own experience and asked, 'Is it ever permissible for an actor to sob at the curtain of a play?' and he replied, 'Never!'

In the poem the lapis and the Chinese scenes, the bombardment and my own advice to the players are all rendered in strict chronological order as though copied from a diary.

> For everybody knows or else should know
> That if nothing drastic is done
> Aeroplane and Zeppelin will come out,
> Pitch like King Billy bomb-balls in
> Until the town lie beaten flat.
>
> All perform their tragic play,
> There struts Hamlet, there is Lear,
> That's Ophelia, that Cordelia;
> Yet they, should the last scene be there,

> The great stage curtain about to drop
> If worthy their prominent part in the play
> Do not break up their lines to weep.

To me, for once, the sequence of ideas is perfectly clear as it is not clear in other poems of Yeats, but is it equally clear to readers who are unfamiliar with the voices speaking in the poem?

Then in 1909 John Synge died, and Yeats' disillusionment was complete. He does not seem to me a great love poet, but as a poet of friendship he is incomparable. Even when he writes about a woman who was also his mistress, what is most moving in the poem is not the love but the friendship. Yeats had the sort of tolerant, amused, enduring affection and the long memory for little kindnesses that go with great friendship, and no other poet in the world but he could have written

> But friendship never ends;
> And what if mind seem changed,
> And it seem changed with the mind,
> When thoughts rise up unbid
> On generous things that he did
> And I grow half contented to be blind!

How deeply he was hurt by the *Playboy* riots and all the controversy they involved him in is hard to tell, but I recently woke up in the middle of the night, wondering what on earth had caused him to write such an intolerable piece of bad manners as that epigram 'To a Poet who would have me Praise certain Bad Poets, Imitators of His And Mine'. A glance at the dates confirmed a guess that it had been written within a month of Synge's death. Even I, who am not very observant, noticed that anyone who had opposed or attacked Synge never received more than a formal welcome from Yeats. His late poem 'The Municipal Gallery Revisited' shows what he still felt about the dead Arthur Griffith — 'Griffith staring in hysterical pride', and Padraic Colum once said to me, 'Yeats had no more time for me after I opposed Synge.' He was a man with no memory for personal injuries or insults [I should know!], but a long memory for injuries or imaginary injuries done to his friends. That I think is the secret of his unremitting hatred of

George Moore, who had satirized Lady Gregory, but was still a bigger man than Yeats admitted.

And yet there is even more than that to it, and this is where our literary history, written by intelligent Americans and Englishmen, breaks down. The death of Synge marks more than the end of a friendship; it marks the end of a historical period. The ten years from 1900 to 1910 must have been one of the most exciting decades of Irish history, and one can still catch some of the excitement from Moore's *Ave, Salve, and Vale* (the three volumes of *Hail and Farewell!*). In the year 1904, for instance, there appeared Yeats' *On Baile's Strand*, *The King's Threshold*, and *The Pot of Broth*; Lady Gregory's *Spreading the News*; Synge's *Riders to the Sea*; Moore's *The Lake*; Russell's anthology, *New Songs*, which contained the early work of Colum; Hyde's *An Cleamhnas* (The Matchmaking); three short stories by James Joyce: 'The Sisters', 'Eveline', and 'After the Race'; and Herbert Hughes' *Songs of Uladh*, which contained the first of Joseph Campbell's songs and ballads. Synge, I suspect, was more than a person; he was a portent and a symbol and his early death was a disaster.

In 1910 the Abbey produced Synge's unfinished *Deirdre of the Sorrows* and Colum's *Thomas Muskerry*, and in the following year George Moore left for London and published the first volume of his history of Ireland's great adventure. The spell was obviously over, and everyone knew who was to blame — the old sorcerer Yeats, who without a penny had conjured up a decade of cultural achievement that suggested not some English provincial town but some state in Renaissance Italy, and now he had lost his magic.

Yeats himself seems to have felt he had lost his magic. That is the theme of 'The Green Helmet' of 1910, with its description of Ireland after the death of Synge.

> Here neighbour wars on neighbour and why, there is no
>   man knows,
> And if a man is lucky all wish his luck away,
> And take his good name from him between a day and a day.

The more despondent he grew, the more contemptuous and arrogant he became, and he left the theatre in the hands of men he patronized and despised. The honeymoon with Ireland was over

— 'this blind and bitter land', 'my fool-driven land', 'this unlucky country that was made when the devil spat'. And yet much of this despondency must have been personal and connected with the loss of Maud Gonne and the death of Synge. I have already referred to the peculiarly political character of Irish literature, and a shrewd critic like Yeats had noticed it for himself. 'It is strange,' he wrote later to Clement Shorter, 'but your wife, like all the rest of us, is most powerful and most simple and touching when she writes of Ireland or of herself, whereas an Englishman is dramatic when at his best, and as a rule at his worst when he speaks of himself or of England.' I would not defend the 'rule', but it is true of himself and Irish writers generally that their work is strongest when it takes a political colouring. Accordingly, when we read a great poem like 'September 1913', we have to make an adjustment of perspective that we should not normally make for an English poem, and allow for a mass of personal as well as political dis-illusionment.

> What need you, being come to sense,
> But fumble in a greasy till
> And add the halfpence to the pence
> And prayer to shivering prayer, until
> You have dried the marrow from the bone?
> For men were born to pray and save:
> Romantic Ireland's dead and gone,
> It's with O'Leary in the grave.
>
> Yet they were of a different kind,
> The names that stilled your childish play,
> They have gone about the world like wind,
> But little time had they to pray
> For whom the hangman's rope was spun,
> And what, God help us, could they save?
> Romantic Ireland's dead and gone,
> It's with O'Leary in the grave.

Yet though Yeats may have been feeling desperate, and though he even told Robert Frost that he did not expect to write poetry again, we can see even from these lines that he had learned back from Synge the lesson he himself had taught. He had devoted his life to a process of simplification — of acting, stage design, play-writing, and now he had himself picked up the knack of placing the dull word, the commonplace phrase to restore the tone of the human voice speaking. Once when we were discussing some translation of mine he said, 'You must write poetry as though you were shouting to a man at the other side of the street and were afraid he wouldn't hear you.' 'And what, God help us, could they save?' is someone shouting to a man at the other side of the street.

Then at Easter 1916, the Three Bad Poets — as Pearse called himself, Thomas MacDonagh, and Joseph Plunkett — led a despairing rising in Dublin, and with them went Maud Gonne's husband. All ended up before English firing squads. I hold no brief for Yeats; I am afraid his first thought was that now Maud Gonne was again free to marry him, so he got permission from the English authorities to visit France, supposedly to write about the battlefields, but really to break the news himself to Maud in her Normandy cottage.

In spite of the dramatic announcement and the chivalrous gesture she would still have nothing to do with him, so he turned to her daughter, Iseult, instead. There was something in the Gonnes that made them mistrustful of Yeats, and Iseult refused him as well.

How could she mate with fifty years that was so wildly bred?
Let the cage bird and the cage bird mate and the wild bird
   mate with the wild.

So, with a breaking heart, the elderly cage bird married, in 1917, an English girl instead — to the great relief of everyone who cared for him. His quarrel with the theatre continued. For himself he now wanted a drawing-room theatre in the Japanese manner, and for it and for a society audience he wrote *Four Plays for Dancers*. Lady Gregory did not see why she should be punished with the Abbey audience, and she disliked Yeats' new manager, Lennox Robinson, and everything he stood for. It is a mistake to convert a woman, because long after you have begun to have doubts about your own faith, she will be trying gently to convert you back to it. In an Open Letter of 1919 he explains to her in an insufferably supercilious and pretentious way why their theatre, which had produced a dozen masterpieces between 1900 and 1910, could produce no more, and why he must have a drawing-room theatre in London. This is Yeats at his most exasperating, and it was very noble of Lady Gregory not to pitch him and his theatre to the devil, but no doubt she knew him well enough to feel that he would come back.

The trouble about the Japanese plays is that they gave no scope to Yeats the dramatist, and he was a very fine dramatist in an old-fashioned way. He had an almost uncanny skill with a scenario, and once when I asked where he had learned it, he told me that he had taken a play of Corneille on holiday with him and torn it to pieces until he had mastered its construction. Once, when he was grumbling to me against the charming plays of Teresa Deevy and muttering that 'she wouldn't let us rewrite them for her', Robinson said rudely, 'Teresa Deevy rewritten by you would be like Chekhov rewritten by Scribe.' But there was no scope in the Noh plays for either Corneille or Scribe.

To take an example, the most beautiful of the dance plays is *The Only Jealousy of Emer*. It is the apologia of every husband to every wife for his straying fancies, and echoes magnificently Cú Chulainn's cry in the eleventh-century scene: 'Emer, why will you not let me have my day off with women?' There is no finer poetry in Yeats than in the scene between the Ghost of Cuchulain and the Woman of the Sidhe and no theatrical effect more muffed.

GHOST OF CUCHULAIN :   O my lost Emer!
WOMAN OF THE SIDHE : And there is not a loose-tongued schemer
But could draw you, if not dead,
From her table and her bed.
But what could make you fit to wive
With flesh and blood, being born to live
Where no one speaks of broken troth,
For all have washed out of their eyes
Wind-blown dirt of their memories
To improve their sight?
GHOST OF CUCHULAIN :   Your mouth, your mouth.
EMER : If but the dead will set him free
That I may speak with him at whiles
By the hearth-stone I am content —

> Content that he shall turn on me
> Eyes that the cold moon or the vague sea
> Or what I know not's made indifferent.

If, instead of giving up her husband, Emer had been giving up chocolate for Lent, she could hardly have done it more flatly. What has happened is that the Yeats of *The Countess Cathleen* has come back; the young poet who wrote long, vague, beautiful speeches that were lost in their own rhetoric, and the years of cutting, of speeding-up, of sharpening have all gone for nothing.

But what happened to this scene some years later when he had returned to Ballylee and was rewriting the play for the Abbey stage is an object lesson in play-writing.

WOMAN OF THE SIDHE : For all have washed out of their eyes
                    Wind-blown dirt of their memories
                    To improve their sight?
GHOST OF CUCHULAIN :   Your mouth, your mouth!
FIGURE OF CUCHULAIN : Cry out that you renounce his love; make
                    haste
                    And cry that you renounce his love for
                    ever.
EMER :   No, never will I give that cry.
FIGURE OF CUCHULAIN :   Fool! Fool!
                    I am Fand's enemy come to thwart her
                    will,
                    And you stand gaping there. There is still
                    time.
                    Hear how the horses trample on the shore,
                    Hear how they trample! She has mounted
                    up.
                    Cuchulain's not beside her in the chariot.
                    There is still a moment left; cry out, cry
                    out!
                    Renounce him and her power is at an end.
                    Cuchulain's foot is on the chariot-step
                    Cry —
EMER :   I renounce Cuchulain's love for ever.

Yeats' reconciliation with Ireland and the Irish theatre figures hardly at all in foreign studies, but it accounts for some of his finest work. The early Yeats had accepted Ireland very much in the spirit in which a young poet anywhere accepts the tradition of his people; the later Yeats accepts responsibility when there no longer was any call for him to do so. It is significant that one of the first indications of this is a new respect for the Anglo-Irish tradition :

> The pride of people that were
> Bound neither to Cause nor to State,
> Neither to slaves that were spat on,
> Nor to the tyrants that spat,
> The people of Burke and of Grattan
> That gave, though free to refuse —

It is the power to refuse that makes the later gift significant. The new Ireland he served gave him a great deal in return. He had been friendly with Kevin O'Higgins, and from O'Higgins' assassination he got 'A great man in his pride confronting murderous men'; he was one of a committee of the Senate that examined school housing and from that he got 'I walk through the long school room questioning'. The movement towards clerical control that began with the forbidding of divorce got under way only after he left the Senate, but his undelivered speech on divorce is a classical statement of the Liberal case.

In his last phase he was, of course, a supporter of the Fascist O'Duffy, for whose party he wrote some unsingable songs and produced a scheme for making Tara the capital of Ireland. But as a fascist he was the least fanatical of men. Mrs. Yeats was on the opposite side, as I was, and one evening he told me a little moral tale to illustrate the virtues of fascism. 'You see, O'Connor, the people next door are Blueshirts. The Blueshirts keep a dog. George is a De Valeraite and George keeps hens. The fascist dog worries the democratic hens. Today her favourite hen disappeared, and George said, "It's that damn fascist dog!" so she wrote to the neighbours to complain. But you see, O'Connor, to Blueshirts the idea of order is sacred and back comes a note that reads, "Dear Madam, Dog Destroyed." And now George, who is English and very fond of animals, is filled with remorse.'

The following week when we met he began to chuckle.

'O'Connor, remember the fascist dog? Remember the democratic hen? The democratic hen has come home! Now, George is full of guilt and insists on apologizing. I won't hear of it. I say, "George, nothing you can do will bring the fascist dog back to life."'

I enjoyed the story, but once more what interests me is the monologue, that telephone conversation of which one hears only part. Could the fascist dog and the democratic hen be the source of the dog and goose of one of his deplorable fascist marching songs — the dog of law drowned by the fierceness of humanitarian sentiments?

> Justify all those renowned generations;
> They left their bodies to fatten the wolves,
> They left their homesteads to fatten the foxes,
> Fled to far countries, or sheltered themselves
>   In cavern, crevice, hole,
>   Defending Ireland's soul.

> 'Drown all the dogs,' said the fierce young woman,
> 'They killed my goose and a cat.
> Drown, drown in the water-butt,
> Drown all the dogs,' said the fierce young woman.

You may, I hope, have gathered from what I have written that there was nothing in Yeats of the figure suggested by that perverse epitaph in Drumcliffe. He was a man who did not know what it was to cast a cold eye on anything: he was always engaged, sometimes wrongly, but always warmly. Yeats himself had chosen for Lionel Johnson's epitaph, 'Lonely unto the Lone I go, Divine to the Divinity', and when I heard of Yeats' death the epitaph for him that came to my mind was a few lines from that beautiful play *The Herne's Egg*.

> Strong sinew and soft flesh
> Are foliage round the shaft
> Before the arrowsmith
> Has stripped it, and I pray
> That I, all foliage gone,
> May shoot into my joy.

CHAPTER SIXTEEN

All the Olympians

Nobody will ever understand much about modern Irish literature who does not grasp the fact that one cannot really deal with any of its three great writers in isolation. Synge and Lady Gregory are as much part of Yeats' life-work as are his plays, and until his death he proudly linked their names with his own. They are converts, not imitators, and what they share with him is a religion as much as an aesthetic. The death of Synge came very close to being the end of the others as writers: Yeats' work between 1909 and his marriage is the least important part of his work, and all Lady Gregory's best work was written during Synge's lifetime. In many ways she was temperamentally closer to him than she was to Yeats, and in a peculiar way he seems to have acted as a challenge to her.

It is because the relationship of the three was a conversion rather than a conspiracy that it does not really affect the originality of Synge and Lady Gregory. That it was a true conversion we can see if we consider what they were like about the year 1895. Lady Gregory was a London literary hostess who seemed to model herself on Queen Victoria. In 1886 the English poet Scawen Blunt wrote of her:

> It is curious that she, who could see so clearly in Egypt when it was a case between the Circassian pashas and the Arab fellahin, should be blind now that the case is between English landlords and Irish tenants in Galway. But property blinds all eyes, and it is easier for a camel to pass through the eye of a needle, than for an Irish landlord to enter the kingdom of Home Rule. She comes of a family, too, who are 'bitter Protestants', and has surrounded herself with people of her class from Ireland, so that there is no longer room for me in her house.[1]

Synge was a shy and sickly young man who was quietly starving

[1] W. S. Blunt, *Land War in Ireland*, 146.

in a Paris attic, producing badly written little articles which editors fought shy of. A couple of years later the London hostess was hard at work learning Irish, writing down folk-stories in the cottages of the poor peasants she had cut Blunt for trying to assist, and indeed was being restrained only by Yeats himself from turning Catholic as well. Synge, dressed in homespuns, was living a comfortless life on a barren island on the edge of Europe. The conversion was complete, but within, both remained very much what they had always been.

Not that I find Synge very easy to understand either before or after conversion. Yeats' autobiography, Lady Gregory's journals, George Moore's gossip, Professor D. H. Greene's Life, Dr. Henn's criticism all leave him completely opaque to me. The only passage I can think of that suggests a real man is in Miss Walker's reminiscences.

> At the first opportunity, he would lever his huge frame out of a chair and come up on the stage, a half-rolled cigarette in each hand. Then he would look enquiringly round and thrust the little paper cylinders forward towards whoever was going to smoke them. In later years he became the terror of fire-conscious Abbey stage managers. He used to sit timidly in the wings during plays, rolling cigarettes and handing them to the players as they made their exits.[2]

At least the shy man in that little sketch is alive, even if one cannot exactly see him as author of The Playboy of the Western World.

So one must fall back on the work, and even here I find myself mystified. In every writer there are certain key words that give you some clue to what he is about. Words like 'friend' and 'friendship' are valuable when one is reading Yeats, but in Synge all I can find are words that suggest carrion.

> Yet these are rotten — I ask their pardon —
> And we've the sun on rock and garden;
> These are rotten, so you're the Queen
> Of all are living, or have been.

[2] M. Nic Shiubhlaigh and E. Kenny, The Splendid Years, Dublin, 1955.

If this is how he usually addressed girls it is hardly surprising that he had to spend so much time rolling cigarettes. When he escaped for a while from this carrion view of life it was into a sort of Wordsworthian pantheism. Clearly he was deeply influenced by Wordsworth, and Wordsworth need hardly have been ashamed of signing some of his poems.

> Still south I went and west and south again,
> Through Wicklow from the morning till the night,
> And far from cities, and the sites of men,
> Lived with the sunshine, and the moon's delight.
>
> I knew the stars, the flowers, and the birds,
> The grey and wintry sides of many glens,
> And did but half remember human words,
> In converse with the mountains, moors, and fens.

How Yeats managed to persuade him at all is a mystery. Yeats had not a glimmer of carrion consciousness. I get the feeling that he carefully avoided the whole subject as being exaggerated, dull, and totally irrelevant. Where he may have managed to communicate with Synge is through Wordsworthianism. Not that Yeats had much time for Wordsworth — 'the only great poet who was cut down and used for timber' — but when he preached about the Aran Islands, the necessity for writing about peasants and for adopting peasant speech, a student of Wordsworth could easily have caught what seemed to be echoes of the English poet.

> Low and rustic life was generally chosen because in that situation the essential passions of the heart find a better soil in which they can attain their maturity, are less under restraint, and speak a plainer and more emphatic language; because in that situation our elementary feelings exist in a state of greater simplicity and consequently may be more accurately contemplated and more forcibly communicated; because the manners of rural life germinate from those elementary feelings; and from the necessary character of rural occupations are more easily comprehended and are more durable; and lastly, because in that situation the passions of men are incorporated with the beautiful and permanent forms of nature. The language, too, of these men

is adopted (purified indeed from what appear to be its real defects from all lasting and rational causes of dislike or disgust) because such men hourly communicate with the best objects from which the best part of language is originally derived; and because from their rank in society and the sameness and narrow circle of their intercourse, being less under the action of social vanity they convey their feelings and notions in simple and unelaborated expressions.[3]

It seems to me possible that when we read Synge's prefaces, which so often seem to echo Yeats, we may find that they are really — saving the syntax — echoing Wordsworth.

The material of Synge's plays is slight, and, for the most part, according to Yeats' formula. What is extraordinary is the impact the plays themselves made by comparison with Yeats' and Lady Gregory's. *In the Shadow of the Glen*, for instance, is a folk-story about a flighty wife whose husband pretends to be dead so as to expose her. At the end of the play she goes off with a tramp who, as so often in these plays, represents the Wordsworthian compromise. It is a harmless little play that barely holds interest on the stage, but Arthur Griffith screamed his head off about it as about everything else Synge wrote. 'His play is not a work of genius, Irish or otherwise. It is a foul echo from degenerate Greece.'

It is hard to understand the ferocity of the Catholic reaction to Synge, so much fiercer than the reaction to Joyce. Though it is doubtful if Yeats himself understood it, instinct seems to have warned him that his theories stood or fell by Sygne's work.

It must have been instinct too that warned Arthur Griffith what to attack. Essentially Synge seems to have been, as everyone describes him, gentle, and I should say with little self-confidence. He was willing to write folk plays, mystery plays, or mythological plays to order, though they always turned out to be much the same play. Yeats describes him somewhere as the most 'unpolitical' man who ever lived, but he was 'anti-political' rather than 'unpolitical'.

Once some group of patriotic people persuaded him to write a really patriotic play about the heroes of 1798 and the wickedness of the English soldiery. In his obliging way Synge came back with

[3] Wordsworth, Preface to *Lyrical Ballads*.

a most extraordinary scenario. The characters were two girls, one Protestant, the other Catholic, who in fear of being raped took shelter in a mountain cave. During the play they discuss the cruel and immoral behaviour of both sides, the Catholic girl defending the rebels and the Protestant the military, till they begin to pull one another's hair out. Finally they separate, the Catholic declaring that she would prefer to be raped by an Englishman than listen to further heresy; and the Protestant that she would prefer to be raped by a rebel than listen to Catholic lies.

Much chance there was that a man like that would write a play to reunite everybody!

In the Shadow of the Glen fails because the story on which it is based is farcical, while the play itself is serious. *Riders to the Sea* succeeds brilliantly because, though it is a Yeatsian miracle, one can watch it without even being aware that a miracle is involved. We can perceive its originality best if we study Lawrence's imitation of it in 'Odour of Chrysanthemums'. A fisherman's death, a miner's death represent the whole of life concentrated in a limited society. Both are anti-political, and in neither is there any reference to the price of fish or coal, or any demand for safety regulations. In these two worlds there is no safety except a clean burial. 'What more can we want than that? No man at all can be living for ever, and we must be satisfied.'

The Tinker's Wedding fails as a play because it has no Synge in it; *The Well of the Saints* because it has too much. The truth is that neither Yeats himself nor any of his followers ever really mastered the problems of extended form, and once they went beyond the one-act play they made the most extraordinary mistakes — I have already pointed out Synge's mistake in the first act of the *Playboy*.[4] In a one-act play dealing with a miracle, it is the miracle which automatically establishes itself as the crisis, the point towards which a playwright must build and then work away from; but in *The Well of the Saints* there are two miracles, neither of which is the real crisis.

The Playboy of the Western World is Synge's masterpiece because it contains more of the real Synge than anything else he

[4] Moore noticed this weakness in Lady Gregory's plays. See *Hail and Farewell!* III, *Vale*, chap. viii.

wrote, and naturally, it created a greater storm. Synge himself is the shy and sickly young man who scandalizes the world by a crime he has not committed at all, but he remains a hero even when he is shown up, because he has at last learned to live with his image of himself. Unfortunately he discovered what life was like only as death caught up with him. When the *Playboy* appeared he was world-famous and dying.

His greatest achievement as a writer was his elaboration of a style. It was he who really came to grips with the problems posed by Hyde in *Beside the Fire* — the problems of adapting folk speech to literary ends. Yet Synge's own ear for folk speech cannot have been very good. Though he describes himself recording the conversation in the kitchen below his bedroom in Wicklow he never seems to have studied Hyde's introduction to *Beside the Fire*, where he points out the most obvious fact about English spoken in Ireland: the absence of the pluperfect. In Modern Irish, unlike Old Irish, there are no perfect tenses, so they rarely occur in spoken English. We do not normally say 'He had been there an hour' or 'I shall have discussed it with him.' If we need to supply the missing tense we use the adverb 'after' with the verbal noun: 'He was after being there an hour' or 'I'll be after discussing it with him.'

Synge could never get this quite straight. He dropped the relative pronoun, as in the lines I quoted earlier, 'Of all are living or have been', a construction that in my experience does not occur at all, and rounded it off with a past perfect; and twice at the climax of *Riders to the Sea* he uses improbable tenses: 'It isn't that I haven't prayed for you, Bartley, to the Almighty God. It isn't that I haven't said prayers in the dark night till you wouldn't know what I'd be saying.' Even in the very opening scene he gives us the English use of 'shall' in 'Shall I open it now?'

What he did succeed in was giving Anglo-Irish speech a strong cadence structure. The dialogue in Lady Gregory's *Spreading the News* is enchanting, but it is prose, and in the passionate moments of real drama there is no reserve of language upon which to draw. Lady Gregory herself must have been keenly aware of what he had achieved because in a play that she obviously intended as a rival to *Riders to the Sea*, *The Gaol Gate*, she used an irregular ballad metre, which she then concealed by writing it as prose; but this is a clumsy device because if the actor becomes aware of the metre he can scarcely avoid falling into sing-song, while if he is not, he is just as liable to break up the cadences as though they were nothing but prose. Hyde had given Irish prose writers a medium by which they could keep their distance from English writers; Synge went one better and invented a medium which enabled them to keep the whole modern prose theatre at a distance.

Nobody that I know of has analysed this cadence structure. One obvious cadence fades out on an unimportant word like 'only' or 'surely'. Another of the same sort ends on a temporal clause, which in modern English would be placed at the beginning of the phrase, and this is emphasized by the modern Irish use of the conjunction 'and' as an adverb. Thus, where an English speaker would be inclined to say, 'When I was coming home it was dark', we tend to say, 'It was dark and I coming home', and Sygne tends to use it for its slightly melancholy colour.

MAURYA: Isn't it a hard and cruel man won't hear a word from an old woman, and she holding him from the sea?
CATHLEEN: It's the life of a young man to be going on the sea, and who would listen to an old woman with one thing and she saying it over?

A notable cadence seems to end on a single accented long vowel, often a monosyllable which is preceded by another long and a short — cretics alternating with choriambs is perhaps how it might be described. Synge makes very effective use of it in the great love scene in the *Playboy* — 'in the heat of noon', 'when our banns is called', 'in four months or five', and 'in his golden chair'.

If Synge remains a mysterious figure, there is nothing whatever mysterious about Lady Gregory. If there is one word that sums her up it is complacency — Victorian complacency at that. To please Yeats she rewrote the early sagas and romances that had been edited by famous scholars in English, French and German, but when she came to a line such as 'Will we ask her to sleep with you?' in 'The Voyage of Mael Dúin', Lady Gregory, remembering what the Dear Queen would have felt, turned it into 'Will we ask her would she maybe be your wife?'

Yet I think the critic in the *Times Literary Supplement* who not so long ago told us that there would be no Lady Gregory revival was probably wrong. If ever we get a national theatre again I should expect more revivals of *Spreading the News, The Rising of the Moon, The Travelling Man,* and *The Gaol Gate* than of *Riders to the Sea* or *On Baile's Strand.* We have to learn to appreciate the work of Yeats and Synge, and in doing so lose something of its original freshness, but anyone can appreciate a Lady Gregory play just as anyone can enjoy watching a children's game. Under the Victorian complacency is the Victorian innocence, and this is a quality that does not easily date.

I do not mean that she is unsophisticated. If Yeats had his Corneille for master and Synge his Racine, she has her Molière, and anyone who knows Molière will notice his little tricks in her comedies; as for instance the slow passages of elaborate exposition that suddenly give place to the slapstick stichomythia.

MR. QUIRKE : The man that preserved me!
HYACINTH :   That preserved you?
MR. QUIRKE : That kept me from ruin!
HYACINTH :   From ruin?
MR. QUIRKE : That saved me from disgrace!
HYACINTH :   (*To Mrs. Delane.*) What is he saying at all?
MR. QUIRKE : From the Inspector!
HYACINTH :   What is he talking about?

But in spite of the Victorian complacency she had a genuine tragic sense. Naturally it was a very limited one. She had a tendency to repeat a phrase of Yeats' : 'Tragedy must be a joy to the man that dies.' Even as stated it is a very doubtful critical principle, because we do not go to the theatre to see Oedipus enjoy himself, but as she applied it it was even more restricting because it tended to turn into 'Tragedy must be a *pleasure* to the man who dies', which is a very Victorian notion indeed and somewhat reminiscent of the Father of All putting his creatures across his knee and saying, 'This hurts me more than it hurts you.'

But within that Victorian framework she achieves remarkable results, as she does for instance in *The Gaol Gate.* When the play opens we see two poor countrywomen, mother and daughter-in-

law, at the gate of Galway Gaol, waiting for the release of a young
man who is supposed to have betrayed his comrades in some
agrarian outrage. Instead, when the gaol gate opens, they are informed that his comrades have been released and that he has been
hanged; and as they walk back through the streets of the town the
old mother bursts into a great song of praise. Lady Gregory had
been studying *Riders to the Sea* and old Maurya's great tragic tirade
at the curtain, and to make certain of a poetic effect has deliberately chosen to write in a loose and ungainly metre. But even more
striking is the contrast between the two climaxes, Synge's haunted
by the imminence of death, Lady Gregory's by the triumph of life.

MARY CAHEL : (*Holding out her hands.*) Are there any people in
the streets at all till I call on them to come hither? Did they
ever hear in Galway such a thing to be done, a man to die for
his neighbour?
Tell it out in the streets for the people to hear, Denis Cahel from
Slieve Echtge is dead. It was Denis Cahel from Daire-caol that
died in the place of his neighbour! . . .
Gather up, Mary Cushin, the clothes for your child; they'll be
wanted by this one and that one. The boys crossing the sea
in the springtime will be craving a thread for a memory. . . .
The child he left in the house that is shook, it is great will be
his boast of his father! All Ireland will have a welcome before
him, and all the people in Boston.
I to stoop on a stick through half a hundred years, I will never
be tired with praising! Come hither, Mary Cushin, till we'll
shout it through the roads, Denis Cahel died for his neighbour!

Apart from the fact that this is as great as anything in classical
tragedy, it is also one of the most astonishing things in the Irish
Literary Revival, for it is the work of a Protestant landowner,
whose own son would die as an officer in the British Air Force
and who had broken off an old friendship with Scawen Blunt
because he himself had occupied a cell in Galway Gaol with the
Denis Cahels of his day. It makes everything else written in Ireland
in our time seem like the work of a foreigner.
There is an even more haunting tragic climax in *Dervorgilla* of
the following year, 1908. Dervorgilla keeps on attracting romantic

writers since Thomas Moore called her 'falsest of women', and in
The Dreaming of the Bones even Yeats denies her forgiveness for
her imaginary crime. According to the chestnut, which is served
up even in the most recent histories and guide-books, she was the
wife of O'Rourke of Breany and eloped with MacMurrough of
Leinster, thus precipitating the Norman invasion. The writers have
most peculiar notions of Irish dynastic marriages : Dervorgilla was
a woman famous for her piety, whose 'marriages' to two unmiti-
gated ruffians like O'Rourke and MacMurrough she had nothing
whatever to say to.

But what we are dealing with in Lady Gregory's play is the
legend of the unfaithful woman who sacrificed Ireland to her
passions, and we see her in retirement and repentance at Mellifont
Abbey, acting Lady Bountiful to the young people of the countryside till her identity comes to light. Her last great speech is as
noble as anything in Irish literature; in a sense we may, I think,
read it as Lady Gregory's own apology for her withdrawal from
Kiltartan Cross.

> DERVORGILLA: Since you were born and before you were born
> I have been here, kneeling and praying, kneeling and praying,
> fasting and asking forgiveness of God. I think my father God
> has forgiven me. They tell me my mother the Church has
> forgiven me. That old man had forgiven me, and he had
> suffered by the Gall. The old — the old — that old woman,
> even in her grief, she called out no word against me. You are
> young. You will surely forgive me, for you are young. (*They
> are all silent. Then Owen comes over and lays down his cup
> at her feet, then turns and walks slowly away.*) It is not your
> hand that has done this, but the righteous hand of God that
> has moved your hand. (*Other lads lay down their gifts.*) I take
> this shame for the shame in the west I put on O'Rourke of
> Breffny, and the death I brought upon him by the hand of
> the Gall. (*The youngest boy, who has hesitated, comes and
> lays down his hurl and silver ball, and goes away, his head
> drooping.*) I take this reproach for the reproach in the east
> I brought upon Diarmuid, King of Leinster, thrusting upon
> him wars and attacks and battles, till for his defence and
> to defend Leinster he called in the strangers that have de-
> voured Ireland. (*The young men have gone. Mamie comes as*

if to lay down her gift, but draws back. Dervorgilla turns to her.) Do not be afraid to give back my gifts, do not separate yourself from your companions for my sake. For there is little of my life but is spent, and there has come upon me this day all the pain of the world and its anguish, seeing and knowing that a deed once done has no undoing, and the lasting trouble my unfaithfulness has brought upon you and your children for ever. (*Mamie lays down her necklace and goes away sadly.*) There is kindness in your unkindness, not leaving me to go and face Michael and the scales of judgement wrapped in comfortable words, and the praises of the poor, and the lulling of psalms, but from the swift, unflinching, terrible judgement of the young.

I have quoted that great speech, partly that you may understand why the first play I insisted on reviving when I became a director of the Abbey Theatre was *Dervorgilla*, partly to pass on the terrible lesson I learned from it. The play was produced by a young English producer I admired, and the part of Dervorgilla acted by an exceptionally intelligent young actress, and I did not attend the theatre until the dress rehearsal. I listened in bewilderment and horror, and it was only in the last few minutes that I could bring myself to moan, 'For God's sake, stop that infernal snivelling!' It was that evening that I asked Yeats if it was ever permissible for an actor to weep at the curtain of a play and he wrote his answer into 'Lapis Lazuli'.

But my mistake, of course, went deeper than production or acting. It was that in post-Civil War Ireland I expected the atmosphere of that whole dazzling decade; a decade in which Kuno Meyer could casually edit 'King and Hermit' and 'Liadan and Cuirithir' and George Moore in the same year produce the Irish version of *The Untilled Field*; when people acted superbly who had never acted before and in a single year one might have joined in the *Playboy* riots and seen *The Rising of the Moon* and *Dervorgilla* itself, while English and American critics wondered what would happen next.

Only a literary historian will ever be able to capture again anything of that magic — 'All the Olympians, a thing never known again.'

CHAPTER SEVENTEEN

Antithesis - I

I have tried to indicate clearly what the thesis of the Irish Literary Movement was, because, like all theses, it produced an antithesis, and this we must understand if we are to understand James Joyce.

One might be tempted to describe it as a Protestant-Catholic antithesis if it were not that Trinity College, which represented the Protestant interest, was scarcely more friendly to the revival than was the National (*né* Royal) University. At the same time the tradition that Yeats, Synge and Lady Gregory had picked up from Petrie, Ferguson and Standish O'Grady, was largely a Protestant one. It was not only that, of course, because if it had been it would have achieved nothing. It was also the tradition of people who had spent a considerable part of their youth in the country, whereas its opponents were mainly people who by circumstances or inclination were townsmen. The thesis gained strength from its connection with the country, as Yeats realized in later years.

> John Synge, I and Augusta Gregory, thought
> All that we did, all that we said or sang
> Must come from contact with the soil, from that
> Contact everything Antaeus-like grew strong.

The opposition on the other hand were people who had been driven from their little holdings by landlordism and finally managed to settle in the towns and cities. With a few drinks in, they sang sentimentally of 'the valley near Slievenamon' or 'the hills of Donegal', but next morning saw them return cheerfully to office and shop. This is not the only thing that reminds us how similar were the positions of Yeats and Joyce in twentieth-century Dublin and those of Shakespeare and Jonson in seventeenth-century London. Shakespeare and Yeats were highly unscholarly men of feeling, full of happy reminiscences of a country childhood; Jonson and

Joyce were men of enormous reading and curious scholarship, who were happiest in Bartholomew Fair and Nighttown. Shakespeare and Yeats appealed most to the country-bred, Jonson and Joyce to the scholars and townees; for that reason alone Joyce's work swept Americans off their feet. In Ireland the townees who had managed to acquire some sort of education could scarcely be expected to hail with enthusiasm 'a commodious vicus of recirculation' that would put them back exactly where their grandfathers had been in the middle of the nineteenth century.

In fact the antithesis had a considerably wider scope than I can describe, nor did it entirely neglect the countryside. Edward Martyn's theatre of ideas failed miserably, but the practical work of the co-operative societies did not fail altogether until the twenties, and one can still see beautiful glass in ugly Catholic churches throughout the country, though no one can any longer remember the names of the young priests who were responsible for commissioning it. That practical, forward-looking excitement of the period with its subsequent disillusionment is recorded very vividly by one of those enthusiastic young priests, Gerald O'Donovan, in novels that are now almost forgotten.

But to most readers its principal justification must be Joyce. In 1902, at the age of twenty, he visited Yeats for the first time, and Yeats was so astonished and amused at his audacity that he recorded the interview.

Then, putting down his book, he began to explain all his objections to everything I had ever done. Why had I concerned myself with politics, with folklore, with the historical setting of events, and so on? Above all why had I written about ideas, why had I condescended to make generalizations? These things were all the sign of the cooling of the iron, of the fading out of inspiration. I had been puzzled, but now I was confident again. He is from the Royal University, I thought, and he thinks that everything has been settled by Thomas Aquinas, so we need not trouble about it. I have met so many like him. He would probably review my book in the newspapers if I sent it there. But the next moment he spoke of a friend of mine (Oscar Wilde) who after a wild life had turned Catholic on his deathbed. He said that he hoped his conversion was not sincere. He did not like to think that he had been untrue to himself at the end. No, I had not understood him yet.

I had been doing some little plays for our Irish theatre, and had founded them all on emotions or stories that I had got out of folklore. He objected to these particularly and told me that I was deteriorating. I had told him that I had written these plays quite easily and he said that made it quite certain; his own little book owed nothing to anything but his own mind, which was much nearer to God than folklore.

'The folk life [Yeats said, and back comes Thesis], the country life, is nature with her abundance, but the art life, the town life, is the spirit which is sterile when it is not married to nature. The whole ugliness of the modern world has come from the spread of towns and their ways of thought, and to bring back beauty we must marry the spirit and nature again. When the idea which comes from individual life marries the image that is born from the people, one gets great art, the art of Homer, and of Shakespeare, and of Chartres Cathedral.'[1]

There, in a nutshell, are thesis and antithesis, and in 1904, in the same year as *The King's Threshold*, *On Baile's Strand*, and *Spreading the News* appeared the first three stories of the book we now know as *Dubliners* — 'The Sisters', 'Eveline', and 'After The Race'. It is ironic that a country with a dwindling peasant population should have produced the greatest folk art of our time; it is much more ironic that a country whose capital was a provincial hole like Dublin should have produced the masterpieces of urban literature.

Not that Joyce was so staggeringly original as he appears in books by students of Joyce. After all, it was only twelve months before that George Moore had published *The Untilled Field*, and it takes a student of Joyce to ignore a simple fact like that. Moore was the only Irish writer of his time who was in touch with continental fiction. He was the first writer in these kingdoms who realized what it was all about and introduced to English fiction the principles of French naturalism. There is no doubt at all in my mind that Joyce was deeply influenced by him.

But in *The Untilled Field* Moore was working with several dis-

[1] Richard Ellmann, *James Joyce* (London, 1959), 106-7.

advantages. First of all he wrote in the main about country people as Yeats felt proper and, being an Irish country gentleman, Moore had a good idea of what country people were like. Second, to complicate things still further, he was a Catholic by birth and writing for an ecclesiastical magazine simple stories in simple English, which could then be translated into Irish to provide models for young writers in that language. A writer can work under one disadvantage; he cannot work under two, and Yeatsianism and Catholicism are two extremely rigorous codes. One can fit the Yeatsian theories into poetry and drama — both primitive arts; but prose fiction is a modern, critical, urbanized art; and Moore, with the best will in the world, cannot conceal that the countryside dominated spiritually by Yeats and practically by the Church was merely a place or state of punishment where some souls suffer for a time before they go to America. As his stories went on they became wilder in both directions. Moore did not believe in Yeats or the Catholic Church. 'They were talking about reviving the Gothic, but Rodney did not believe in their resurrections or in their renaissance. "The Gael has had his day. The Gael is passing." '

In one beautiful story, 'Home Sickness', a Bowery barman returns to Ireland, falls in love with a local girl, and plans to settle down where he belongs, but at last, realizing that all his neighbours are terrorized by a stupid parish priest, he slips back to his New York saloon, leaving the girl and Ireland behind him.

> There is an unchanging, silent life within every man that none knows but himself, and his unchanging, silent life was his memory of Margaret Dirken. The bar-room was forgotten and all that concerned it and the things he saw most clearly were the green hill-side, and the bog lake and the rushes about it, and the greater lake in the distance, and behind it the blue line of wandering hills.

In Joyce as in Moore there is the realization of the prose writer as opposed to the poet that there *is* a way out. As an advertisement I once saw in my youth said: 'If they don't sell Suxo in your neighbourhood, leave the neighbourhood.' The hero of 'Home Sickness' feels 'He must go away from this place — he must get back to the bar-room.' Similarly Joyce's Eveline feels 'If she went, tomorrow she would be on the sea with Frank, steaming towards Buenos Ayres.' But Joyce's heroine was more trapped than Moore's hero, because for her there was no 'bog lake and the rushes about it'; nothing but a number on a terrace. Joyce is probably the most exclusively urban writer who ever lived. To him 'country' was Sandymount Strand, two miles from the town centre. The figure that in *Ulysses* echoes the artist, Stephen, is Leopold Bloom, because, owing to historical circumstances, the Jews for close on two thousand years have been townsmen. Because of much less drastic, though not less imperative, historical circumstances, Irishmen of Joyce's generation were equally cut off from the country. Whatever figures there were in their mythology, Antaeus was not one of them. Jewish literature is the literature of townsmen, and the greatest Jew of all was James Joyce. Never once in all his work, so far as I know it, do we get a hint of what life was like in Ireland outside of Dublin.

Within the limits of that extraordinary first decade of the twentieth century — roughly between the ages of twenty and thirty — Joyce had written an autobiographical novel and the group of short stories he published as *Dubliners*. It would seem from the portion of the novel that has been preserved under the name of *Stephen Hero* that he wrote about himself very differently from the way he wrote about others. *Stephen Hero* is immature, imitative, and hysterical; the early short stories are absurdly mature and clever. At the same time the novel is deeply felt as nothing in the short stories is felt. I think one can see this best in the passage from *A Portrait* that I quoted earlier. This is almost certainly a passage from *Stephen Hero*, which, except for the slight dolling-up to fit it into a new attitude to literature required in *A Portrait*, does not seem to have been submitted to much rewriting. It is a moving, angry, eloquent outburst, which suggests profound depths of feeling in the characters described. In *Dubliners*, on the other hand, the death of Parnell is treated with an icy, clinical touch. As in most of the other stories there is a deliberate tawdriness of material, which is underlined by the symbolic popping of corks from three stout bottles to suggest the volleys over the hero's grave and a recitation of threadbare sentiment to suggest the funeral march.

How remarkable the contrast between the two episodes is we can see if we imagine 'Ivy Day in the Committee Room' as a chapter of *A Portrait of the Artist* or the Christmas Day scene as a short story in *Dubliners*. Nowhere is Joyce more obviously an urban writer than in the brooding emotion with which he deals with himself and his family and the contemptuous detachment with which he deals with everyone else. Intense subjectivity and intense objectivity alternate in his work, and in his later work he makes a desperate effort to fuse the two sides of his mind.

What he obviously believed would be the key to this came to him some time during the writing of *Dubliners*, for, as I have pointed out in another book, the first paragraph of 'Two Gallants' and the paragraph describing the harper in the same story — both apparently late additions to the story — are in an entirely new style. This is certainly influenced by Flaubert and Pater, but it is more deliberate and selfconscious than anything they attempted. There is a careful repetition of key-words, sometimes with a slight variation of form and order, which is intended to affect the reader subconsciously.

> He plucked at the wires heedlessly, glancing quickly from time to time at the face of each new-comer and from time to time, wearily also, at the sky. His harp, too, heedless that her coverings had fallen about her knees, seemed weary alike of the eyes of strangers and of her master's hands. One hand played in the bass the melody of *Silent, O Moyle*, while the other hand careered in the treble after each group of notes. The notes of the air sounded deep and full.

This is the beginning of an entirely new attitude to style not only in Joyce himself but in people like Hemingway and Faulkner who were influenced by him. Up to this, style had represented a relationship between writer and reader concerning the object, which was regarded as a third party. In the new style which Joyce is attempting to fashion, the relationship is between the writer and the object, and it is now the reader who is the third party, present only by courtesy. This is the magical as opposed to the logical approach to language. When we approach language logically we are always aware that it is a crude and clumsy method of communication. We take something we call a root, stick a preposition by way of a head on it and a suffix by way of a tail and by a sort of gentlemen's agreement decide that it expresses an idea common to all of us. Since the gentlemen's agreement is necessarily vague the word itself usually changes its meaning within a couple of generations. But when we approach language magically we realize that words like 'crash' or 'flash' derive in some peculiar way from the object itself, though we have no idea why two consonants should represent the effect of sound and another two the effect of vision.

Poetry always inclines towards this magical approach to language, and we realize that though the words have a perfectly good logical context, the real meaning is being supplied by unanalysable collocations of images and sounds. This was the quality that Flaubert and Pater tried to add to prose, but in Joyce the desire for a magical approach to language goes deeper than any aesthetic. It is the passion of a man who had wished to be a Catholic priest, and who is trying to transfer to his idea of the writer everything he valued in his idea of the priest, from the forgiveness of sins to the power of changing bread and wine into the body and blood of Jesus Christ. In Joyce the change in the idea of style from one of a relationship between the writer and reader to one of a relationship between writer and object implies the mystery of transubstantiation. This is what V. S. Pritchett really meant when he called Joyce 'a mad grammarian' and what I meant when I described his work originally as 'a rhetorician's dream'.

It was when he reached this point in his development that Joyce threw most of Stephen Hero into the fire and began again, with his new attitude to style and form. The rewriting involved a vast reconstruction, and though I think I was the first to point out the peculiarities of this, I cannot pretend that I have ever identified more than a small number of them. One of the peculiarities was that the book seems to be based on Aristotle's De Anima and Aquinas' commentaries, tracing the development of the individual from babyhood to maturity in terms of physical differentiation and mental and spiritual differentiation, but always in terms of what I called 'dissociated metaphor'; metaphor that is never apparent and sometimes carefully disguised.

Thus, when Stephen wets the bed, and first it is hot and then cold, Joyce clearly differentiates the sense of touch, which, according to Aristotle, is the primary sense and distinguishes the animal from the vegetable. But the sentence has a further significance for it shows the child as capable of judgement. 'The mean is capable of judgement, for it becomes in reference to each of the extremes another extreme. And as that which is to perceive white or black must not itself be actually white or black, but both of these potentially . . . so also in the case of touch it must not be either hot or cold in itself.'

The sense of touch is that which predominates throughout the book, and this is emphasized by Joyce's use of verbs. It is never sufficient for him merely to indicate which sense is being dealt with; the significant verb is repeated again and again.

> Stephen felt his own face red too, thinking of all the bets about who would get first place in elements, Jack Lawton or he. . . . Then all his eagerness passed away and he felt his face quite cool. He thought his face must be white because it felt so cool.

And again:

> And though he trembled with cold and fright to think of the cruel long nails and of the high whistling sound of the cane and of the chill you felt at the end of your shirt when you undressed yourself yet he felt a feeling of queer quiet pleasure inside him to think of the white fattish hands, clean and strong and gentle.

I fancy that the metaphorical construction is represented in the text by a small vocabulary in which certain key words are repeated with the intention of creating a magical aura around the text, particularly words of sensory significance like 'feel', 'touch', and 'hands' in the passages we have been considering, 'eyes', 'gaze', and 'smell' in others. No doubt there are many words used in this way which I have not identified, but one — the word 'pass' — is repeatedly introduced, I think to suggest the continuing movement of the individual through time and space. The example of Joyce's mechanistic prose which I gave twenty-five years ago is still the most illuminating for me.

> The soft beauty of the Latin word touched with an enchanting touch the dark of the evening, with a touch fainter and more

persuading than the touch of music or of a woman's hand. The strife of their minds was quelled. The figure of a woman as she appears in the liturgy of the church passed silently through the darkness: a white-robed figure, small and slender as a boy, and with a falling girdle. Her voice, frail and high as a boy's, was heard intoning from a distant choir the first words of a woman which pierce the gloom and clamour of the first chanting of the passion.

Et tu cum Jesu Galilæo eras.

And all hearts were touched and turned to her voice, shining like a young star, shining clearer as the voice intoned the pro-paroxyton and more faintly as the cadence died.

In the folds of this style, fire and ice, subjectivity and objectivity, are being merged. Joyce is the most extreme example in literature of the power of insulation. Somewhere in his twenties, with a crude and powerful novel and half a dozen brilliant short stories completed, he left for the Continent and returned to Ireland only for brief visits. In exile he began to write in an altogether new way with a complete and selfconscious mastery of his medium. By the time he had finished *A Portrait of the Artist as a Young Man* he was not only better equipped than any writer of his time. He was also the greatest master of rhetoric who has ever lived.

There is no doubt that living abroad made this possible, because not only did each year of exile carry farther into the background the anger and grief of his youth, with its loathing of Catholicism and English rule, it kept the material itself from developing along with him. It remained living, but imprisoned in a great block of ice. Yeats' material kept on changing as he changed, facing him with new challenges from decade to decade, and precisely at the point when Joyce was beginning to feel full confidence in himself as a writer, Yeats was beginning to lose his.

Strange as it may seem, Joyce's retreat to the Continent has much about it that suggests a saint's retreat to the monastery of some enclosed order, and it fed in him that element that I have tried to isolate — the element of the would-be priest. For the later Joyce rhetoric was no longer merely a technical exercise; it was a sacrament in which the living substance was to be changed into something different and new.

CHAPTER EIGHTEEN

Antithesis - II

Joyce's masterpiece, *Ulysses*, seems to have begun life as a short story for *Dubliners* entitled 'Mr. Hunter's Day' and it may even then have been remotely based on the story of Ulysses, just as 'Grace' is supposed to be based on Dante's *Divine Comedy*. *Dubliners* was a completely objective book, as *A Portrait of the Artist* was a completely subjective one, so that *Ulysses* would have carried on the characteristic Joycean alternation of ice and fire, passion and detachment. But somewhere along the way of composition Joyce revolted against the idea of a large book in the manner of *Dubliners*, even with all the new rhetorical devices he had discovered to conceal his schizophrenia, so the character of Stephen Dedalus from *A Portrait of the Artist* was added to the dramatis personae, and at once the conflict in Joyce himself became a conflict that needed to be resolved within the narrative. Joyce skilfully avoided it as long as possible, and Bloom and Dedalus meet and pass, meet and pass, until at last they are left alone in Nighttown. Then, as in 'Ivy Day in the Committee Room', when Mr. Henchy, the worldly old trimmer, suddenly calls to the Parnellite 'Come in, Joe!', the whole drama of *Ulysses* concentrates upon the moment when the Jew forgets himself and calls Dedalus 'Stephen'. In real life the use of Christian names was a point of etiquette over which Joyce fussed endlessly, and to him it was clearly the indication of a moment of abandonment. In *Ulysses* as in the early story it seems to be a matter that had no great conquences, because all that happens is that Bloom brings Stephen to his home; they have a chat over a cup of cocoa and then separate, so far as the reader knows, forever. As I shall endeavour to show, Stephen and Bloom are one and the same man, a man young and old or a man considered subjectively and objectively, as you prefer to put it.

The book contains eighteen episodes; the first three associated with Stephen in particular, the rest centring mainly on Bloom. But now the technical development has reached what I think we may call a manic stage. Not only is each episode related to a corresponding episode in the *Odyssey*; it is also associated with an organ of the body, an art, a colour, a symbol and a literary technique. This is achieved by what I have called 'dissociated metaphor', metaphor that is not supposed to be perceived by the reader and that lies concealed in the text in the form of analogies, parallels, and puns — principally puns.

The whole process was explained by Mr. Stuart Gilbert in his book on *Ulysses*. He had the advantage of Joyce's assistance, but like other exhibitionists, Joyce not only reveals but conceals; and Mr. Gilbert does not seem to have been informed about some of the most important examples of dissociated metaphor. For instance, in the fourth episode, when we first meet Bloom and his wife, Molly, they represent a modern Ulysses and Penelope, so we find them discussing the transmigration of souls. The metaphor for this is the transmutation of matter, and as matter is transmuted through the intestines of animals, the first line tells us that Bloom 'ate with relish the inner organs of beasts and fowls'. Pursuing the metaphor further, Bloom goes out to buy a kidney for his breakfast — the kidney being the organ symbolized in the chapter — receives a letter from his daughter, Millie, who is improbably employed in a photographer's shop in Mullingar, which is the centre of the Irish cattle industry, and so the place where the greatest transmutation of matter occurs, and finally, instead of going to the upstairs water-closet, which would have played the deuce with the metaphor, Bloom goes to an earth-closet outside the house and returns to earth the matter that will come back as food for cattle and sustain future generations of Ulysseses and Penelopes. It is all almost incredibly neat.

In the sixth episode, 'Hades', which describes the funeral to Glasnevin, the associations are almost entirely with death, and very remote some of them are. There is, for instance, the word 'mortgage', with its echo of the French word for death, and the shop called Todd's, which echoes the German word *Tod*. The most abstruse I have found is the passage in which Molly looks out at the two dogs copulating in the street and Bloom thinks: 'And the sergeant grinning up. She had that cream gown on with the rip she never stitched.' Shakespeare's 'grim sergeant Death' is easily identified but it is not so easy to understand the gown with the R.I.P. in it.

One of the most amusing episodes is the seventh, 'Aeolus', which takes place in a newspaper office. Its organ is the lungs, its art is rhetoric, and its technique is described by Mr. Gilbert as 'enthymemic'. The *Shorter Oxford* abjures the word, but gives instead 'enthymematic', which probably leaves you as wise as it leaves me. Not that it makes much difference, because the technique here as elsewhere is based mainly on puns about the word 'wind', from the correspondence column in which a reader solemnly asks 'Dear Mr. Editor, what is a good cure for flatulence?' to Bloom's meditations on 'influence', 'gale days' and 'windfalls'.

As entertainment for hospital patients with a long, slow, but not too distressing illness *Ulysses* is insurpassable. Joyce is a wonderful man against whom to pit one's wits, and not only will they fail to notice the days passing, but they will return to ordinary life as well informed as the editor of an encyclopedia.

But with the eleventh, twelfth and thirteenth episodes Joyce begins to run into serious trouble, and with the fourteenth he is in it up to the neck. Ezra Pound was the first person to notice that something had gone wrong, and when he read the 'Sirens' episode he commented sourly : 'A new style per chapter not required.' 'Not required' is polite, because a new style per chapter was now becoming the bane of the book. In the eleventh chapter Bloom is with the Sirens in the Ormond Restaurant, in the twelfth with the Cyclops in Davy Byrne's public-house, and in the thirteenth with Nausicaa on Sandymount Strand.

The technique of the 'Sirens' is described as 'Fuga Per Canonem' ('canon fugue', to you), which, by the nature of canon fugues, it cannot possibly be. At a performance of *Die Walküre* Joyce modestly asked a friend : 'Don't you find the musical effects of my Sirens better than Wagner's?' and when the friend rudely said 'No', Joyce stamped out of the opera house. So Mr. Gilbert is clearly giving us the Master's view when he says that

the devices of suspension and resolution are frequently employed, as in the passage 'Upholding the lid he (who?) gazed in the coffin (coffin?) at the oblique triple (piano) wires.' (In-tellection is suspended till the last word resolves the mystery.) Examples of the 'hollow fifth' (quinto vuoto) are such words as 'Blmstup' where the thirds, the letters oo and ood ('Bloom stood up') are omitted, and such sentences as 'Why did she me?' and 'Milly no taste' where the central verb is omitted between subject and object. Thus the hearer of an 'empty fifth' instinctively fills up the gap with a major third.

The only intellection suspended in this passage seems to me to be Mr. Gilbert's. If I am the 'hearer' of one of Mr. Gilbert's 'empty fifths', I do not instinctively or otherwise fill up the gap with a major third. Here metaphor has ceased to be a servant and become a master. Oo and ood are not thirds any more than they are kicks, runs or entrechats. Joyce the story-teller is giving up the job, and his place is being taken by Joyce the magician, tinkling his little bell and putting another spoon of incense in the censer.

It is interesting to watch the thickening and clotting of the technical processes in those three chapters leading up to 'The Oxen of the Sun'. 'Cyclops' has the marvellous running commen-tary in Dublin argot which I still reread with delight, ignoring the puns and analogies, but I never allow my eye to stray any longer over the gigantesque parodies with which it is broken up. 'Nausicaa' is in a style that Joyce calls 'Tumescence and Detumes-cence', which is largely a parody of Home Chat and the Irish Messenger of the Sacred Heart, and I find it very difficult to get through something that would be amusing enough in the humorous column of a daily newspaper.

But with 'The Oxen of the Sun' my patience gives way alto-gether. Joyce describes its style as 'Embryonic Development', and this is symbolized by an anthology of parodies of English prose from Anglo-Saxon to modern American. To begin with, parody is an extremely limited form, which appeals almost entirely to the intelli-gence. It is an aspect of literary criticism, and done supremely well as it is in Housman's 'O suitably attired in leather boots' or in a few pieces of Beerbohm's, it gives us a pleasure similar to that which we get from an essay of Matthew Arnold's. But Joyce is a mimic, not a parodist, and scarcely ever does he give me the feeling that he is commenting upon the author he is guying.

Anyhow, this is not my principal objection to the chapter, and here I must refer you to Joyce's play *Exiles*. The hero of this is an imaginary and somewhat flattering self-portrait. It describes an Irish writer, Richard Rowan, who has had a tragic relationship with a pious Catholic mother from which he is trying to break free. At the same time he is trying to procure his wife for his friend Robert Hand, a journalist who seems to have been modelled on Oliver Gogarty. He reveals this perverted desire to Hand himself.

> Because in the very core of my ignoble heart I longed to be betrayed by you and by her — in the dark, in the night — secretly, meanly, craftily. By you, my best friend, and by her. I longed for that passionately and ignobly, to be dishonoured for ever in love and lust.

As I have explained in another book this is not a unique perversion because we also find it in the work of Dostoevsky and D. H. Lawrence. There I called it the Unnatural Triangle, the triangle in which a man attracted by another man uses the woman he loves for sexual bait, and then derives an intense pleasure from imagining the sexual intercourse of friend and mistress. It is not easy to disentangle the complicated threads that make up the obsession, and in all three writers it takes a slightly different form. Of course, all of them have a fundamental homosexuality and a fundamental masochism which is linked with voyeurism. Joyce's masochistic fantasies seem to indicate that it was not enough for him to be himself corrupt in order to free himself from the ties of Christian morality represented by his dead mother; he had to prove his own corruption by depraving someone he loved. The notes to the second edition of *Exiles* seem to describe a situation in which he tried to manoeuvre his wife into becoming the mistress of an Italian friend and then by feeding her word-tests, endeavoured to discover whether she had in fact deceived him.

But as Dostoevsky's masochism is perceptibly altered by the fact that he was mainly attracted by children, Joyce's is altered by his Messianism. It was not only that he tried to manoeuvre his wife into the position of a physical link with a man who attracted him; he also tried to manoeuvre the man into the position of Judas. He

found no difficulty in discovering Judases; he provided a characteristic paragraph to be added to Gorman's biography of him which
revealed his true identity to the percipient reader. This paragraph
is an extraordinary production.

> Several times in Joyce's career this brusque and unexplained
> attitude of certain admirers of his has taken place. There were
> at least two instances of it in Dublin — one before he left and
> one during his last visit there, another in Trieste after he had
> become famous, and it has happened in Paris also. There is no
> single explanation so far as these different admirers are con-
> cerned that will fit all these cases, but the fact remains that all
> through his life he seems to have had admiration both in its
> spiritual and its material form spontaneously and suddenly
> offered him and subsequently just as suddenly transformed into
> passive or open hostility.[1]

The conclusion is obvious. When in the Nighttown episode
Lynch goes out with Kitty we have the revealing phrase. '*Exit
Judas. Et laquaeo se suspendit.*' When in real life the character described under the name of Lynch did commit suicide, Joyce's messianism was clearly justified.

Exiles shows us the true reason why Stephen Dedalus appears
in the book at all. Stephen is haunted by his dead mother, as
Richard Rowan was. Leopold Bloom is obsessed by the desire to
be degraded in the degradation of his wife, just as Richard Rowan
was. Stephen and Bloom are the same person, fire and ice, subjectivity and objectivity; both represent different aspects of the
author, and the book is a heroic attempt to reintegrate them. But
in 'The Oxen of the Sun', the very point where they are drawn
together, a violent disturbance is created in the technical processes,
and the focal point of the narrative is obliterated in a storm of
parodies — most of them inferior.

In criticizing any book, particularly a book of such enormous
importance as *Ulysses*, one must always ask oneself if what one is
complaining of was not actually intended by the writer. It is just
possible that Joyce intended his style to grow progressively more
clotted from the brilliant opening chapters that describe morning

[1] H. S. Gorman, *James Joyce* (London, 1941), 262 n.

in Dublin. Apparently he told nobody, but if it was not intended, Joyce has become a victim of his own mannerisms; if it was, it seems to me an artistic error of the first magnitude.

The sixteenth chapter, which follows the two chapters in which Stephen and Bloom are getting themselves tight, clearly represents an after-midnight hangover. To suggest this, the technique is described as 'Narrative (Old)' to distinguish it from the first chapter of the book, 'Narrative (Young)', and the 'Calypso' chapter, 'Narrative (Mature)'. This scarcely means more than that it includes every known form of grammatical, syntactical and verbal error as well as cliché. Old or young, mistakes dragged out at such intolerable length lower a reader's spirit, though our imaginary hospitalized student will find plenty to work on.

The first sentence runs : 'Preparatory to anything else Mr. Bloom brushed off the greater bulk of the shavings and handed Stephen the hat and ashplant and bucked him up generally in orthodox Samaritan fashion, which he very badly needed.' Our student will, of course, note, along with the grammatical error, that 'bulk' is not a quality of shavings and that Samaritans by definition are not orthodox.

The confusion becomes worse in the scientific catechism of the 'Ithaca' episode. In the last great chapter which most of us read carefully at some time for pornographic reasons, we finally discover that Molly Bloom is not only the wife of Leopold Bloom *and* Penelope: she is also the earth. Like the earth she needs sun, and this is provided by a character whose name is Blazes Boylan. I can only hope that my readers are more capable of detecting the obvious than Joycean scholars are, because so far none of them seems to have done so.

Nothing that I or anyone else can say will change the fact that *Ulysses* is one of the great monuments of Irish literature. What I would suggest to you is that it is at its greatest not in its construction, which is haphazard, nor in its rhetorical experiments, which are frequently otiose, but in its description of the poetry of everyday life in Dublin in the first decade of this century; and as that Dublin fades into history, this aspect will seem more and more important. That is to say, the first ten — at most, the first twelve — episodes are what will endure. The streets, the shops, the

public-houses recorded for ever by a man with an uncanny eye
and a splendid ear are unique in the literature of the world.

Once, when I was lecturing at a Hundred Best Books college in
America, a bright student asked serenely: 'Mr. O'Connor, you can
hardly deny that faced with the choice between recovering a lost
dialogue of Plato's and a description of daily life in Athens at the
time, any reasonable man would choose the Platonic dialogue.'
The question took my breath away for a moment, but at last I
was able to reply: 'I doubt if there is a classical scholar in the
world who wouldn't sacrifice every lost work of Plato's for one
single minute by minute description of daily life in Athens.' Knowing no Greek, I still do not know whether I was right or wrong,
but I know what my own choice would be.

This unique quality of Joyce's work is, I think, what makes it
impossible for anyone except a native Irishman — or, as Joyce
himself seemed to think, Jew — to understand what underlies it.
It is, as I have said, the antithesis to Yeats' thesis of the return
to the country, but it is an antithesis which is conceivable only in
Ireland where the population has been forcibly driven off the land
into the towns and cities with no prospect of return and with no
desire to return. Joyce's Dublin is a walled town of the Middle
Ages, or, if you prefer it, a sentinelled ghetto. And this, it seems
to me, is the supreme irony, the perfect example of the operation
of a literary dialectic, for it seems that the great monument of
urban life does not come from any of the famous cities of the
world, like Athens, Rome, Paris, London or New York, but
from a glorified market town where droves of cattle can still be
seen in the streets and which is populated by an imperfectly
urbanized peasantry of whom Joyce was one.

This part of Joyce's work, I think, will never date. What will
date, and has probably begun to date already, is the spoiled priest,
the magician, making passes and muttering spells. I met Joyce
once only, after the completion of *Ulysses*, and when I came back
to Ireland Yeats asked: 'What did you think of him?' Being young
and rude, I replied: 'I thought he was as mad as a hatter.' Yeats
grew angry and said: 'You should be ashamed to say such a thing
of a great Irish writer.' Then I told him the story of the picture of
Cork, which has got me into trouble with every admirer of Joyce

since Desmond MacCarthy published it twenty-odd years ago. I had admired an old print of Cork in the hallway and wondered what the frame was made of. 'That's cork,' said Joyce. I said, 'I know it's Cork, but what's the frame made of?' 'That's cork,' Joyce repeated, and it was. Yeats looked at me frowning for quite a while and then tweaked his nose irritably. 'You're right, of course,' he muttered. 'That *is* insanity.'

Not that I worried then whether it was or not. Later, it mattered more, when I realized how rare true sanity is. Nowadays Joyce reminds me of the character in one of V. S. Pritchett's stories who keeps on saying: 'Of course, I'm only putting God's point of view.' Joyce is equally modest. In *A Portrait* he only puts God's point of view about himself; in *Ulysses* God's point of view about life; in *Finnegans Wake* God's point of view about the universe.

Twenty years ago no one could have dismissed *Finnegans Wake* like that without my rising to defend and expound it. Today, I can do neither: 'I cannot pay its tribute of wild tears.'

CHAPTER NINETEEN

Transition

In writing about Irish literature from 1900 to 1910 I have been writing of a war and naturally I have had to ignore a number of campaigns, any one of which might keep the serious student of literature happy through years of research. I should like to have discussed Emily Lawless, whose *With the Wild Geese* appeared in 1902 and gave to young Irishmen of my own generation the pleasure that Kipling's best verse must have given to English youths of my own time; and also Thomas Boyd, who appeared on the Irish scene in the year 1906 and then seems to have disappeared entirely. No one seems to know where he came from or where he went to, though he wrote two or perhaps three of the best poems written in that incomparable decade. Let me quote only a couple of verses from his poem on the Bull of Cooley.

> The shadows of the primal wars
>   Darken his giant sides,
> And his harness gleams with glimmering stars
>   That light his mighty strides.
>
> His voice is of the Deep; his path
>   With the fair dead is strewn;
> Awful, upon his brow he hath
>   The great horns of the moon.

Above all, I have had to ignore Padraic Colum, who wrote some of the great poems of the period as well as one of the plays I like best — *Thomas Muskerry*. George Russell described him well; for one evening when I had complained of my indigestion, Russell went into a roar of laughter and said : 'Every serious Irish writer has a pain in his belly. Yeats has a pain in his belly; Joyce has a terrible pain in his belly; now you have a pain in your belly. Padraic Colum is the only Irish writer who never had a pain at all.'

But I must speak of James Stephens, whose first important works appeared in 1912, for both — *The Charwoman's Daughter* and *The Crock of Gold* — are masterpieces. Stephens, like Colum, is a hangover from the great decade; he was a friend of Synge as well as of Russell, and one might almost say that after 1912 he no longer wrote masterpieces. If Boyd is a problem, Stephens is a mystery. All we really know of him is what Miss Hilary Pyle has unearthed, which is that at the age of six he was arrested for begging on the Dublin streets and committed to a Protestant home; and all we can say without fear of contradiction is that he knew the facts of life in this Christian land of ours as Yeats, Synge and Joyce never knew them. I was brought up in the slums of Cork and know something of the facts of life as they appeared, perhaps, to Sean O'Casey. Stephens believed that in our great Christian civilization people died of hunger, and I fancy he knew what he was speaking about.

Just think! In 1912 two masterpieces; in the following year some fine stories which are rather less than masterpieces; in the year after, *The Demigods*, which is not even good; and then a succession of books all uneven in quality and none up to that early, fantastic standard.

In describing Stephens as a genius I use the word deliberately, more deliberately than of any other Irish writer except perhaps Patrick Kavanagh. When I talked with George Russell I always referred to Joyce as a genius, and Russell usually said: 'You mustn't use the word "genius" about Joyce. An enormous talent, of course, but not a genius. Now Stephens is a genius.' I disagreed violently, but now that I am almost as old as Russell was when he spoke to me, I know exactly what he meant. If genius means anything it means the power of a natural force, and this was what Stephens had. In fact it was all that Stephens had, for though Joyce, when he forgot to be a talent might be a genius, Stephens, when his genius deserted him, was no talent. The genius was obvious in the conversation — that of a man who felt that if he stopped he might starve. Stephens sang for his supper; he sang for his breakfast and lunch as well. He sings like a bird through those two early books — through *The Charwoman's Daughter* more than through *The Crock of Gold* though the latter has acquired the reputation.

Like Stephens' conversation, *The Charwoman's Daughter* is life-giving. Without using clichés, I do not know how to describe this quality, but it is the book I prescribe for friends who are ill. I do this not because it is hearty and cheerful, but because it reminds me of Mozart's best music, written over an abyss of horror in which I should perish. By some special grace, both men suffered and survived. You have only to wait for the second paragraph to catch the powerful beat of some archangel's wings.

> Her mother seldom washed at all. She held that washing was very unhealthy and took the natural gloss off the face, and that, moreover, soap either tightened the skin or made it wrinkle. Her own face was very tight in some places and very loose in others, and Mary Makebelieve often thought that the tight places were spots which her mother used to wash when she was young, and the loose parts were those which had never been washed at all. She thought she would prefer to be either loose all over her face or tight all over it, and, therefore, when she washed she did it thoroughly, and when she abstained she allowed of no compromise.

The Charwoman's Daughter is as much a masterpiece as *Ulysses*, though there is no further resemblance. Joyce does almost everything except sing; Stephens either sings or dithers. In the later books the singing note fails, and yet, just as a man who can swim never really loses his skill, a man who can sing never loses his, and even in the radio talks he gave during his last miserable years in London we suddenly hear the pure ringing tone as in his account of how some rough youths once thrust him through the bars of the rhinoceros cage in the Dublin Zoo.

> [The rhinoceros] was very fat, but it wasn't fat like stomachs, it was fat like barrels of cement, and when it moved it creaked a lot, like a woman I used to know who creaked like an old bedstead. The rhinoceros swaggled over to me with a bunch of cabbage sticking out of its mouth. It wasn't angry, or anything like that, it just wanted to see who I was. Rhinos are blindish: they mainly see by smelling, and they smell in snorts. This one started at my left shoe, and snorted right up that side of me to my ear. He smelt that very carefully; then he switched

over to my right ear, and snorted right down that side of me to
my right shoe: then he fell in love with my shoes and began to
lick them. I, naturally, wriggled my feet at that, and the big
chap was so astonished that he did the strangest step-dance
backwards to his pile of cabbages, and began to eat them.
I squeezed myself out of his cage and walked away. In a
couple of minutes I saw the two boys. They were very
frightened, and they asked me what I'd done to the rhinoceros.
I answered, a bit grandly, perhaps, that I had seized it in both
hands, ripped it limb from limb and tossed its carcase to the
crows. But when they began shouting to people that I had just
murdered a rhinoceros I took to my heels, for I didn't want to
be arrested and hanged for a murder that I hadn't committed.[1]

'Ach, Seumaisín! bhi gach aon mhadra 'sa mbaile buidheach
dó' — 'Ach, Jamesey, every dog in the townland was grateful to
him', a Kerrywoman said of his stay in her house; and he always
writes superbly of animals, not in O'Flaherty's remote and poignant
way but as though they were somewhat like himself — weak and
kind and muddled and for ever in danger of starvation. Here, for
instance, is a glimpse of the cow.

I had a row with her a couple of weeks after, for I put my
mackintosh on the fence so that I might be free to pet her. You
pet a cow by putting your cheek up against her nose. You do the
same with women. Well, Mogue pulled my mackintosh over the
fence and she ate every bit of it except one sleeve. That was
serious, for I was on my way to school and my lunch was in
the mackintosh, so she got that too. To be without your lunch
at twelve o'clock and watch the other kids wolfing theirs is as
desolating a thing as can happen. The way everybody except
yourself eats like wolves is very distressing.[2]

The laughter, of course, is characteristic, but it is the whistling
of a child walking through a graveyard at night. There is no
laughter in some of the other stories he wrote and told to his
friends, like the one about how he fought the swan for the hunk

[1] James Stephens (ed. L. Frankenberg), *James, Seumas and Jacques* (London,
1964), 4-5.
[2] Ibid., 279.

of bread and about the sick old dog who fed him for days while he was starving. Whether or not he ever really starved is beside the point. The point is the fear, the abyss of horror on the edge of which he teeters. The most unbearable of his stories, 'Hunger', describes the extinction of a whole Dublin family through starvation.

What makes *The Charwoman's Daughter* a masterpiece is that it is all an enormously delicate, witty variation on the themes of hunger and fear. Mrs. Makebelieve, the poor old charwoman, lives in an imaginary world of absolute security, but the horror is always there, implicit in every fantasy and reminiscence. For instance, her only memory of the brother who she hopes will come back some day from America and make her and her daughter rich is that even as a baby 'he would always say "no" if only half a potato remained in the dish or a solitary slice of bread was on the platter'. In other books and stories, even in the middle of gaiety the horror will suddenly swoop down, as in the dreadful incident of the unemployed man that jolts us in *The Crock of Gold*.

Of all the Irish writers Stephens had the most agile mind. He is a sort of literary acrobat, doing hair-raising swoops up in the roof of the tent. The most laborious, leaden-footed, ham-fisted mind was also in Dublin during those strange ten years. Sean O'Casey probably knew poverty in the same way as Stephens, but he did not feel it in the same way. The reason was probably that while Stephens had a thoroughly bad mother, O'Casey had a devoted one, who spoiled him and whom he exploited shamelessly. (Since I suspect that I did more or less the same thing myself I am not inclined to take a lenient view of the case.) O'Casey was an idealist, and he was going to be nothing but an idealist, even if he had to do so at his mother's expense.

He had a strong sense of justice, which might even be described as a permanent grievance, and he attempted to brain the schoolmaster who punished him in the wrong. As a result he had no education except what he could pick up from the books he borrowed or stole. He was secretary of the St. Laurence O'Toole Pipers' Band and dressed in a kilt, which apparently did not suit him. He was a member of a hurling club, though he was so blind that he could not see the ball. He was a member of the Gaelic League and taught Irish, though he never mastered the grammar of it. Considering the standard of Irish in Dublin, one can only assume that when his contemporaries say his Irish was not good it must have been terrible. He was also (like Yeats) a member of the Irish Republican Brotherhood and one of the founders of the Irish Citizen Army. He wrote popular songs of a really remarkable awfulness and political articles of an even more deadly eloquence. His neighbours called him 'Irish Jack', a typical example of the hostility with which everything national was viewed in the cities and towns.

What was worse, he saw through everybody. He showed them up for what they were, liars, humbugs, hypocrites and exploiters, and they did not even perceive the greatness of soul that inspired him. He noticed sourly that even Lady Gregory, who had been so kind to him, read cheap romances on the side, and Yeats did not even bother to conceal that he enjoyed detective stories and Wild Westerners. (Once, in delirium, he even shouted to his wife, 'George! George! Call the Sheriff!') And here was poor Sean, with the cardboard soles in his broken boots, half blind, reading the immortal works of Shakespeare! The time, as the immortal Shakespeare had said, was certainly out of joint, and it was hard luck that there was no one but himself to set it right.

Then something extraordinary happened to O'Casey. I have no idea what it was, though I suspect it was the death of his mother. After this he went to live with his friend Micheál O Maoláin in Parnell Square, wrote in succession three of the most remarkable plays in Irish or any other literature, and then tapered off in a manner even more extraordinary than that of Stephens.

There are two ways in which we have to regard these plays; first in relation to O'Casey himself, then in relation to the development of Irish literature. A good many years ago I suggested that what made the plays so remarkable was that in them O'Casey was castigating an aspect of his own character about which he felt particularly guilty. His biographer, Saros Cowasjee, quotes this suggestion, and then goes on to prove it (as I think) from *The Shadow of a Gunman*.

This is generally regarded as lightweight O'Casey, which it is not. It has a shocking bit of construction in the first act in which a man called Maguire appears, leaves for a place called Knocksedan, thirty miles away, joins with some other Republicans there in an attack on a British column, is killed, identified and reported dead in a Stop Press edition which is on sale in the Dublin streets ten minutes after his departure. Apart from this — the neatest trick in theatrical history — there is nothing in the least immature about the play. Its title, *The Shadow of a Gunman*, might be the title of the whole trilogy. The men are uniformly drunkards, hypocrites and cowards, and the only decent characters are the two women, Mrs. Henderson and the heroine, Minnie Powell, who dies heroically, saving the poet Dan Davoren from the British police.

The scorn that O'Casey heaps on the men in this play is the same that we find in his early political writings, and yet there is a profound difference, because this time there is also scorn of himself.

> SEUMAS (with a gesture of despair): Oh, this is a hopeless country! There's a fellow that thinks that the four cardinal virtues are not to be found outside an Irish Republic. I don't want to boast about myself — I don't want to boast about myself, and I suppose I could call meself as good a Gael as some of those that are knocking about now — knocking about now — as good a Gael as some that are knocking about now, — but I remember the time when I taught Irish six nights a week, when in the Irish Republican Brotherhood I paid me rifle levy like a man, an' when the Church refused to have anything to do with James Stephens, I tarred a prayer for the repose of his soul on the steps of the Pro-Cathedral. Now, after all me work for Dark Rosaleen, the only answer you can get from a roarin' Republican to a simple question is 'goodbye . . . ee'.

This is not only Seumas — or Micheál O Maoláin, who kindly posed for the part — it is Sean O'Casey, thinking unhappily and guiltily about his own days in the Gaelic League and the Irish Republican Brotherhood, the rifle levy and the kilts and the bagpipes and the hurleys he could afford while his poor mother fretted over rent and food. Because what unifies these three great plays and distinguishes them from all O'Casey's later work is the bitter recognition that while the men dream, drink, drivel, dress up and go play-acting, some woman with as much brains and far more industry sacrifices herself to keep the little spark of human life from going out altogether. They are hymns of praise to women, hymns, I should say, above all to his dead mother.

Of the three, the play that still affects me least is *Juno and the Paycock*, because in this what I take to be O'Casey's inspiration is partly diverted. This could easily be no more than a tragi-comedy about a feckless family set on the downward path by the mere whisper of a windfall; but the windfall has nothing whatever to do with the essential tragedy, which is that of poor Johnny Boyle, the informer, nor indeed has it much to do with Mary Boyle's becoming pregnant. The men are the same useless types, but their patriotism, their theosophy, their socialism, are more remote, more caricatured than the patriotism and poetry that are savaged in *The Shadow of a Gunman*. Bentham is a dig at George Russell and the Dublin Theosophists, but O'Casey was no theosophist, and we can never imagine ourselves behaving as Bentham and Jerry Devine behave, so the lash cracks in the air.

On the other hand, the more I see of *The Plough and the Stars*, the more I am inclined to think it the greatest of modern plays, and for the excellent reason that it comes closest to O'Casey's own experience. It deals with the Irish Citizen Army, the organization O'Casey gave the biggest part of his big heart to, and is more directly political than any other play he wrote, particularly in the tremendous second act, which is a play within a play, a masterpiece within a masterpiece.

It is here that national history and literary history link up again. The break-up of a political movement results in the formation of an intellectual movement, and when this in turn breaks down, it is followed by yet another political movement. Yeats soon realized that the Rising of 1916 had been the culmination of his own efforts at creating a cultural identity for Ireland. But when the political movement, driven underground, turned into a fight between two groups of terrorists, and later, when the British had withdrawn, produced a vicious civil war, it became clear that it was at an end. The nationalist thesis was hopelessly discredited, and was discredited in literature by O'Casey, who was himself a nationalist, and idealist and knew that however shop-soiled they might be, his Seumases, Pethers and Fluther Goods were idealists too.

> FLUTHER : . . . an' I said to meself, 'You can die now, Fluther, for you've seen th' shadhow-dhreams of th' past leppin' to life in th' bodies of livin' men that show, if we were without a titther o' courage for centuries, we're vice versa now. Looka here. . . . The blood was BOILIN' in me veins!
> PETER : I was burnin' to dhraw me sword, an' wave an' wave it over me —
> FLUTHER : Will you stop your blatherin' for a minute, man, an' let us hear what he's sayin'!
> VOICE OF THE MAN : Comrade soldiers of the Irish Volunteers and of the Citizen Army, we rejoice in this terrible war. The old heart of the earth needed to be warmed with the red wine of the battlefields. . . . Such august homage was never offered to God as this : the homage of millions of lives given gladly for love of country. And we must be ready to pour out the same red wine in the same glorious sacrifice, for without shedding of blood there is no redemption!

As I have said, it is the greatest scene in O'Casey, this contrast between Patrick Pearse, the out-and-out idealist, and the shop-soiled idealists of the pub, but there is no use pretending that O'Casey himself did not thrill to the characteristic words he puts into the mouth of Pearse. And yet the thesis breaks down; the reality is too harsh for it, and nothing remains at the end but the heroism of a handful of women.

What happened to O'Casey after this is another story, and not mine. One night at Lennox Robinson's house someone — perhaps myself — commented on the fact that O'Casey had written no good plays after leaving Dublin : the remark was not quite so trite then as it is now. Robinson replied wearily, 'And I don't care if he never writes another. All that matters to me is that Sean is happy at last.' I thought it a magnificent reply, because I suddenly saw what I thought was wrong with O'Casey's later work. It was the work of a man who was intensely happy in his new-found country, in his marriage, his children and a whole new world of books and pictures and music. It had never struck me before that the three great plays for all their wonderful moments of laughter were the work of a deeply unhappy man, nor did it strike me until a long time after that the same explanation might hold true of James Stephens. I am not even sure that it is correct, but it does seem to me possible that two men whose early lives had been a nightmare out of which they had broken with a group of masterpieces should ever afterwards dread the writing of masterpieces because of the suffering that gave birth to them, and would seek other, more impersonal forms.

Unfortunately for them, their genius is unique and specialized, and tied to a particular combination of circumstances, and they do not so easily discover new forms that will express it.

CHAPTER TWENTY

'And now that our story . . .'

'And now that our story approaches the end' my own position becomes anomalous, because it becomes my own story, which must be classed as autobiography, not as literary history or criticism; and yet to keep the narrative all in one tone and pretend a detachment I do not feel would merely falsify the record.

The Shadow of a Gunman was produced in 1923. In 1924 Liam O'Flaherty published *Spring Sowing*, and at once we are back to an interrupted pattern that began in 1903 with Moore's *The Untilled Field* and was briefly resumed in 1914 in Joyce's *Dubliners*— the search for what Samuel Ferguson had called the 'facts'. The romantic thesis had broken down; the antithesis did not seem to have got far, and there was nothing else for writers to do.

It is almost a relief to be quit of the romantic thesis. After the passion and grief of *The Plough and the Stars* it is wonderful to open a book of stories by Liam O'Flaherty and find something like 'Four Lambs' glowing with a sort of primal innocence. Like Stephens, O'Flaherty is at his best when he writes of animals, though he writes in a way very different from that of Stephens. After this, his best stories are about children, and then about country people who have the docility and innocence of animals and children. Not that O'Flaherty himself is quite so innocent. His is a divided character, and his secondary personality blows up into outrageous, uproarious and sometimes absurd novels, like *The Martyr*, in which, if I remember rightly, a Free State officer is described leading a Republican to a mountain-top with his cross, crucifying him there, setting fire to him and his cross, and finally hurling the blazing sacrifice into the mountain lake below.

The great O'Flaherty of the short stories is a man without ideas, ideals, or opinions, concerned only with the 'facts'. 'Going into Exile' describes a boy and a girl setting out from their Connemara home to America with no hope of ever seeing their parents again. O'Flaherty knew all the reasons for emigration far better than

George Moore did, but in this great story he ignores everything that is merely incidental and plunges straight into what exile really is — a state of things like love and death that all men must in some way endure.

One might have thought of his work and that of the writers who followed him as a new phase in Irish literature, but already the clouds were gathering. Early in 1925, less than a year after the publication of *Spring Sowing*, the Irish Parliament asked its Committee on Standing Orders to frame an order making it impossible to introduce a bill of divorce *a vinculo matrimonii*. In June of that year in a fine speech Yeats, then a senator, drew the conclusions from this step.

> It is perhaps the deepest political passion with this nation that North and South be united into one nation. If it ever comes that North and South unite, the North will not give up any liberty which she already possesses under her constitution. You will then have to grant to another people what you refuse to grant to those within your borders. If you show that this country, Southern Ireland, is going to be governed by Catholic ideas and by Catholic ideas alone, you will never get the North. You will create an impassable barrier between South and North, and you will pass more and more Catholic laws, while the North will gradually assimilate its divorce and other laws to those of England. You will put a wedge into the midst of this nation.[1]

Yeats proved an excellent prophet. The Minister for Justice, Kevin O'Higgins, was opposed to the censorship of literature, and it was not until after his assassination in 1927 that a censorship bill could be introduced. However, when it came in the following year, it was worth waiting for because it banned not only 'evil' literature, but the literature of contraception as well. Changes of government had no effect on this. I have a very painful memory of an afternoon when Yeats, Russell, Higgins and myself interviewed Mr. De Valera's Minister for Justice, Patrick Ruttledge by name, in an attempt to get him to remove the ban from Shaw's *Black Girl in Search of God*.

[1] Donald R. Pearce (ed.), *The Senate Speeches of W. B. Yeats* (London, 1961), 92.

We failed; and Shaw went, Clarke went, O'Faolain, O'Flaherty
and O'Casey went, and meanwhile the international clock struck
not Shaw, Clarke, O'Faolain or O'Flaherty, but Stalin, Mussolini,
Franco and Hitler.

Catastrophe was precipitated by two events that were almost
simultaneous — the death of Yeats and the outbreak of the Second
World War. Now we had censorship of newspapers as well as
censorship of books, and the intellectual darkness of the country
was almost palpable. In 1940 O'Faolain began the publication of
The Bell as a shop window for new writers, but within a very few
months the most important feature of the magazine became
O'Faolain's own leading articles in which he mocked at the
obscurantists and the cowardly press which meekly accepted in-
structions from the ecclesiastical authorities as to what it might
print. (For instance, no law case that reflected on a priest.)

Curiously, O'Faolain's influence is most strongly marked not on
any novelist, but on the poetry of Patrick Kavanagh. Kavanagh's
early work was lyrical and rural — an Irish John Clare, as he was
called — but in *The Bell*, and particularly in his long poem 'The
Great Hunger', of 1942, his poetry turned sharply critical.

> Sitting on a wooden gate,
> Sitting on a wooden gate,
> Sitting on a wooden gate
> He didn't care a damn.
> Said whatever came into his head,
> Said whatever came into his head,
> Said whatever came into his head
> And inconsequently sang.
> Inconsequently sang
> While his world withered away,
> He had a cigarette to smoke and a pound to spend
> On drink the next Saturday.

It was typical of the period that he was visited by members of
the Vice Squad who threatened him with what would happen if
he went on in this way. The issue of Cyril Connolly's magazine
Horizon which contained selections from the poem was seized.

You will find, I believe, that the year 1940 is the crucial year
for any study of modern Irish literature. By that time Mr. De

Valera's government had complete control inside the country and
nothing whatever to fear from liberal opinion abroad. In 1942, the
same year that saw the publication of 'The Great Hunger', while
Jews were being massacred by the million in concentration camps,
and London, Coventry and Plymouth were in ruins, *The Tailor
and Ansty* appeared. It was a collection of folk-tales and country
anecdotes taken down by a young man called Eric Cross from my
old friend Timothy Buckley, the tailor of Gougane Barra. It was
promptly banned. The ban was contested by Sir John Keane, a
Protestant landowner who was also a Senator, and since there was
no one, Protestant or Catholic, in the Irish Senate prepared to
support him, his motion was seconded 'by courtesy' by a professor
in Trinity College.

The four-day debate that raged about *The Tailor and Ansty* is
an indispensable document for any student of our literature because it shows better than anything that I can say to what depths
the intellectual life of the country had sunk. Sir John Keane insisted on reading the passages from the book that had been objected
to, but the Senate retorted by having all quotations stricken from
the record, so that, as its spokesmen quite seriously argued,
pornographers could not buy the House reports for the purpose
of reading indecency.

The debate, as I have said in the new edition of *The Tailor and
Ansty*, is like a long slow swim through a sewage bed. Senator
Goulding said that 'any man who dared to use the language used
by the character in the book referred to would be thrown out
from their firesides. Any man who dared to sit at an Irish country
fireside and use the language used by these two characters would
be forbidden to enter the house again.' Senator O Buachalla said
that 'the general feeling of the House as a result of Senator Sir
John Keane's quotations was one of disgust', and Senator Mrs.
Concannon displayed her wide knowledge of European literature
by saying, 'If Dante could come to life again and wanted to think
of a really cruel punishment for his political enemies, if he condemned them for all eternity to read a book like *The Tailor and
Ansty* there could not be any torture that would get at their
"innards" more fiercely.' Senator Kehoe said that 'Case-hardened
and all as they may be, the individual conscience and the collective

conscience still baulk at laying bare the sores of moral leprosy';
and the spokesman of the De Valera Government, Professor William
Magennis, of whom Senator Mrs. Concannon had testified that
'Gifted with a mighty intellect and a great store of knowledge, he
could if personal ambition had been his guiding star, have stayed
in his study and written one of those great philosophical works
that would have made his name shine forever', said of the Tailor:
'The man is sex-obsessed. His wife, Anastasia — called here
"Ansty" — is what in the language of American psychology is
called a moron — a person of inferior mental development, who
may be 30 or 40 years of age, but has reached only the mental stage
of a child of 4 or 5.' However, with his 'mighty intellect and great
store of knowledge', Magennis was able to explain it all. 'There is
a campaign going on in England to undermine Christianity. It is
financed by American money. The society that is the main agent
in the endeavour to put in paganism instead of the Christian creed
and practice includes Professor Joad and George Bernard Shaw.'

I have given so much space to that preposterous debate because
it seems to me a remarkable indication of the level of education
and political morality in the year 1943. Another of the same kind
was the discussion on the banning of my translation of Bryan
Merryman's *The Midnight Court*, which took place in the *Irish
Times* in 1945 and would make a substantial and informing book-
let. This time the Government spokesman was Professor James
Hogan, like Magennis an ornament of the National University but
an infinitely abler man. He was an atheist and blasphemer of the
rowdy kind, but he had just seen the light and after a close comparison of my translation with the German one he discovered that
I had intruded a blasphemous line into my text that was not in
the original. It was, and I replied urbanely enough that Professor
Hogan did not know sufficient German to read an Irish text in the
original. He then wrote to a friend, a famous Celtic scholar, for
support, and the Celtic scholar replied that the only blasphemies
that had ever shocked him were Hogan's own, and added with
bleak irony:

Ask for this great deliverer now, and find him
Eyeless in Gaza, at the mill with slaves.

This ended another old friendship. The literature of the period can, I think, still be read, but it is obviously not the sort of literature that one would predict from O'Flaherty's *Spring Sowing*. It was being gradually diverted by pressure from outside, becoming critical and caustic. Naturally, different pressures affect different writers. One can see the effect on O'Faolain's work in *Teresa and other Stories*, which appeared in 1947, though most of the stories in it belong to a slightly earlier period. 'The Silence of the Valley' is a fictionalized account of the death of Tim Buckley, the Tailor, and in the conversations which counterpoint the death of a figure from the older Ireland there is contempt for the newer with its intellectual dishonesty, its vague words and vaguer ideas.

'We,' the Celt went on, dark with anger, 'envisage an Ireland both modern and progressive. Christianity,' he went on, proud both of the rightness and intellectual tolerance of his argument, 'is not opposed to modernity, or to comfort, or to culture. I should not mind,' his voice was savage, for she was chuckling like a zany, 'if seaplanes landed on that lake outside. Why should I? All this admiration for backwardness and inefficiency is merely so much romantic nonsense. Ireland has had enough of it.'

She groaned comically.

'Fascist type. Definitely schizoid. Slight sadistic tendency. Would probably be Socialist in Britain, if not —' she wagged her flaming head warningly and made eyes of mock horror — 'dare I say it, C.P.?'

I was living in County Wicklow at the time and became aware that all round me there were farmed-out illegitimate children, many of whom were cruelly ill-treated. High-spirited girls who left home in a hurry were trailed by plain-clothes policemen to see whether or not they had a baby and if so, what they did with it. Once I saw a dozen of them appear in succession in Green Street court-house to be indicted and sentenced to death for the murder of their babies. Out of that experience I must have written a dozen stories. Austin Clarke has summarized some similar experience in six deadly lines.

The hasty sin of the young after a dance,
Awkward in clothes against a wall or crick-necked
In car, gives many a nun her tidy bed,
Full board and launderette. God-fearing state
Provides three pounds a week, our conscience money
For every infant severed from the breast.[2]

The most representative figure of the period is Clarke, because he covers the greatest trajectory between the Yeatsian romanticism of —

When the black herds of the rain were grazing
In the gap of the pure cold wind
And the watery hazes of the hazel
Brought her into my mind,
I thought of the last honey by the water
That no hive can find.

— and that brutal, stinging poem on the burial of Douglas Hyde, the President of Ireland. By the time war broke out Catholics were no longer permitted to attend Protestant funerals or funeral services, and I have described in *An Only Child* the rage of my mother, then eighty-five, when she realized that not one Catholic neighbour was following the coffin of the Protestant who lived next door.

At the last bench
Two Catholics, the French
Ambassador and I knelt down.
The vergers waited. Outside
The hush of Dublin town;
Professors of cap and gown,
Costello, his Cabinet,
In Government cars, hiding
Around the corner, ready
Tall hat in hand, dreading
Our Father in English. Better
Not hear that 'which' for 'who'
And risk eternal doom.[3]

[2] and [3] Austin Clarke, 'Flight to Africa'.

Of the principal Irish writers of the period only Mary Lavin has come out of it unmarked. Her work seems to be in a class by itself. It is deeply personal, and there are a great many doors in it marked 'Private'. Only once has she written about Irish nationalism; this was in a story called 'Patriot Son', and from my point of view it was once too often. Like Whitman's wild oak in Louisiana, she has stood a little apart from the rest of us, 'uttering joyous leaves of dark green', but like Whitman I know that I could not do it.

O'Faolain, myself, and I suspect Clarke and Kavanagh are merely the strayed revellers of the Irish literary revival, and by the early 1940s this was all over and done with.

> The great shocked art, the gross great enmity
> That roamed here once, and swept indoors, embalmed
> Their lesson with themselves.[4]

This is precisely the sort of situation Yeats dreaded when he turned to Fascism and wrote, 'Fail, and that history turns into rubbish, all that great past to a trouble of fools.' Logically I can see no way out of it. Brendan Behan's *Borstal Boy* was banned in Ireland, and Behan, though more involved politically than any writer of his time, developed into an excellent entertainer of English and American audiences. Edna O'Brien's novels of girlhood in Ireland have been banned, but she seems to be doing very nicely for herself abroad. In an American review I have just read a beautiful short story about life among young people in Dublin today, but it is anonymous and I cannot imagine that the author of it will ever settle down in Ireland. What have we to offer a young writer as a substitute for 'the great shocked art, the gross great enmity'?

If one could imagine the revival of Irish as a spoken language, it would give writers a centre, a viewpoint sufficiently different from those of other writers in the English language, but the paradox of Irish is that its revival coincided with the emergence of a strong literature in English, and its rapid decline since the establishment of a native government with the official attempt at destroying Irish literature in English. It too is part of 'the great shocked art, the gross great enmity', and if it is to survive at all it can only do so as part of some equivalent to this.

[4] Thomas Kinsella, 'Downstream'.

But what can we find by way of equivalent? Logically, as I have said, nothing; but if I were being entirely logical I should not have attempted the task I have attempted, of outlining for you the history of the literature of Ireland. Obviously, whether logically or not, I should not have done this if I did not feel that closer acquaintance with it might be an inspiration to another generation, enabling them in the words of Samuel Ferguson 'to live *back* in the land they live *in*, with as ample and as interesting a field of retrospective enjoyment as any of the nations around us'.

This is the thing we have never yet been able to do, in spite of the efforts of Ferguson and Yeats. Literature in Irish is still a subject unknown, nor except in America is there such a thing as a chair of Irish literature.[5] The great monuments of our past are almost as filthy and neglected as they were in Ferguson's day and infinitely less complete. I am not sure that any country can afford to discard what I have called 'the backward look', but we in Ireland can afford it less than any other because without it we have nothing and are nothing, and we must not cease to remember Yeats' final words:

> Cast your mind on other days
> That we in coming days may be
> Still the indomitable Irishry.

[5] The new chair of Irish literature at University College, Dublin, has been established along the lines advocated by Frank O'Connor for years. (*ed.*) *Dublin, 1965.*

Early Irish Story-telling

I

From the eighth to the twelfth century Ireland had a most remarkable literature. It had a fine poetry and an even finer prose, which was not equalled until the rise of the Icelandic story-tellers in the thirteenth century. By this time Irish poetry was in a bad way and Irish prose was dead. Their rise and fall correspond so closely with the rise and fall of a particular kind of Irish intellectual that the work and the men must be connected.

The men are the Irish ecclesiastical families, an institution unique in Europe. They have never been studied with any detachment because Protestant historians cannot help hailing them as Protestants born before their time, while Catholic historians, though refusing to regard them as Protestants, suspect they were not quite as Catholic as they should have been. They have been described as lay impropriators of Church property who emerged as a result of the Viking invasions. Almost certainly they existed long before Christianity; they didn't impropriate Church property, and up to the seventeenth century they still described themselves as *ecclesiastici*.

They probably owed their origin to the simple fundamental fact that in Irish law land belonged not to the individual, but to the family, and accordingly it was almost impossible to alienate it. Up to the twelfth century, when Muircheartach O'Brien made an outright gift of Cashel to the Church, the Church had no land; it had only cattle, precious stones, and precious metals. Certain great families *lent* land, first to the druids, then to the churchmen, and, in the sixth and seventh centuries, when the little monasteries became places of pilgrimage and instruction and a single monastery might be wealthier than any state, they saw the bread they had cast on the waters return to them, miraculously multiplied. Naturally they took advantage of this; they brought up their children,

instead of verse. But twenty years ago I drew attention to the un-
likelihood of anything of the kind having occurred with a story
like 'The Boyish Feats of Cú Chulainn'. This is a long episode in
'The Cattle Raid of Cooley', which the abbot in 'Mac Con Glinne's
Dream' carried in one of his fishing boots. It is told as a flashback,
which by itself is highly improbable in a story orally transmitted,
because in oral story-telling — and this is as true of radio and tele-
vision as it is of the folk-story teller — the voice is merely a single
point of light in a dark expanse, while in literary story-telling the
whole expanse is lighted; the reader's attention is permitted to
stray, and the story-teller's art is an art of digression. Besides, it is
dramatized among a group of Ulster exiles with the Connacht
hosting (which is still more improbable, because the traditional
story-teller does not have the command of quotation marks that
we have); and it is rendered in a form of dialogue that is still
frowned on by my friends in the *New Yorker*. ('He has not', said
Janet, lighting a cigarette as she peered down the dark avenue
where the trees were already turning a deep autumnal brown,
'arrived yet.') And this, of course, is completely impossible. It does
not even survive my telling of it, much less the rough and tumble
of two hundred years of oral transmission, which is what Rudolf
Thurneysen asks us to accept.

Here, for instance, is Fergus mac Roich speaking.

There was war between the Ulstermen and Eogan mac Durthacht. The Ulstermen went to battle. He (Cú Chulainn) was left
asleep. The Ulstermen were defeated. Conchobar and Cuscraid
the Stammerer of Armagh and a great number of men were left
behind. Their wailing waked him. He stretched himself so that
he burst the two pillarstones at the head and foot of his bed.
'This happened in the presence of Bricriu here,' said Fergus.

He got up then. I met him in the gate of the yard when I was
badly wounded.

'Phew! Welcome home, Uncle Fergus!' he said. 'Where is
Conchobar?'

'I don't know,' I said.

He went out then. The night was dark. He went in the direction of the battlefield. He saw a man coming towards him with
half a head and half another man's body on his back.

'Help me, Cú Chulainn!' he said. 'I have been wounded, and I have brought half my brother on my back. Give me a hand.'
'I will not,' said he.
Then *he* tossed the burden to him. He threw it off. They wrestled. Cú Chulainn got a fall. Then the Scaldcrow's voice was heard from among the corpses.
'This is no makings of a soldier under a ghost's feet.'
Then Cú Chulainn rose and cut off his head with his hurley and started pucking the ball before him across the battlefield.
'Is my Uncle Conchobar in the battlefield?' he said.

The very first thing we notice about a passage like this is how very literary it all is. 'This happened in the presence of Bricriu here' is one of those sly literary touches that mark a high point of implausibility. Cú Chulainn's line when he meets the wounded Fergus in the doorway of the yard is equally sly. 'Fuit! Dia do bethu, a phopa, a Fhergais. Cate Conchobar?' Of course, a translator can knock the stuffing out of it as Miss Faraday does when she renders it as 'Alas! God save you, friend Fergus, where is Conchobar?' but that doesn't seem to me to represent very accurately the tone of the original. Above all, we notice that the storyteller is a born picture-maker; he never consciously leaves a piece of narrative empty but fills it with some detail like that of the small boy pucking his ball on the battlefield.

In the last few years a view completely different from that of Thurneysen has been expressed by Professor Carney, who tends to see literary influences everywhere, as when he argues that an eighth-century Irish story, 'The Cattle Raid of Froech', has been influenced by an otherwise unknown seventh-century life of St. Kentigern. This seems to me even more far-fetched. The quality these early stories have is that of a primary literature. By 'primary' I mean in the main uninfluenced by other literatures, as Greek and Hebrew are uninfluenced. When a Greek poet says, 'There are wonderful things on earth, but none more wonderful than man', there is no need to look for a source. This was how the Greeks saw things, as though they were looking at them for the first time. When a Hebrew poet writes, 'The heavens declare the glory of God', we know that this was how the Jews saw things.

Sometimes — perhaps always — a primary literature develops

accidentally as it did in Ireland and, I should say, in Iceland. A sophisticated civilization gives a hint, just sufficient to make a more primitive race selfconscious and articulate, but not enough to destroy the originality of its thought, as Latin destroyed the originality of thought in Gaul.

It is not, of course, a literary criterion because Latin, English, and French are in the main all secondary literatures, and none the worse for it, but it is a critical criterion, and it seems to me to dispose of Professor Carney's theories. Of course, there are in early Irish episodes which do not come from man's original experience but from books. For instance, before Cú Chulainn goes out to his last great fight his horse weeps on his shoulder. A similar incident occurs in St. Adomnán's life of St. Colum Cille. St. Adomnán was a student of Virgil, and I think it is fair to assume that both he and the author of 'The Death of Cú Chulainn' got the theme from the episode of Mezentius' horse in the *Aeneid*. The same is true of the classical suicide—falling on one's sword. This occurs twice in Irish literature; once in a story called 'The Siege of Howth', once in a Leinster saga called 'Rónán's Kin-slaying'; and it also occurred in a now lost version of a beautiful story called 'The Death of Derbfrorgaill'. Here, and in a few other passages, we can recognize the existence of the bookish writer. Elsewhere it is a complete waste of time to look for him. The Irish story-tellers were no mere transcribers of folk-lore; nor were they mere imitators of the few Latin authors they knew. The author of 'The Destruction of Dinn Ríg' did not find either in folk-lore or Latin the words of the anxious mother who wakes her husband in the middle of the night with the cry, 'Your daughter breathes like a woman! Listen to that sigh now that her lover has left her!'

The earliest of our stories—those that describe the gods and their relations with Man—have been badly obscured in the literature; not, I fancy, because the monks—those pious, celibate, dull transcribers of folk-lore we have heard so much about—omitted or distorted them. They were not so easily shocked. The reason was probably that in the last half of the seventh century there appeared a long historical romance, 'The Cattle Raid of Cooley'. The Irish had learned history from Latin writers and been unhappy because they had no history of their own. 'The Cattle Raid' gave them a history they could understand and which they then tried to relate to world history. One eighth-century story-teller took the story of Conchobar mac Nessa's death and rewrote it so as to make it coincide with the Crucifixion. (Fortunately for the literary critic he forgot to omit the passage of the old text that described not only the death but the burial of Conchobar.)

But not only did the writers force traditional events into the framework of 'The Raid', they forced their religious traditions into it as well. All the stories incidental to 'The Cattle Raid' — 'The Dream of Óengus,' 'The Cattle Raid of Froech', 'The Adventures of Nera', and 'The Sick-bed of Cú Chulainn' — are myths, distorted (sometimes in the most brutal way) into historical romances. 'The Story of Macha' is an excellent example of what I mean, because it really gives us a glimpse into the mind of an Irish story-teller in the eighth century.

The legend of Macha must be one of the oldest things in Irish. She was the Ulster horse goddess, the local version of Epona, and in Armagh cathedral there is a stone figure of her, which cannot be later than the fifth century and which shows her with horse's ears and wearing a runner's slip. The Ulster capital was called Emain Machae — the Twins of Macha — presumably in reference tò its two great forts. The legend would seem to have been that the horse goddess was compelled to race the king's horses and in doing so gave birth to twins, after whom the capital was named. The opening of the story is one of the most beautiful things in Irish. Incorporated in the text is a gloss that runs 'Macha was the woman's name *ut periti dicunt*', but this only shows that the copyist was puzzled by the technique of the story-teller who never mentioned the goddess by name at all.

There was a rich peasant of the Ulstermen among the hilltops and lonely places. Crunnchu mac Agnoman was his name. He accumulated great wealth in his deserted state. He had many sons about him. The woman who had lived with him, the mother of his children, was dead. He was a long time without a wife.

One day he was lying on his bed in his house alone when he saw a young woman walk in who had fine looks and dress and bearing. The woman sat in a chair at the fireplace and lit the fire. They were there until evening without speaking. Then she took a kneading trough and sieve and began to prepare the supper. When evening came she took buckets with her and milked the cows without being asked. When she returned she walked righthandwise around the house, and went to the kitchen and instructed the staff, and sat in a chair beside Crunnchu.

Everyone went to bed, but she remained after them all, and she raked the fire and walked righthandwise round the room and went under the blanket to him and placed her hand on his crotch. They had sexual congress and she was pregnant by him. As a result of their union his wealth increased further. She loved to see him well dressed and equipped.

Here a couple of lines have clearly been dropped in which the woman surprises her husband by capturing a runaway horse. One day, the story goes on, Crunnchu decides to go to the fair, presumably to show off his fine attire. His wife warns him not to go because she fears that in his simple vanity he will boast of her and their marriage will end. This is what happens. When someone praises the king's horses, Crunnchu cannot resist boasting that his wife can run faster than they, and the king threatens him with death unless his wife proves him right. She is brought to the fairground and this is how the story ends.

'It is not right to stare at me', she said, 'in my condition. Why was I brought?'

'To race the king's horses,' said they all.

'I am exempt', she said. 'because my labour pains are on me.'

'Take the sword to the peasant!' said the king.

'Wait for me a little while so till I rest,' she said.

'No,' said the king.

'Shame on you then!' she cried. 'Not to give me a little respite! Because of that I shall bring shame on you later. Now,' she said, 'set the horses loose beside me.'

This was done, and she was ahead of the horses at the end of the fairground. Suddenly she raised a scream because of the fierceness of her labour. God relieved her at once, and she brought forth a son and daughter in one delivery — Fír and Fial (True and Loyal). When the crowd heard the woman scream they were seized as though all strength had gone from them but that of a woman in labour.

'From now on', she said, 'the foul play you showed me will

be a shame to you. When your need is greatest those of you who inhabit the province will have only the strength of a woman in childbirth, and the time a woman suffers in childbirth you shall suffer — five days and four nights — and it will afflict you for nine generations.'

This came true. It afflicted them from the time of Crunnchu to the time of Fergus mac Domnaill. This illness did not affect women or boys, or Cú Chulainn because he was not an Ulsterman, or anyone who was outside the province.

Now, this story is a neat example of the Irish mind at work. The goddess' oath when she goes to bed with a mortal is probably based on a popular etymology of the Latin word, *testis*, but the principal problem the eighth-century editor has to solve is what the Ulstermen were doing while Cú Chulainn defended the province single-handed in 'The Cattle Raid'. The story said they were suffering from *noinden*, but what on earth was a *noinden*? Twenty years ago I suggested that it was the Latin *nundinae*, which came into Irish with the meaning of 'assembly', and that the Ulstermen were really at a holiday gathering in Emain Machae, but my etymologies are liable to be quite as erratic as those of earlier storytellers. They derived it from *noídiu* — baby — and decided that it was probably in some way connected with childbirth. 'God relieved them at once' because they saw that it was probably some disease that afflicted Ulstermen for their impiety to the goddess. Our story-teller was too good a scholar to accept the derivation from *noídiu*, and treated the word exactly as Thurneysen did, making it mean 'nine days', but he had that *je ne sais quoi* of Irish husbands, which Thurneysen lacked, and realized the inconvenience it would cause if wives were encouraged to spend nine days over a little transaction like that, so he rationalized his 'nine days' into 'nine periods of time' — five days and four nights or four days and five nights, which was as much as a reasonable Irish husband could be expected to allow.

But the really remarkable thing about this story which seems to escape everyone's attention is that it is unfinished. We are never told what happened either to Crunnchu or Macha, though in a late version among the T.C.D. manuscripts it is said that Macha died as a result. But even this is not enough. The whole point of the story is in the first sentence: 'Boí aithech somma di Ultaib i mbendait slíab ocus dithrab' ('There was a rich peasant of the Ulstermen among the hilltops and lonely places'); the brilliant opening, which builds up the picture of an elderly man, living in a wild place, after his wife's death, is what makes possible his marriage with a goddess; and his vanity, which makes him boast of it in a public place, is the climax. After it he can only return to his old lonely life, but that conclusion, which must have been so heart-rending, is omitted to build a fresh one about the so-called 'Debility of the Ulstermen'. The whole end of the story has been distorted, and not only its religious but its human significance has been lost.

Something similar has happened to that magnificent story 'The Wooing of Étaín' — another of the masterpieces which the abbot in 'Mac Con Glinne's Dream' had stuffed into his boots. This looks like a ninth-century reconstruction of three stories about Étaín, the first of which at least is much older than that; probably late seventh century. The first paragraph of that first story brings us right into the heart of religious teaching in the Bronze Age.

There was a famous king over Ireland; he was of the tribes of the Goddess: Eochaid the Supreme Father was his name. Another name for him was the Good God, because it was he who wrought miracles and safeguarded the weather and the crops. It is said that this was why he was called the Good God.

Elcmar of the Settlement had a wife. Eithne was her name. Another name for her was Boann ('The Boyne' or 'The White Cow'). The Good God desired her sexually. The woman would have yielded to the Good God but for fear of Elcmar, so great was his power.

How different this is from the opening of the second story, which is clearly the work of the ninth-century editor!

Eochaid the Ploughman took the kingship of Ireland. The five provinces of Ireland were subject to him, and each provincial king. Their kings at the time were Conchobar mac Nessa and Mess Gegra and Tigernach Tétbannach and Cú Roí and Ailill mac Mata Muirisc.

The opening of the first story is timeless, as mythology and cosmology must be; that of the second has been distorted to fit into the historical framework of 'The Cattle Raid'. In the original tradition, on which the seventh-century story is based, Eochaid the Supreme Father (the Irish Zeus) certainly owned the Settlement of the Boyne, because well into historical times the Irish name for Newgrange was Uaim Echdach Ollde — the Cave of Eochaid the Supreme God. According to the usual folk-lore pattern of the Old God dispossessed by the Young God — the old year giving place to the new — Eochaid must have been dispossessed by his son Óengus, who was also the son of the cow goddess, the river Boyne. But this did not suit the seventh-century writer, who may himself have been a member of a druid family, and who was certainly interested in druidic doctrine. The ninth-century writer probably did not know what druidic doctrine was about; he wanted to put those old gods and goddesses into a historical framework that included the death of Our Lord; and above all, he was a born writer of romances with a wonderful love story to tell —

> *Ich will von Atreus Soehnen,*
> *Von Kadmus will ich singen;*
> *Doch meine Saiten toenen*
> *Nur Liebe im Erklingen.*

Accordingly he preferred to play down the part of the Irish Zeus and his son, Óengus, and concentrated on Óengus' foster-father, Midir, who was a lover after his own warm heart. Midir — we are still in the first story — marries a girl called Étaín Echraide — Étaín of the Horse Troops — another horse goddess, like Macha. Midir's previous wife, Fuamnach, turns Étaín into a pool of water; the water then turns to a worm, and the worm to a fly. The fly is swallowed by a woman in her drink and is reborn as Étaín — another Étaín. After a beautiful passage in which Étaín and her maids are watched while bathing by a mysterious horseman, who is her husband from another life, the remaining two stories tell how this husband, Midir, pursues her through various incarnations until he wins her back to live with him in his otherworld kingdom. The mortal husband of a later incarnation, Eochaid the Ploughman, believes he has won her back from Midir, but it is really his own daughter — another Étaín — whom he has won back; and his daughter by her is exposed and brought up by herdsmen until in time she becomes the mother of Conaire, King of Tara. Thus the whole timeless story of reincarnation has been brought round once more to fit into the pseudo-historical framework of 'The Cattle Raid', for at the end of the story of Conaire he is defended by Cú Chulainn's foster-father, Conall Cernach, the Irish Cernunnos.

But the real cultural-historical level of the story is revealed in the episode in which the child of an incestuous union is exposed and brought up by herdsmen. Tribal societies had two great terrors — incest and parricide — and this is part of the Oedipus theme emerging. What the story really describes is the experience of the Bronze Age invaders among the monuments of a Neolithic civilization, which they could neither understand nor imitate. The love affair of Eochaid, the horse god, with the cow goddess, Boyne, may well represent a reconciliation between these two civilizations. I suspect, too, that the trick by which Eochaid enables his son Óengus to obtain possession of Newgrange from Elcmar, the husband of the cow goddess, is a resurrection myth, profounder in its implications than the usual folk-lore story of the old god replaced by the new, which also attached to Newgrange. Here, I think, Newgrange is regarded as the kingdom of the dead, and it is occupied by the Divine Son, who represents youth and beauty. There is no doubt whatever that Fuamnach's changing of Étaín into a pool of water is a myth of the origin of life, because life is assumed to emerge from water and to pass through lower forms of life until it appears in human form, and that reincarnation never ends, and the Étaíns we loved so long ago return to earth again and again if, like Midir, we have the courage to seek them out —

> A brighter Hellas rears its mountains
>   From waves serener far;
> A new Peneus rolls its fountains
>   Against the morning star.
> Where fairer Tempes bloom, there sleep
> Young Cyclads on a sunnier deep.

When I read it first, that great story gave me the same sort of shock that I got when I first read, 'There are wonderful things on earth but none more wonderful than man' and 'The heavens declare the glory of God.' Not the same shock, but the same sort of shock, for the Irish looked at things with eyes very different from those of the Greek and the Jew. While the Greek triumphed in the glory of man and the Jew abased himself before the glory of God, the Irishman was fascinated by the mystery. He saw that Time was relative because what to one man is a day is nine months to another; matter was relative because what was solid earth to one was to another a wild sea; identity was relative because Étaín never dies, and all life, as a later Irishman has put it, is no more than 'a commodious vicus of recirculation back to Howth Castle and environs'.

III

As you will have gathered, the story of early Irish literature is very confused, and the situation is not improved by the fact that Irish literature is not taught in our universities.

The surprising thing is perhaps that we should ever have expected it to be other than confused. We cannot help thinking of a small country called Ireland, with a capital and a centralized government; but to the Irishman of the early Middle Ages Ireland was a very large place indeed, as I discovered when I tried to make a verse translation of a seventh-century hymn to St. Colum Cille that Professor Greene has edited and found that in early Irish there was no word for 'Irishman'. To the author of the hymn 'Irishman' meant a member of the Uí Néill, the Tara dynasty that had successfully invaded Ulster, and nothing else — though the vast majority of Irishmen were certainly not Uí Néill. So, when St. Adomnán speaks of *Rex totius Hiberniae*, he means the Uí Néill king, and nothing else, and when he himself turns up in a story written south of O'Connell Bridge it is as a sinister warlock. In fact, as I have said already, when we deal with early Irish literature, we are dealing with a number of literatures, and it would be just as well from the point of view of criticism if we recognized which literature we are dealing with.

This was brought strongly to my mind some months ago when I was glancing at an Old Irish text that has not, to my knowledge, been translated — 'Nuallguba Emere' or 'Emer's Elegy'. When I was a young man I fell in love with a story called 'The Siege of Howth', which had a superb climax. On the surface one would say that the story was the work of a story-teller suffering from acute schizophrenia, who needed what my wife would call 'hospitalization'. It describes a horrible Ulster poet, Athirne Ailgesach — Athirne the Exacting — who goes through southern Ireland humiliating everyone by demanding the impossible from local kings: from one a family heirloom that has been lost for generations, from another his right eye, from a third his wife. By the traditions of Irish hospitality his demands have to be met until you manage to get the brute outside your own front door, which, for Leinstermen, meant at the other side of O'Connell Bridge. The Ulstermen, who also know the rules of Irish hospitality, come to escort him home, and are besieged at Howth. After a bitter fight the Ulstermen break the siege and the Leinstermen retreat across the river.

So far, any responsible teacher of composition would consider himself soft-hearted in merely telling the author that higher education would be wasted on him, but suddenly an astonishing change occurs, and the story breaks into wonderful narrative prose. I am not making this up, because Thurneysen, in his own fine German translation, omits the whole story up to the precise point at which the miracle happens. Conall Cernach, the Ulster hero, sets off in pursuit of Mess Gegra, the King of Leinster, to avenge the death of his two foster-brothers, one of whom has never been mentioned at all in the story. Their heads have been carried off by the Leinstermen. In these Leinster stories, by the way, the fighters carry their enemies' heads slung from their belts. My translation follows Thurneysen's except for the omission of one brief passage, which is clearly an interpolation.

Conall Cernach set out alone in pursuit of the Leinstermen to avenge his two brothers who had been killed in the battle — Mess Dead and Loegaire. He went by Dublin, through Drimnagh, past Hy-Gavla in Forchartan, past Oughterard and Naas to Clane.

When the Leinstermen reached their own country, they scattered, each to his own place. Mess Gegra, however, remained alone by Clane pathway after the hosting with his charioteer.

'I want to sleep for a while,' the charioteer said to Mess Gegra. 'Then you can sleep.'

'That suits me,' said the king.

As Mess Gegra watched the water he saw a nut coming towards him on the river. It was the size of a man's head. He climbed down, caught it, and split it with his knife and left half the kernel for the servant. Then he saw how the servant raised himself from the ground in his sleep and waked him.

'What ails you, boy?' said the king.

'A bad dream I had,' said the boy.

'Harness the horses, boy!' said the king.

The servant harnessed the horses.

'Did you eat that nut?' said the boy.

'I did,' said the king.

'Did you leave half for me?' said the servant.

'I ate a little of it first,' said the king.

'Who ate a little on me ate a lot,' said the servant. And as the king reached out his hand with the kernel in it the servant struck at it with his sword and cut off his hand.

'Shame on you, boy!' said the king. 'Open my fist: half the kernel is inside.'

When the servant saw this he turned the sword against himself and it pierced his back.

'Pity, boy!' said the king. Then he hitched the horses to the chariot himself and placed his hand inside before him. As he left the ford going west Conall reached it coming from the east.

'Aha! Is this Mess Gegra?' said Conall.

'I am he,' said the other.

'Well, then?' said Conall.

'What more can you ask, but, as the saying goes: The man who owes you anything, catch him where you can.'

'You have my brothers with you,' said Conall.

'Not in my belt.'

'You will pay,' said Conall.

'That is no honourable fight. I have only one hand.'

'I shall see to that,' said Conall. 'I shall have my hand tied to my side.'

His hand was tied three times over to his side. They fought till the river was red with them. But Conall won the game.

There follows the wildest, most moving poetry, as in the head that blushes for breaking its word, and then grows heavy so as not to leave the corpse of a wife.

'That is enough, Conall,' said Mess Gegra. 'I know you will not leave without my head; so add my head to your head and my glory to your glory.'

Then Conall mounted his own chariot and his charioteer Mess Gegra's chariot and went through Uachtar Fine. There fifty women met him; they were Buan, Mess Gegra's wife, and her followers, coming south from the border.

'Whose wife are you, woman?' said Conall.

'The wife of Mess Gegra, the King of Leinster.'

'You are ordered to come with me,' said Conall.

'Who ordered it?'

'Mess Gegra.'

'Have you brought a sign?' said the woman.

'These are his chariot and his horses.'

'He gives treasures to many,' said the woman.

'And here is his head.'

'This time I am lost to him,' said the woman.

The head blushed and paled, turn by turn.

'What ails the head, woman?' said Conall.

'I know,' the woman said. 'A dispute he had with Athirne. He said no Ulsterman would ever carry me away single-handed. Breaking his word is what ails his head.'

'Come into the chariot with me,' said Conall.

'Wait for me till I lament my husband,' she said.

Then she raised her cry till it was heard in Tara and Allen, threw herself backwards and was dead. Her grave is on the road. Buan's Blackthorn: a blackthorn tree grew through her grave.

'Bring that with you, boy,' said Conall.

'I cannot bring the head with me,' said the servant.

'Then cut out the brain. Use your sword and bring the brain, mix it with lime and make a ball of it.'

He did so and left the head with the woman, and they went on until they reached Emain. The Ulstermen were jubilant at having killed the King of Leinster.

What an extraordinary episode this is! On the one hand there are the Leinster head-hunters, on the other the classical scholars who know the Roman way of dying — 'as in wild earth a Grecian vase'.

Now in *Irische König-und-Heldensage* Thurneysen argues that the passage I have read to you is an imitation of a similar passage in 'The Death of Cú Chulainn', a text so deservedly famous that it has never been edited at all. The episode that corresponds with the scene in which Mess Gegra opens the nut runs like this — (I have omitted a couple of passages that deal with Cú Chulainn's infernal horse, which seems to have obsessed the writer).

'I should wish', said Cú Chulainn, 'to go to that lake and get a drink from it.'

'You may', they said, 'so long as you come back to us.'

'If I do not come', said Cú Chulainn, 'I shall summon you to come for me.'

Then he gathered his guts into his belly and went to the lake. When he reached the lake he drew his hand across his belly and tossed away what was in it. Then he took a drink and washed himself there. Then he called out and signalled them to come for him.

He went a good distance from the lake westward and lost his sight, and he went to a stone pillar on the plain and tied himself with his belt, so that he should not die sitting or lying down, but standing. It was after that the men gathered round him and they did not dare to approach him. They thought he was alive. 'It is a shame for you', said Erc mac Cairbre, 'not to take that man's head in revenge for my father's head that he took and buried in Nia Fer's Neck.' Then the birds lit on his shoulder. 'There used be no birds on that pillar,' said Erc mac Cairbre. Then Lugaid gathered back Cú Chulainn's hair and chopped his head off. The sword fell from Cú Chulainn's hand and struck Lugaid's right hand, and it fell to the ground. Cú Chulainn's right hand was cut off then in revenge.

Then the hosts set off and they brought Cú Chulainn's head and his right hand with them as far as Tara.

After that wonderful passage the story follows the main outline of 'The Siege of Howth'. Conall pursues Lugaid; he has his arm

248 A SHORT HISTORY OF IRISH LITERATURE

tied to his side, and they fight until Lugaid tells Conall to 'add
his own head to Conall's head and his own kingship to Conall's
kingship'. The main difference is that this particular author, who
seems to have thought that the horse was the principal character
in every story and to have had a passionate preoccupation with
guts, sees the opportunity of writing in another scene to feature
Conall's horse. The horse bites Lugaid in the crotch and scatters
his guts about the field. But there are two things to observe about
the story. Twenty-odd years ago I disagreed with Thurneysen's
view that 'The Siege of Howth' was an imitation of 'The Death
of Cú Chulainn', because, as a writer myself, it seemed to me
obvious that the author of that first great passage did not need
to imitate anyone. Since then I have found evidence that suggests
that my guess was right. This is in a lament for Cú Chulainn supposed to be spoken by his wife, Emer, to his horse. (Did I say that
the man was mad on animals?) It runs: 'Orphans will be left
desolate by the hero's death, women's fate will not be joyous,
Mess Gegra the formidable, who wrought the great revenge, will
die.' The text is very old, and the passage I have quoted may
originally have been in archaic verse, but it shows quite clearly
that in the story of Cú Chulainn's death as the author knew it,
the killer was not Lugaid, but Mess Gegra, the King of Leinster.
     Is this a Leinster version as opposed, for instance, to a Mun-
ster one? Are we again dealing with different literatures? 'The
Death of Cú Chulainn' is not all of a piece. There are several strata,
clumsily heaped on one another, and if, as I fancy, one of these is
a Munster stratum that introduces Lugaid the son of Cú Roí as Cú
Chulainn's killer instead of Mess Gegra, there is definitely another
stratum that suggests other Leinster stories, and above all the
presence of a classical school in the neighbourhood — possibly the
classical school of Kildare. I have already drawn your attention
to the theme of the weeping horse in 'The Death of Cú Chulainn'
which comes straight out of the Aeneid. But you will also, I hope,
have noticed the prominence given to the theme of the chopped-
off hand. It occurs again in another Leinster story — the best of
them all regarded as literature — 'Mac Dathó's Pig'. 'Lám made a
cast with a large spear at me. I threw it back and struck off his
hand, so that it lay on the ground.' The same words almost as in

'The Death of Cú Chulainn' — 'so that it fell to the ground'. This was something of an obsession with Virgil, because in the *Aeneid* we have a man's hand cut off in exactly this way by a spear cast, and another passage addresses a fighter whose 'severed hand seeks its master and whose dying fingers twitch and clutch again at the sword'. Even more striking is the classical suicide in 'Rónán's Kin-slaying' and in 'The Siege of Howth', and these are again linked with 'Mac Dathó's Pig', because in this Conall throws Anluan's head at his brother's chest, and in 'Rónán's Kin-slaying' Donn throws the heads of her father, mother and brother at the chest of Eochaid's daughter.

Those four stories are linked (possibly careful examination would show that other stories are also linked with them), and they represent (if not one original author) a distinct school of literature, quite different from the West Munster school that produced the great poetry of the eighth century, but as distinctive as it.

After the Viking period the existence of different schools of literature added to the chaos already produced by the invasions. One is struck by the frequent references in our remaining manuscripts to one called the Book of Drumsnaught, which Thurneysen has shown to have been an eighth-century compilation. Later copyists write, 'According to the version in the Book of Drumsnaught' or 'the Book of Drumsnaught says the song of the fairies was . . .' Now Drumsnaught was not a famous monastery, and it is impossible to understand the authority attributed to this manuscript, unless it was one of the very few books of early Irish literature to survive intact. The only reasonable explanation for the chaotic condition of Irish texts after the year 900 is that the later copyists were not so much dependent on alternative versions of the same story from which they chose episodes at random, but on stray leaves of vellum picked up here and there, and for which those unfortunate and unscholarly men had to provide some sort of context. It must have been like trying to patch up an imperfect text of Molière from an equally imperfect text of an English adaptation. Names change, incidents are dragged in or omitted, whole scenes are duplicated.

That is the picture presented to us by the earliest text of 'The

Cattle Raid of Cooley', which, as I have told you, dominated Irish literature and Irish thought for hundreds of years. It was once a great masterpiece, it is now a great mess; and I believe that literary criticism could do a great deal in restoring it, which philological criticism, no matter how inspired, can never do.

The problems begin with the very first line. The story is ace-phalous; it has no beginning, and I am convinced that if one were to read the story in the Strachan–O'Keeffe edition or Miss Faraday's translation, knowing no other version, one wouldn't even know what the story was about. In fact, we all read it with a very clear recollection either of the Book of Leinster text or of one of the versions based on it. The Book of Leinster text has a perfect opening.

> Once Ailill and Medb were in their kingly bed in the fort of Croghan of Connacht, and they had a pillow talk.
> 'It's a true word, girl,' said Ailill, 'a good man's wife is a lucky woman.'
> 'Of course she's lucky,' said the girl. 'What do you mean?'
> 'What I mean', said Ailill, 'is that you're better off now than the day I married you.'
> 'I was well off enough before,' said Medb.
> 'You were well off in a way I never heard or knew of,' said Ailill, 'but as a lone woman and the enemies on your border taking your spoil and cattle in raids from you.'

They argue about which of them is the richer, but when an inventory is taken their property is practically identical in value except that Ailill has a magnificent bull, which had once belonged to the queen, but which, scorning to be a 'kept bull', had trans-ferred itself to the king's herd. There is only one bull like it in Ireland; that is in Ulster, and since the Ulster landowner refuses to give it up to Mac Roth, the queen's messenger — even though Medb offers to sleep with him — she starts the great war of the provinces against Ulster. 'There is no need to polish the knots, Mac Roth,' says Medb, 'because it was known that what was not willingly given would be unwillingly taken, and taken it shall be.'

A perfect opening, caustic and convincing, but it is written in the deplorable narrative style that seems to have developed in the eleventh century, so scholars dismiss it as a contribution of the Book of Leinster editor. From the point of view of a literary critic, this is impossible. It is as unlikely that a rude mechanical editor like the Book of Leinster editor could fit an acephalous text with such a striking beginning as that a rural stone mason could carve a head for a classical statue.

Not only does this opening answer the questions that are left by the original 'Cattle Raid'; it seems to answer a number of other questions that no one had asked at all. One is the problem of the very first scene of what the Copyist calls 'The Story in Order'. Medb returns from an inspection of the hosting and announces that it would be foolish for the rest to go if the Gaileóin — the Leinstermen — are permitted to go.

> 'What is wrong with the men?' said Ailill.
> 'There is nothing wrong with them,' said Medb. 'They are fine soldiers. When the rest were building their huts they had thatched their own and cooked their supper; when the rest were at supper, they had finished theirs, and their harpers were playing to them. It is silly for them to go. They will get all the credit of the victory.'
> 'They *are* fighting on our side,' said Ailill.
> 'They are not going to come with us,' said Medb.
> 'Let them stay behind so,' said Ailill.
> 'They are not going to stay behind,' said Medb. 'They will attack us when we move on', she said, 'and seize our land from us.'
> 'What is to be done with them so?' said Ailill. 'Since they can neither stay nor go?'
> 'Kill them,' said Medb.
> 'That certainly is a woman's advice,' said Ailill.

As it stands in the text, this simply has no meaning. All that Thurneysen can extract from it is that the author was a Leinster-man, which is not very convincing. But read it in the immediate context of the Book of Leinster opening and it makes very good sense indeed. Not only has Medb started a great war for the most trifling of whims; she is now proposing to conduct it in a series of whims.

Her lover, Fergus mac Roich, protects the Leinstermen from her, but now another incident occurs which reads very peculiarly. Fergus sends warning to Cú Chulainn of what the Irish hosting is doing and then leads it astray. Instead of taking advantage of the warning Cú Chulainn goes to spend the night with a girl called Feidelm Noichride at Tara. (The name has been selected at random; Feidelm Noichride was Loegaire's wife, and it is not clear what she was doing in Tara.) As a result, the Irish hosting slips by, and Cú Chulainn says, 'I wish I had not gone there and betrayed the Ulstermen; I have let the hosting upon them unawares.' On the one hand we have Fergus, as Medb's lover, betraying Ulster; on the other, Cú Chulainn, as Feidelm Noichride's lover, doing the same thing. I find it hard to believe that this peculiar juxtaposition was not deliberate — at one stage of the story at least — and that a puritanical story-teller did not intend us to see two good men betraying a cause for the sake of two light women.

Shortly afterwards occurs the episode of 'The Boyish Feats of Cú Chulainn', the long flash back in skilful narrative prose that I have already described to you. The only trouble about it is that for all its charm, it is out of key with those portions of 'The Raid' that I am trying to isolate for you as part of the original story. It is like the *Iliad* rewritten by Hans Christian Andersen; and one can admire Andersen without comparing him with Homer.

Then, all at once, we return to the early story again in a brief passage of prose and a long scene in unrhymed verse, which is in an Irish so archaic that it has not been translated yet. The prose passage, which is linked with the verse, describes how Medb detains Fergus mac Roich during the advance of the army so that they can make love. It is an extraordinary scene — there is no other word for it — more reminiscent of eighteenth-century French fiction than Irish of the early Middle Ages.

Then Ailill said to his charioteer, Cuillius: 'Find Medb and Fergus for me today. I do not know what is keeping them together. I should like you to bring me a sign.'

Cuillius arrived when they were in Cluichre. The pair of them had stayed behind when the troops went by. Cuillius crept up on them and they did not observe the spy. Fergus' sword happened to be beside him. Cuillius drew it from its sheath and left the sheath empty. Cuillius came to Ailill.

'Well?' said Ailill.

'Well!' said Cuillius. 'There is your sign.'

'Excellent!' said Ailill.

The two men smiled at one another.

'As you guessed,' said Cuillius, 'that is how I found them, making love.'

'She has to do it,' said Ailill. 'It is for his help on the raid that she has done it. See that the sword is kept in good condition. Put it under your seat in the chariot with a linen cloth round it.'

After this Fergus got up and looked for his sword.

'Oh!' he said.

'What ails you?' said Medb.

'A bad thing I have done, Ailill,' he said. 'Wait here while I go into the wood,' said Fergus. 'And don't be surprised if I am some time.'

As it happened, Medb did not know of the loss of the sword. He left and took his charioteer's sword with him in his hand. He made a wooden sword in the wood.

'Let us go after the others,' said Fergus.

All their battalions met in the plain. They pitched their tents. Fergus was summoned by Ailill to play chess. When Fergus went to the tent Ailill began to laugh at him.

This scene is quite clearly part of the original 'Cattle Raid', because as a result of it Fergus, goaded and bribed by Medb, has to face his foster-son, Cú Chulainn, in battle unarmed. He persuades Cú Chulainn to run away from him, for the sake of old times, and promises to do as much for Cú Chulainn on another occasion. This, of course, occurs during the last great battle of the 'Raid' when Ailill returns his magic sword to Fergus to use against the Ulster hosting. Consequently the whole defeat of the Irish hosting is brought about by one of Medb's amorous whims, as irresponsible in their own way as her military ones.

But how much more the scene really tells us about the original 'Raid' we do not know, because it continues in unrhymed verse that cannot yet be translated. All 'Constant Reader' like myself can really make out is that Ailill, still amused in a highly modern,

BBC–3 manner at Medb's misbehaviour, is mocking Fergus, who is in a suicidal frame of mind over Medb's original proposal to massacre the Leinstermen and the loss of his sword. He refers to her bitterly as 'a woman of evil counsel', which is what Ailill himself charged her with — 'Ní chélam is ban-chomairle' ('That is certainly a woman's advice'). Medb has also drawn up new plans for the organization of the march, which Fergus regards as foolish and dangerous. Of course, the fact that the episode of the Leinstermen and that of the lost sword are dealt with in the archaic verse is positive proof that they formed part of the very earliest version of 'The Raid'.

The harsh treatment of Medb is characteristic of these original episodes. Even in the eleventh-century 'pillow talk' one can feel that the author, though he is reinterpreting a scene from the original, is really rather sympathetic to Medb as a character. When she says, 'If my husband were jealous, it would not be fitting, because I was never without one man in another man's shadow', the author rather approves of her and approves of Ailill for his forbearance, but there is no approval in the little scene between Ailill and his charioteer — 'The two men smiled at one another'; the note is one of contempt. There is contempt, too, in the episode in which Medb arranges a truce with Cú Chulainn and then puts fourteen men in hiding to kill him. One of the key scenes in the original story must have been that Medb would seduce some foster-brother of Cú Chulainn into fighting him, but this scene has now been obscured by being rewritten as an independent story in the manner of 'The Boyish Feats', but in that dreadful, inflated, gushing style of the post-Norse period. But even in this there are a few lines in an entirely different style, the style of the original writer. We find Medb micturating in her tent as Fer Diad rides by.

'Are you awake, Ailill?' said Medb.
'Not at all,' said Ailill.
'Do you hear your new son-in-law greeting you?'
'Is that what he is doing?' said Ailill.
'It is,' said Medb, 'and I swear by what my people swear the man who greets you there will not come back to you on the same feet.'

The last pages of 'The Raid' must once have been magnificent in a wild, Wagnerian way. Cú Chulainn, badly wounded, is tied to his bed while the final battle rages outside. Ailill gives Fergus back his sword, and he cuts his way through the Ulster ranks till he reaches his old enemy, Conchobar. He is saved from killing his king by Cormac Connlongas who directs his fury on to the hills around him, and then Cú Chulainn, maddened by the noise of battle, bursts his bonds and emerges to face him. He reminds Fergus of his promise, and Fergus runs away from him, thus precipitating the rout of the Irish hosting. But the climax of Medb's adventure was too much for the good taste of the Clonmacnois monks, and they omitted the passage entirely. Fortunately, in Terryglass they were not so dainty. During the battle Medb begins her monthly period, and Fergus mac Roich is compelled to fight a rearguard action to protect her. After the battle she blames her defeat on 'faults and factions', but Fergus retorts in archaic chant that this is only to be expected in 'a drove of horses led by a mare'. Then the story ends symbolically with the battle of the Connacht and Ulster bulls, the undefeatable images of masculinity. Dying and broken, but victorious, the Ulster bull sets out for home and dies on the border.

It is one of the great climaxes of literature, and we can understand why Mac Con Glinne's abbot went about with 'The Raid' stuffed into one of his high boots. But what I have tried to suggest is that not only was the story once a masterpiece; it was a masterpiece of a quite different kind. The passages I have isolated for you have a strong anti-feminist trend, which is most unusual in Irish literature, and one would like to know why. I can only guess, but I think that opening scene between husband and wife in Croghan might be a clue. Between the earliest period of our history, when women had no legal status, and the later period, when they had all the status their wealth could buy, there was an intermediate period — some time before the year 700 — when they were entitled only to strict equality with their husbands. This seems to me to be what Medb is trying to reach in that opening scene. At no time could Medb have led an army, but the author seems to be implying that if women can have property equal to that of their husbands, they will not stop there but go on until an army is no more than 'a drove of horses led by a mare'. There were many who felt in that way during the Renaissance, and again and again I get the feeling that our author is anticipating John Knox and his *Monstrous Regiment of Women*. At least it is a point worth considering.

That great literature I have spoken of ended with what I may call the Cistercian Invasion, which in intellectual matters was direr than the Norman Invasion. There was no longer any place for the little monasteries, which represented a typical friendly compromise between the monks and the squire. Muircheartach O'Brien could shock Ireland by appropriating Cashel to the Church; when Donagh O'Carvill appropriated land for Mellifont it was on a colossal scale, which made Cashel look like a flea-bite. When he cut down the King of Ireland at the roadside he was asserting the authority of the Church as no one in England or France dared to do it. The Hildebrandine Reformation in Ireland had no time for poetry or stories, more's the pity. And suddenly, after the year 1200, Irish poets ceased to write about nature and nobody any longer wrote good Irish prose. Both had perished with the class that produced it, and only about the year 1900 did a group of writers arise to continue the great literature they had created.

Selected Bibliography

Note: For a more detailed bibliography of the Irish works, see R. I. Best, *Bibliography of Irish Philology and Printed Literature,* 2 vols. Dublin, 1913, 1942.

Alspach, R. K., *Irish Poetry from the English Invasion to 1798.* London and Philadelphia, 1943.
d'Arbois de Jubainville, H., *Cours de litterature celtique,* 8 vols. Paris, 1883-1899.
—— *L'Épopée celtique en Irlande.* Paris, 1892.
Arensberg, C. M., *The Irish Countryman.* London, 1937.
Arnold, Matthew, *On the Study of Celtic Literature.* Everyman ed. London.
Bergin, Osborn, 'Bardic Poetry.' *Ivernian Journal,* 1913.
—— 'Unpublished Irish Poems.' *Studies.*
Bieler, Ludwig, *The Irish Penitentials.* Dublin, 1963.
—— *Ireland: Harbinger of the Middle Ages.* London, 1963.
Binchy, D. A., *Críth Gablach.* Dublin, 1941.
—— 'Some Celtic Legal Terms.' *Celtica,* 1953.
—— 'Patrick and his biographers.' *Studia Hibernica,* 1962.
—— 'The Passing of the Old Order.' *Proceedings of the International Congress of Celtic Studies,* 1959, Dublin, 1962.
—— 'Ancient Irish Law.' *Irish Jurist,* 1 (1966).
—— 'Bretha Déin Chécht.' *Eriu,* xx (1966).
Brooke, S. A., and Rolleston, T. W., *A Treasury of Irish Poetry.* London, 1900, 1915.
Calder, George, *Auricept na nÉces.* Edinburgh, 1917.
Carleton, William, *Traits and Stories of the Irish Peasantry,* ed. D. S. O'Donoghue. London, 1834.
Carney, James, *Studies in Irish History and Literature.* Dublin, 1955.
Clarke, Austin, *Poetry in Modern Ireland.* Dublin, 1951.
Colum, Padraic (ed.), *A Treasury of Irish Folklore.* New York, 1954.
Corkery, Daniel, *Synge and Anglo-Irish Literature.* Cork, 1966.
Cross, T. P., and Slover, C. H. (ed.), *Ancient Irish Tales.* London, 1937.
D'Arcy McGee, Thomas, *The Irish Writers of the 17th Century.* 1846.
Davitt, Michael, *The Fall of Feudalism in Ireland.* London, 1904.
Dillon, Myles, *The Cycles of the Kings.* London, 1946.
—— *Early Irish Literature.* Chicago, 1948.
—— *Irish Sagas.* Dublin, 1959.
—— (ed.), *Early Irish Society.* Dublin, 1954.
Ellis-Fermor, Una, *The Irish Dramatic Movement.* London, 1954.
Ferguson, M. C., *Sir Samuel Ferguson in the Ireland of his Day,* 2 vols. London, 1896.
Flanagan, Thomas, *The Irish Novelists, 1800-50.* London, 1958; New York, 1959.

258 A SHORT HISTORY OF IRISH LITERATURE

Flower, Robin, *The Irish Tradition*. Oxford, 1947.
Gavan Duffy, Charles, *The Ballad Poetry of Ireland*. Dublin, 1845.
—— *My Life in Two Hemispheres*. London, 1898.
Greene, David (ed.), *An Anthology of Irish Literature*. New York, 1954.
—— and O'Connor, Frank, *A Golden Treasury of Irish Poetry*, A.D. 600-1200. London, 1967
Gregory, Lady A., *Journals*, ed. Lennox Robinson. London, 1946.
Gwynn, Stephen, *Experiences of a Literary Man*. London, 1926.
—— *Irish Literature and Drama*. London, 1910.
Haslip, Joan, *Parnell*. London, 1936.
Healy, John, *Ireland's Ancient Schools and Scholars*. Dublin, 1908.
Healy, T. M., *Letters and Leaders of my Day*, 2 vols. London, 1928.
Hughes, Kathleen, *The Church in Early Irish Society*. London, 1966.
Hull, Eleanor, *The Poem-Book of the Gael*. London, 1912.
Hull, Vernam (ed.), *Longes Mac n-Uislenn*. New York, 1949; London, 1959.
Hyde, Douglas, *A Literary History of Ireland*. London, 1903.
Kenney, J. F., *The Sources for the Early History of Ireland*, I. New York, 1929.
Kiely, Benedict, *Poor Scholar*. New York, 1948.
—— *Modern Irish Fiction*. London, 1950.
Knott, Eleanor, *Irish Syllabic Poetry*, 2nd ed. Dublin, 1957.
—— *Irish Classical Poetry*, 2nd ed. Dublin, 1960.
Loftus, R. J., *Nationalism in Modern Irish Poetry*. Wisconsin, 1964.
MacBride, Maud, *A Servant of the Queen*. Dublin, 1950.
McHugh, Roger, *Dublin 1916*. London, 1966.
Mangan, J. C., *Poems of James Clarence Mangan*, ed. John Mitchel. New York, 1859, 1870.
Maxwell, C., *A Stranger in Ireland*. London, 1954.
Mercier, Vivian, *The Irish Comic Tradition*. Oxford, 1962.
—— and Greene, David, *One Thousand Years of Irish Prose*. New York, 1952.
Meyer, Kuno, *Selections from Ancient Irish Poetry*, 2nd ed. London, 1913.
—— *Uber die älteste irische Dichtung*, pts. I and II, in *Preussische Akademie der Wissenschaften*, Berlin, 1913-14.
—— *Bruchstücke der älteren Lyrik Irlands*. Berlin, 1919.
—— (ed.), *Liadain and Curithir*. London, 1902.
Moore, George, *Hail and Farewell*, 3 vols., London, 1911-14, 1947.
Murphy, Gerard, *Saga and Myth in Ancient Ireland*. Dublin, 1955.
—— *The Ossianic Lore and Romantic Tales of Medieval Ireland*. Dublin, 1955.
—— *Early Irish Lyrics*. Oxford, 1956.
—— *Early Irish Metrics*. Dublin, 1961.
Nicholson, Asenath, *Ireland's Welcome to the Stranger*. London, 1847.
—— *Lights and Shades in Ireland*, 3 pts. London, 1850.
O'Brien, William, *Recollections*. London, 1905.
O'Casey, Sean, *Autobiographies*, 2 vols. London, 1963.
O'Connor, Frank, *A Book of Ireland*. London, 1959.
—— *Kings, Lords, & Commons: An Anthology from the Irish*. New York, 1959; London, 1961.
—— *The Lonely Voice*. Cleveland, 1962; London, 1963.
—— *The Little Monasteries: Poems translated from the Irish*. Dublin, 1963.
O'Donoghue, D. J., *The Poets of Ireland*. London, 1892-3; Dublin, 1912

O'Donoghue, D. J., *Literary and Historical Essays*. Dublin, 1846.
O'Faolain, Sean, *The Irish*. London, 1947.
O'Farachain, R., *The Course of Irish Verse in English*. New York, 1947.
O'Grady, Standish, *The Bog of Stars and other stories and sketches of Elizabethan Ireland*. London, 1893.
O'Hanlon, John, *The Life of St Malachy O'Morgair*. Dublin, 1859.
O'Malley, Ernest, *On Another Man's Wound*. Dublin, 1936.
O'Rahilly, T. F., *Dánta Grádha*, 2nd ed. Dublin, 1926.
—— *Measgra Dánta*. Cork, 1927.
—— *Early Irish History and Mythology*. Dublin, 1946.
O Tuama, Sean, *An Grá in Amhráin na nDaoine*. Dublin, 1960.
Price, Allan, *Synge and Anglo-Irish Drama*. London, 1961.
Robinson, Lennox, and MacDonagh, Donagh, *The Oxford Book of Irish Verse*. Oxford, 1958.
Skelton, R., and Clark, D., 'An Irish Gathering.' *Massachusetts Review*, Winter 1964.
Strachan, J., and O'Keefe, J. G., *Táin Bó Cúailnge*. Dublin, 1912.
Sullivan, A. M., *New Ireland*. London, 1877.
Thurneysen, Rudolf, *Sagen aus dem alten Irland*. Berlin, 1901.
—— *Die irische Helden- und Königsage*. Halle, 1921.
Windisch, Ernst, *Irische Texte mit Wörterbuch*. Leipzig, 1880.
Windisch, Ernst, and Stokes, Whitley, *Irische Texte mit Ubersetzengen*, 4 pts. Leipzig, 1884-1909.
Yeats, W. B., *Autobiographies*. London, 1961.
—— *Collected Poems*, 2 vols. London, 1933.
Zimmer, Heinrich, 'Über den compilatorischen Charakter der irischen Sagentexte im Sogonannten Lebar na hUidre.' *Zeitschrift für vergleichende Sprachforschung*, XXVIII (1883-6).

PERIODICALS: *The Bell*, Dublin, 1940- ; *Dublin Magazine*, Dublin, 1923- ; *Dublin Penny Journal*, Dublin, 1832-6; *Eigse: A Journal of Irish Studies*, Dublin, 1939- ; *Eriu: Founded as the Journal of the School of Irish Studies*, Dublin, 1904- ; *Etudes Celtiques*, Paris, 1936- ; *Irish Statesman*, Dublin, 1919-30; *Irish Writing*, Tralee, 1946- ; *Journal of the Ivernian Society*, Cork, 1908-15; *Kilkenny Magazine*, Kilkenny, 1960- ; *Revue celtique*, Paris, 1870-1934; *Studia Hibernica*, Dublin, 1961- ; *Studies: An Irish Quarterly Review*, Dublin, 1910- ; *Zeitschrift für celtische Philologie*, Halle a S., 1899-

Index